The Spaces of Violence

The Spaces of Violence

James R. Giles

THE UNIVERSITY OF ALABAMA PRESS

Tuscaloosa

Typeface: ACaslon

∞

The paper on which this book is printed meets the minimum requirements of American
National Standard for Information Sciences-Permanence of Paper for Printed Library
Materials, ANSI Z39.48-1984.

Library of Congress Cataloging-in-Publication Data

Giles, James Richard, 1937–
The spaces of violence / James R. Giles.
p. cm.
Includes bibliographical references and index.
ISBN-13: 978-0-8173-1502-3 (isbn-13 : alk. paper)
ISBN-10: 0-8173-1502-0 (isbn-10 : alk. paper)
1. American fiction—20th century—History and criticism. 2. Violence in literature.
3. Space (Architecture) in literature. 4. Space and time in literature. 5. Personal space in
literature. I. Title.
PS374.V58G548 2006
813′.54093552—dc22

2005022265

To Gustaaf Van Cromphout and James Mellard

Contents

Preface

One afternoon when I was in high school in Bowie, Texas, I left the Bowie Drug Store, where I had spent an hour or so drinking a Coke and reading James Jones's *From Here to Eternity* from the paperback books rack, and saw, across the street, on the post office steps, a man step out of a car carrying a rifle. The armed man proceeded to shoot a man who was walking up the post office steps and then drive away. Of course, a crowd immediately gathered around the wounded man, and I had only a glimpse of one blood-stained leg awkwardly sprawled across several steps before my view was completely blocked.

I later learned that the two men had quarreled over the ownership of a tree that grew on the boundary of their adjoining properties and that the wounded man had died. I realized in retrospect that the two were (re)creating the dynamic of the movie Westerns and the high school football games I had grown up on; there was, however, nothing heroic about this very real shooting. In fact, football stars and movie cowboys lacked any true relevance to the scene on the post office steps. It was as if the space of Hollywood noir had somehow materialized in front of me, that the savage violence that I had just been reading about in the Jones novel had become most assuredly real. As I have done with virtually everything since, I turned to literature to help me comprehend, to find some defining equation in, all this; and I am probably searching in fiction for the explanation of why one man would in broad daylight fatally shoot another on the steps of a small-town post office. Perhaps my fondness for naturalistic fiction and its affinity for random, senseless violence was born as the dying man tumbled down the concrete post office steps.

I would later have a more immediate, in fact life-threatening, experience with violence. In 1966, I was a graduate student at the University of Texas in Austin and, on August 1 of that year, started to leave the Student Center only to be told that someone was shooting at people from the top of the Tower, a 307-foot-tall structure that serves as the university's central library. That such an absurd thing could actually be happening was impossible to believe, and I proceeded to push my way outside, turning back only when I heard a bullet go past my head. I spent the next ninety minutes in the Student Center as the gunman, Charles Whitman, with a clear view not only of the campus but of the surrounding area, continued to fire at random.

Then word began to spread throughout the Student Center that the gunman had been captured and subdued, and I, along with virtually everyone else, raced outside to see the person who had attempted to kill me and who apparently killed a number of other people (only later did I learn that fourteen were dead and scores wounded). To be honest, I was also impelled by the kind of morbid curiosity that draws people to car wrecks and other disastrous events. I felt the crowd surrounding me surge forward when two policeman exited the Tower followed by someone dressed in everyday clothes before the policemen waved everyone back, proclaiming that their companion was not the shooter (he turned out to be an off-duty cop who had been one of the two people who subdued and killed Whitman). For a moment, though, I had an immediate, though mercifully brief, experience of what mob violence must feel like. Later other people appeared carrying a stretcher on which lay a woman who, for a moment, seemed to be wearing red stockings. The stockings were in fact her blood.

This experience left me, as it did much of the rest of those on campus, shaken and depressed for several weeks. Paradoxically, though, for me, its long-range effects proved to be less than the murder on the steps of the Bowie Post Office. It was then that I lost a major part of my innocence, the Tower shootings only confirming that loss. In addition, I began to understand that the post office shooting had simply been an inevitable result of the cultural dynamic in which I was raised.

During the 1940s and 1950s, Bowie was a town of between four and five thousand people. It was, at least from my youthful perspective, a place of stability and innocence. My father did not serve in World War II, and even though I had uncles who did, that horrendous and historically decisive conflict seemed distant and unreal, at least until popular culture periodically brought it home to me through graphic and, I now realize, often racist im-

ages. The racism was most blatant in the 1940s war movies. I especially remember *Gung Ho!* (1943), starring Randolph Scott and Robert Mitchum,
which depicted the creation of a special forces marine unit recruited on the
basis of their bloodthirstiness and hatred of "the Japs" for a mission to retake
a Pacific island from the Imperial Japanese Army. In one scene, a platoon of
Japanese soldiers comes across a wounded and dying American soldier, who
begs for water and is promptly bayoneted to death. In addition, a native of
Bowie was one of Jimmy Doolittle's pilots in the 1942 U.S. bombing raid of
Tokyo. The pilot's plane was shot down, and he was reported missing. Postcards of the dead pilot were sold at various stores in Bowie, including the
Bowie Drug Store. I have, as an adult, sought one of these postcards, but they
are now virtually forgotten in Bowie.

Probably because I was so young during the war, bayoneted film marines
and real missing pilots seemed unrelated to my world, and I was ignorant of
the lynchings of African Americans that were still taking place in Texas and
the rest of the South. Bowie is the largest town in Montague County, which
was, when I was a boy (and in fact remains), an all-white and overwhelmingly Protestant fundamentalist county. The biological inferiority of all races
except the Caucasian, the corruption and "unsaved" state of all Catholics, and
the greed and capacity for sinister plotting of all Jews were accepted beliefs
during my Bowie childhood. I still remember the principal of my high
school sending out a memo suggesting that we cheer for Southern Methodist
University to beat the University of San Francisco in a 1956 NCAA basketball Final Four game because the Southern Methodist players were from
Texas (some of them were, but not their All-American Jim Krebs) and were
white (that was unmistakable), while the San Francisco players were "Ne-
groes" (including Bill Russell) and Chinese (not as I remember) and "everything in the world except white" (wrong). Russell and San Francisco won. I
was thus hardly aware of the distortion and implicit violence of exclusion
that characterized my youth or of how much that denial of cultural diversity was limiting my understanding of the full richness and complexity of
American culture and, for that matter, of the world. (Novelist John Rechy
once pointed out the cultural limitations of my privileged background: "Jim,
I feel sorry for you. You have never been any kind of minority.") In school we
were regularly told how lucky we were to live in a small town and not a
"dangerous city with its temptations," a designation that presumably included all cities, except possibly Dallas, a city whose potential for truly
world-shaking violence would not be realized until November 1963.

My discovery in high school of twentieth-century American literature and of such African-American writers as Richard Wright and James Baldwin gave me some sense, despite the prejudice and cultural denial in which I grew up, of the affirming essence, the redeeming diversity, of the United States. Of course, it was far too early for me to be aware of Latino, Native American, and Asian-American writers. Bowie and Montague County were thus caught in a kind of cultural time warp—it was as if the scientific and philosophical innovations of the early twentieth century had not quite arrived there, though it was, like the rest of the country, paradoxically enamored of technological innovation.

The town had two principal outlets for entertainment, one more universally accepted than the other. Friday-night high school football was the venerated cultural ritual of the community—and of all of the communities surrounding it. The high school team, called the Jackrabbits (I'm not making that up), played in a small "stadium" with metal stands; Friday evenings in the fall evoked the most intense communal emotions. I did not play football (too thin and uncoordinated) but nevertheless fell in love with the ritualized violence of the sport, never considering its implications for society as a whole (I'm still a football fan, though I have subsequently considered those implications a lot). The implicit message of Friday-night football in Bowie, and it is important to understand the town's typicality in this respect, was that violent competition was an essential element in communal identity, that there was something suspicious and, in some vague way, unmanly about any boy who did not play the game, or at least enjoy and talk about it. Thus, aggressive violence was accepted as a defining aspect of masculinity in Bowie—and in all of Texas, for that matter. No one seemed to find any difficulty in reconciling it with fundamentalist religion, and in fact the games were preceded by prayers offered by the local ministers over the public-address system.

Though not approved by the more rigid fundamentalists, movies rivaled football as an entertainment source, having the distinct advantage of being available for twelve months rather than just ten weeks in the fall. Saturday afternoon was our time for the movies (at either the Majestic or the Ritz or the Texan theater); for a quarter we got to see two feature-length films (always one Western), a cartoon, a serial chapter, a comedy short (with luck, the Three Stooges), and a newsreel (which again threatened to bring the complex world outside Montague County home to us but consistently muted that threat by concluding with images of a college football game or the bathing suit portion of a beauty pageant).

In the Westerns—and, for that matter, in the Stooges shorts—violence was again sanitized. Moe, Larry, and Curly somehow managed to never actually hurt each other, and the cowboy heroes only shot and killed the "bad guys," who clearly deserved it and whose demise was essential for the triumph of justice. Furthermore, they would probably appear intact the following Saturday. Good and evil were depicted as being clear and distinct binaries, recognizable by the color of hats and the presence or absence of vocal talent. The recurrent plot featured outsiders who came into a previously peaceful community and, motivated by greed or compelled by some genetic disposition to evil, "took over" a previously peaceful community and "framed" the hero, who was genetically predisposed to reckless bravery. My personal favorite, Bob Steele, who customarily beat the "bad guys" to a pulp before killing them, usually had the personal motivation of avenging a murdered father to go with his essential "good guyness." Imagine my state of confusion when I accidentally saw an "adult" and hysterically Freudian Western, *Duel in the Sun* (1946), the sheer perversity of which was manifest in the casting of Gregory Peck as a "bad guy" and Jennifer Jones (now a long way from Lourdes) as a "half-breed" nymphomaniac (a medical condition I had previously known nothing about except that it only affected women in noir films and even then not the female leads unless they were played by Jane Greer).

In the Majestic or the Ritz or the Texan, reality would threaten to intrude through war films and the occasional film noir with its vision of a black-and-white urban America haunted by a pervasive and sinister evil. But once again we had never seen anyone who talked or dressed like Bogart or Mitchum and certainly no women who looked or talked anything like Bacall or Veronica Lake or Jane Greer. We knew no landscape of shadowy urban alleyways and palm trees. We loved to be scared by the Universal horror films of the 1940s, but of course manmade monsters, wolfmen, vampires, and mummies existed only in some space of the imagination that had nothing to do with a reality of small brick store buildings, automobiles, and mesquite trees (on a few occasions, Hollywood tried to mix the Western and horror genres, always with laughable results, the one depending as it did on enclosed, even claustrophobic space, the other on the illusion of "frontier openness").

In the late 1940s, in movie newsreels or in *Life* or *Look* magazine, images of the Holocaust or Hiroshima intruded into our consciousness and threatened our innocence. But these images invoked a dimension of horror that seemed as distant as the landscape of the Universal horror films. Television was not yet a presence in American lives, and Hollywood tried resolutely to ignore the reality and the implications for the future of the concentration camps and the bomb (I knew nothing about the U.S. internment of Japanese Americans until sometime in college). That a level of violence unprecedented in, even unimagined by, human history had occurred in what was a rapidly shrinking world was not something we as kids comprehended. Moreover, the American right wing quickly translated the Holocaust and the bomb into "the danger of Communist subversion," and I can remember adults in Bowie speculating about which of their neighbors might be "reds." Of course, those so identified were people who were suspected of some form of unconventionality (God knows we could have used more of that!). The odds of finding someone in Montague County who had read Marx were roughly the same as those of discovering someone who regularly corresponded with George Bernard Shaw.

In the late 1940s and early 1950s, a generation of American writers—often writing about World War II—began to challenge a widely accepted American self-righteousness and to depict the complex interrelationship of sexuality and violence with a frankness revolutionary for this country. I discovered and read, much to my high school English teacher's dismay, Norman Mailer's *The Naked and the Dead*, with its evocations of totalitarian U.S. military officers and murderous sergeants who tortured Japanese prisoners of war. In school we passed around copies of Mickey Spillane's *I, the Jury* with its transposition of a "Wild West" morality to a contemporary urban landscape and its valorization of violence against seductive and rapacious women. Spillane shattered some kind of literary barrier by making the color of pubic hair the irreducible signifier of the lethal female. Bob Steele now drove a car instead of riding a horse, wore a slouch hat instead of a Stetson, and possessed esoteric knowledge about women and sex. I usually lacked the money to buy hardcover copies of these novels, which weren't available in Bowie anyway (the town didn't have a bookstore; the last time I was there it had a small "Christian books and tapes" store), and the Bowie Public Library certainly did not keep them, but mass-market paperbacks had begun to revolutionize American publishing.

These novels intensified my already-ingrained tendency to approach the inexplicable and the truly frightening indirectly, from a mediated distance. When I wrote my first book about violence in contemporary American fiction (*Violence in the Contemporary American Novel*) I treated only urban texts, probably because of their long-standing historic association with naturalistic violence. But as I became suddenly aware one afternoon outside the Bowie

Drug Store, and as the contemporary novel illustrates, violence resides in every kind of American space, including the small town, which is no longer, and can never again be, as isolated or as deceptively innocent as it once was. A peculiarly American violence, essentially technological in nature, has over the past four decades come to dominate much of the world. (Of course, Henry Adams saw the potential for this in the late nineteenth century.) It increasingly seems to me that, despite the traumatic upheavals of the 1960s, the kind of dangerously xenophobic and self-righteous innocence that I grew up with has never left America and is, in fact, increasingly in ascendance. It is as though men with blood-stained legs are once again tumbling down cement stairs, and I have sought explanations for the blood in the novels treated in this study.

Acknowledgments

The encouragement and editorial suggestions of Wanda H. Giles were essential to the development of this manuscript. I also want to acknowledge the generous encouragement of Jackson Bryer, Doris Macdonald, James M. Mellard, Gustaaf Van Cromphout, and Keith Gandal. The interlibrary loan and research departments of Founders Memorial Library at Northern Illinois University (NIU) provided invaluable assistance throughout the research and writing stages of this book, while Eric Hoffman and the Network Writing and Research Lab in NIU's English department made possible the production of a final manuscript. The suggestions of Dr. Arthur Redding at York University in Toronto and Dr. Robert Rebein, Associate Professor of English at Indiana University-Purdue University Indianapolis, external readers of the manuscript for the press, made this a significantly better book, as did the sensitive copy-editing of Jonathan Lawrence.

Spaces of Violence

1
Violence and Space

Michael Kowalewski writes that "American fiction is not for hemophobics. . . .
In studying fictional violence one must explore the power of words to sicken
and befoul as well as freshen and redeem" (11). Slave narratives, captivity narratives, the late-eighteenth- and early-nineteenth-century novels of Charles
Brockden Brown, the nineteenth-century fiction of James Fenimore Cooper,
Herman Melville, and Edgar Allan Poe, and works of the turn-of-the century literary naturalists cumulatively explore virtually every conceivable violent act. In the modernist period, Ernest Hemingway was obsessed with war,
even while romanticizing it, while William Faulkner focused on the psychological ramifications of a peculiarly southern violence. Scott Fitzgerald, John
Dos Passos, and Richard Wright, among others, investigated the brutal and
dehumanizing nature of American urban life. Subsequently, Norman Mailer
has proclaimed the centrality of violence to a male identity rooted in existen-
tialist philosophy.

   Given the history of the United States, the obsession of our fiction writers
with the origins and ramifications of violence is hardly surprising. Sanctioned, even institutionalized violence against the socially marginalized (e.g.,
slavery and genocide of Native American tribes) played a central role in the
formation of the United States. The nation was born out of a violent revolu-
tion, and the Civil War and U.S. participation in World Wars I and II, the
Korean War, the war in Vietnam, and the two recent wars against Iraq have
continued and intensified the national legacy of violence. In the last three
decades, government and educational leaders and cultural analysts have been
concerned with the degree to which violence has begun to assault and plague
supposedly safe middle-class American spaces and institutions (e.g., political

assassinations, school shootings, sexual assaults, violence against children), and they have devoted considerable time, energy, and money to trying to understand the phenomenon.

In this dual context, the contemporary American novel is an obvious place to look for insights into the origins and ramifications of the national plague of violence. Recent American writers have been, if anything, even more obsessed with violence than their predecessors. The texts that shed some light on the blood-stained nature of contemporary American society are numerous, and in a study of this length it would be impossible to cover even most of them in any depth. Thus, selection of a few representative texts offers the most promising approach. The ten novels upon which this study focuses contain contrasting visions of the interaction of violence and space in contemporary America. Published over a period of nearly three decades—from the late 1960s, the decade increasingly seen as inaugurating revolutionary changes in American society and literature, to the mid-1990s—they illustrate widely contrasting visions and modes of narration. In approximate chronological order, they are Cormac McCarthy's *Outer Dark* (1968) and *Child of God* (1973), Don DeLillo's *End Zone* (1972), Robert Stone's *Dog Soldiers* (1974), Denis Johnson's *Angels* (1983), Russell Banks's *Affliction* (1989), Bret Easton Ellis's *American Psycho* (1991), Dorothy Allison's *Bastard Out of Carolina* (1992), Lewis Nordan's *Wolf Whistle* (1993), and Sherman Alexie's *Indian Killer* (1996).

Obviously, other novels by the nine writers examined here might have been chosen. Few contemporary American novels are as saturated with violence as Cormac McCarthy's suggestively entitled *Blood Meridian* (1985), arguably the ultimate anti-Western in American literature, and the three novels that constitute McCarthy's Border trilogy are perhaps better known at present than *Outer Dark* and *Child of God*. But these early novels evoke in their (re)creation of a simultaneously naturalistic and surreal Appalachia a kind of space unique in American literature. Like *Blood Meridian*, Russell Banks's retelling of the John Brown story in *Cloudsplitter* (1998) is a powerful deconstructive American historical novel, and the settings of Banks's other fictions cover a wide range of space, from New England to Florida to Jamaica. But in its probing of a strain of violence peculiarly rooted in small-town New England, *Affliction* evokes an important space that would not otherwise be present in this study. Don DeLillo's controversial (re)creation of Lee Harvey Oswald, *Libra*, deconstructs the genres of both history and biography, while *Underworld* (1977) caps off the exploration of the links between language, violence, consumerism, sports, governmental spying, and waste that characterize the ambitious scope of his fiction. But the early *End Zone* concisely situates these tropes in a setting that grafts the worlds of football (now the dominant spectator sport in the United States and naturally one of the most violent) and academia onto the barren west Texas desert, itself a peculiarly inhuman kind of space. In the bleakness and anger of its tone, *Indian Killer* is a departure from Sherman Alexie's earlier fictions such as the story cycle *The Lone Ranger and Tonto Fistfight in Heaven* (1993) and the imaginatively multicultural comic novel *Reservation Blues* (1995). Still, *Indian Killer* creatively (re)imagines the historic violence against Native Americans in a contemporary urban setting.

As he does in *Dog Soldiers,* Robert Stone focuses on the exploration of American violence through nationalist political agendas in *A Flag for Sunrise* (1981), but in its vision of interpenetrating American and Vietnamese spaces, *Dog Soldiers* evokes a unique trope of space. Equally original is Denis Johnson's vision of "Greyhound space" in *Angels,* which is particularly relevant to this study in a way that neither the dystopian fantasy *Fiskadoro* (1985) nor the impressive collection of stories *Jesus' Son* (1992) are. By reconstructing the 1955 murder of Chicago teenager Emmett Till in Mississippi and placing his narrative focus on the white murderers and incorporating elements of magic realism and an irreverent and satiric vision of Mississippi and (by extension) southern history, Lewis Nordan also evokes a unique trope of space in his best-known novel, *Wolf Whistle.* Another small-town southern narrative, Dorothy Allison's *Bastard Out of Carolina,* has by now emerged as a seminal exploration of abusive treatment of women. In sharp contrast in many ways is Bret Easton Ellis's *American Psycho* with its urban setting.

The ten novels cumulatively cover a wide range of social, cultural, and geographic spaces. Socioeconomic levels from the decidedly marginalized to the upper middle class are depicted in them. A systemic approach to violence is present to some degree in all of them; and, taken together, they offer a powerful critique of the pervasive injustices of contemporary American capitalism. Yet while social protest is a distinct aspect of *Angels, Affliction, Wolf Whistle,* and *Indian Killer,* the protest in all four is muted either by emphases on mythology or through narrative innovation. *Bastard Out of Carolina* is the closest of the ten texts to a traditional social protest novel, and even it contains significant elements of mythology, or at least bricolage. *Dog Soldiers* critiques the U.S. legacy in Vietnam as an imperialist (mis)adventure, but its concern is with exploring the tragic legacy of the war for the domestic space of America; and, while it would be hard to imagine a more devastating analysis of the practices and values of American capitalism than *American Psycho*, Ellis's narrative mode increasingly becomes so surrealistic that it is impossible to be certain what actually happens in the novel. The geographic settings of the novels include New York City, Seattle, San Francisco, Los Angeles, Pittsburgh, Chicago, and Phoenix, along with small towns in New England and the South. Set respectively in Appalachia and the west Texas desert, the McCarthy novels and DeLillo's *End Zone*, for different reasons, often seem to be happening in some space outside the strictly geographic.

Thus the spatial diversity of the texts discussed is both geographic and extra-geographic. On the geographic level, the organizing principle is a progression from the barren and desolate west Texas desert to a culturally and historically isolated Appalachia to New England and southern small towns to contrasting dimensions of urban spaces. On the extra-geographic level the movement is from realistic and naturalistic to metaphoric and surreal visions of space(s). The multilevel diversity of the texts is one of the three organizing principles of this study. The wide-ranging innovation of their approaches to familiar spaces was a central factor in their inclusion. Appalachia is the setting for other American novels, but not the surrealistic Appalachia envisioned by McCarthy. Since the novels and stories of Faulkner and Eudora Welty, small-town Mississippi has been one of the most commonly explored of American spaces; yet in *Wolf Whistle* Nordan's magic realism brilliantly reimagines it, while Allison views it through the perspective of an angry feminism. Academic institutions are a familiar target of satiric novels, while the west Texas desert has been a favorite setting of Western writers and filmmakers, but no one has merged these two spaces by emphasizing their inherently linguistic nature as DeLillo does in *End Zone*. In *Affliction*, Banks views the New England small town, a favored setting for the nineteenth-century female realists Sarah Orne Jewett and Mary E. Wilkins Freeman, through an imaginative narrative perspective that combines elements of literary naturalism with a disturbing regional mythology. Johnson's *Angels*, Alexie's *Indian Killer*, and Ellis's *American Psycho* discover new dimensions of urban space. Banks envisioned the American city and an isolated space as being haunted by the tragic international experience of the Vietnam War.

Violence is a much more complex thing than most people assume. *The American Heritage Dictionary* offers six meanings for the word:

1. Physical force exerted for the purpose of violating, damaging, or abusing. . . .
2. An act or instance of violent action or behavior.
3. Intensity or severity, as in natural phenomena; untamed force. . . .
4. The abusive or unjust exercise of power.
5. Abuse or injury to meaning, content, or intent. . . .
6. Vehemence of feeling or expression; fervor.

Ironically, the contradictory nature of these entries further illustrates the difficulty of pinpointing the precise meaning of the word. In the first entry, violence is willed and physical and malignant, while the second introduces the concept of behavior, which may be conscious or unconscious. Moreover, "behavior" does not necessarily imply a specific physical action. The third entry equates violence with a natural and thus hardly willed "force" (most of us do not, I assume, ascribe intentionality to floods and earthquakes), while the fourth limits it to an abusive, and one assumes primarily political, hegemony. The fifth entry introduces a linguistic dimension to the concept of violence, thereby largely removing it from the realm of the physical, while the sixth, in equating it with "fervor," leaves open the possibility of a positive, reforming violence.

Violence seems comparable to pornography in being difficult to identify but nevertheless a phenomenon most people claim to be able to recognize when they see it. Arthur Redding argues convincingly that violence inherently eludes definition: "Violence is that which by definition cannot be grasped; it is excessive. Language—however violently we will come to know speech acts—falls short" (34). Excess seems to be the one universal characteristic of violence, which in itself can be oppressive, even destructive, or affirmative, even redemptive. By inevitably shattering linguistic boundaries, the excessive will escape any system of signs designed to contain it. The sheer excess of violence is perhaps its chief fascination for Georges Bataille. Still, as Bataille, Redding, and René Girard, among others, eloquently demonstrate, the fact that we cannot define violence does not mean that we cannot, or should not, examine its representations in literature. While language may be inadequate to grasp violence, language nevertheless constitutes one of our most important modes of access to it.

At one point in *Raids on Human Consciousness*, Redding states the essence of his systemic approach to violence:

A more critical "structural" or "systemic" theory of violence, marked by the insistence that violence—occasionally subsumed under bureaucracy or ideology, under economic, gender, and class configurations, or under the micropolitics of power—forms an integral, vitiating ground of any dynamic system whose purported equilibrium is merely a pretense. Under this rubric I align Darwin, Nietzsche, Marx, and perhaps, Foucault. Here violence is understood as the ballast of ideologies; as in the semisecret cargo of a slave trader's ship, there is blood in the hold of every way of seeing. (4–5)

Crucial to this study is Redding's comment that violence is "the ballast of ideologies"—it is what gives hegemonic structures stability. Structural oppression is always dependent upon violence, whether overt or latent, and the reference to the "semisecret cargo of a slave trader's ship" recalls the link between violence and race that has historically been central to American culture.

Even though in the passage just quoted Redding qualifies the inclusion of Foucault, the French thinker's ideas underlie Redding's book from beginning to end. Early in *Raids on Human Consciousness,* Redding quotes the following from Foucault's *Power/Knowledge:* "One's point of reference should not be to the great model of language and signs, but to that of war and battle. The history which bears and determines us has the form of a war rather than that of language: relations of power, not relations of meaning. Neither the dialectic, as a logic of contradictions, nor semiotics, as the structure of communication, can account for the intrinsic intelligibility of conflicts" (1–2). A view of social structures as modes of implementing power, and inevitably of oppressing the powerless, is central to Foucault's work and is made especially overt in *Discipline and Punish.* Oppression of the powerless always involves physical or psychological violence, or at least its imminent threat, and in this context Foucault describes social structures as being warlike. His reference to "the history which bears and determines us" is also relevant for this study, especially in the context of the literary naturalism that is present to some extent in all of the novels to be discussed.

In a majority of the novels, mythological concepts of the origins of violence supplement, if not dominate, systemic analyses of it. Girard's ideas are especially helpful in approaching this pervasive mythological dimension. In *Violence and the Sacred,* Girard, through extensive discussion of violence, first as it is depicted in classical Greek drama and folklore and then as it is analyzed by Freud, Lévi-Strauss, and other philosophical structuralists, discovers a "sacred" role for violence. It is, he argues, inextricably linked to the practice of ritual sacrifice of surrogates:

> Violence is frequently called irrational. It has its reasons, however, and can marshal some rather convincing ones when the need arises. Yet these reasons cannot be taken seriously, no matter how valid they appear. Violence itself will discard them if the initial object remains persistently out of reach and continues to provoke hostility. When unappeased, violence seeks and always finds a surrogate victim. The creature that excited its fury is abruptly replaced by another, chosen only because it is vulnerable and close at hand. (2)

Taken by itself, this passage appears to offer a concise analysis of the horrific American tradition of lynching that had its roots in the post-Reconstruction American South and, as witness Jasper, Texas, has not yet completely died out. Mobs of economically disadvantaged whites—predominantly adult males, though women and even children were sometimes present—frustrated in their inability to challenge the "creature" of their own socioeconomic exploitation, objectified surrogate victims, usually African Americans, before first torturing and then murdering them.[1]

Still, Girard envisions human violence as being universal and rooted in an undiscoverable act of original violence. Thus, for him, violence transcends specific instances of social and political exploitation. Moreover, at least until the advent of Freud, if not since, it necessarily existed, Girard argues, outside human comprehension: "Men cannot confront the naked truth of their own violence without the risk of abandoning themselves to it entirely. They have never had a very clear idea of this violence, and it is possible that the survival of all human societies of the past was dependent on this fundamental lack of understanding" (82). According to Girard, human beings have historically feared outbreaks of what he calls "reciprocal violence," in which unchecked acts of revenge would threaten to destroy the social order.

In primitive societies, Girard argues, such a period of excessive reciprocal violence and resultant disorder constituted a "sacrificial crisis" that could be alleviated first through the communal identification, and then the ritual killing, of a surrogate. Such sacrifice was validated by the immediate chaos within, and the threatened disintegration of, the social order itself. In times of "sacrificial crisis," Girard argues, "the institutions lose their validity; the protective façade of the society gives way; social values are rapidly eroded; and the whole cultural structure seems on the verge of collapse" (49). Girard's ideas about mythological violence are especially relevant to the Appalachian texts of Cormac McCarthy.

Inevitably, given the ancient Greek texts that Girard writes about, his concern throughout *Violence and the Sacred* is with an essentially masculine violence. Bataille's study of violence and excess in *Erotism*, Walter Ong's theory of contest and male "adversativeness" in *Fighting for Life*, and Lawrence Kramer's discussion of the links between sexuality and violence in *After the Lovedeath* continue this emphasis. Bataille, Ong, and Kramer are central to this study, as various forms of ritualized male violence appear in the ten novels discussed here. In *End Zone*, DeLillo turns to football and its specialized language for a narrative focus; deer hunting is central to Banks's *Affliction;* and Nordan envisions lynching as a depraved male ritual in *Wolf Whistle*. Child abuse is seen as originating in practices that reinforce male supremacy in *Affliction* and *Bastard Out of Carolina*. Finally, rites of male competition rooted in consumerism and the commodification of women recur throughout Ellis's *American Psycho*.

An inherent contradiction between Redding's sytemic analysis of violence and Girard's mythological approach to the phenomenon must be acknowledged. Girard is a central target of Redding's book. If violence originated in some universal and mythological space, it seemingly exists outside human comprehension and agency. Again, Girard posits some forgotten primal violence as unleashing acts of sacrificial violence that, in primitive and classical societies, could be appeased only through ritual sacrifice. This constitutes, Redding argues, a profoundly conservative position: when the origins of violence are perceived as transcending human understanding, there would seem to be little anyone can do to control or combat it. In Girard's thesis, the injustices residing in social structures diminish in importance.

Despite the undeniable logic of Redding's argument, the present study will opt for an intermediate position in the implicit binary between his systemic analysis of violence and Girard's mythological approach. After geographic and extra-geographic diversity, the relative positions of these texts on a hypothetical naturalistic-mythological continuum is the second major organizing principle of this study. Since the late nineteenth century, American literary naturalism has been a favorite genre for depicting violence, especially systemic violence. McCarthy's *Outer Dark* and *Child of God* occupy the mythological extreme of the hypothetical continuum, while *Dog Soldiers, Angels,* and especially *Bastard Out of Carolina* represent the naturalistic extreme. Because of its linguistic emphasis, DeLillo's *End Zone* exists both within and outside this continuum. Of course, simply positing such a continuum leaves unanswered the question of what can be done about the plague of violence afflicting contemporary society. But the assumption here is that fictional texts are essentially reporters of social and human conditions and are under no obligation to discover cures for them. As with any art, the creation of lasting literature requires many things, but perfect logic is not one of them. As Henry James pointed out, "the alchemy of art" reveals and *conceals* a great deal.

In *Domby and Son,* Harriet Carker, an embodiment of lower-middle-class virtue living on the outskirts of London, watches, from the window of her small cottage, the unceasing flow of lost and desperate strangers into the city. What she sees allows Dickens one of his not-uncommon editorial comments about the monstrous nature of urban life: "Day after day, such travellers crept past, but always, as she thought, swallowed up in one phase or other of its immensity, towards which they seemed impelled by a desperate fascination, they never returned. Food for the hospitals, the churchyards, the prisons, the river, fever, madness, vice, and death, they passed on to the monster, roaring in the distance, and were lost" (480). Here Dickens, in 1848 England, concisely expresses what was then and would continue to be a popular middle-class assumption in Great Britain and in the United States: that crime, vice, and violence were the peculiar conditions of urban industrial culture. This view of the city as an inherently dangerous, even unsafe space continued on both sides of the Atlantic for the next century and continues to some degree today. One could hardly imagine television programs based on the kind of cultural assumptions central to *NYPD Blue, The Sopranos,* and *Law and Order* being set anywhere but the city.

Ironically, this image of the "dangerous city" has long been reassuring for people residing in suburbia, small-town America, and more rural spaces. Violence, they assumed, was inextricably linked to urban diversity; if they simply avoided the city, they could feel immune from the threat of human, if not natural, violence. Such assumptions were, of course, always mistaken, and to an extent they were also inherently racist; and as recent events have graphically demonstrated, they are increasingly difficult to defend. In recent years, the peace and security of an exclusive western suburb (Columbine, Colorado) and a southern small town (Jonesboro, Arkansas) have been shattered by horrific shootings in public schools. In fact, next to its invasion of non-urban spaces, perhaps the most threatening implication of contemporary American violence for the middle class is that it cannot be dismissed as the behavior of a social or racial Other. In Columbine and, admittedly to a lesser extent, in Jonesboro, the killers *were* the children of the middle class. Violence could no longer be dismissed as some external, urban phenomenon.

Thus, paradoxically, American violence seems to become more mysterious as it accelerates and expands. The more familiar violence becomes, the less its origins and essential nature seem comprehensible. Of course, everyone from professional sociologists and psychiatrists to television commentators, television evangelists, and authors of letters to the editor regularly offer solutions to the problem. But as Norman Mailer, no insignificant commentator on American violence himself, prophesied in *The Armies of the Night* (1968), the flood of "information" in technological, postmodernist America often drowns genuine understanding.

Since violence increasingly expands outside urban areas into other American spaces, theories of urban life are no longer adequate as a context in which to discuss it. More generalized concepts of space are necessary to supplement the theoretical approaches to violence proposed by Redding, Girard, and others. Two such spatial studies are central to this study. Henri Lefebvre's *The Production of Space* (1974) was, upon its first appearance, a ground-breaking investigation of the nature of space. In it, Lefebvre posits three essential forms of space: "first, the physical—nature, the Cosmos; secondly, the *mental*, including logical and formal abstractions; and, thirdly the *social*" (11).

From his Marxist perspective, Lefebvre progresses to "a conceptual triad" of space based on the interrelated history of production and commodification:

> *Spatial practice*, which embraces production and reproduction, and the particular locations and spatial sets characteristic of each social formation. . . . *Representations of space*, which are tied to the relations of production and to the "order" which those relations impose, and hence to knowledge, to signs, to codes, and to "frontal" relations. . . . [and] *Representational spaces*, embodying complex symbolisms, sometimes coded, sometimes not, linked to the clandestine or underground side of social life, as also to art (which may come eventually to be defined less as a code of space than as a code of representational spaces). (33)

Especially relevant to this study is Lefebvre's evocation of representational spaces, according to which art (including, one assumes, literature) can be seen primarily as "a code of representational spaces." Language is central to Lefebvre's ideas about how space is produced: "Perhaps what have to be uncovered are as-yet concealed relations between space and language: perhaps the 'logicalness' intrinsic to articulated language operated from the start as a spatiality capable of bringing order to the qualitative chaos (the practico-sensory realm) presented by the perception of things" (17). In effect, Lefebvre proposes a complex interaction of language and space: language creates space, which in turn influences language. In this context, he summarizes his triad as being "the perceived, the conceived, and the lived" (39).

As he was with Redding, Foucault is an influence on Lefebvre. *The Production of Space* emphasizes the importance of power and knowledge in defining "mental" and "social" spaces; and, rooted as it is in Marxism, Lefebvre's study emphasizes capitalism's control over both power and knowledge. Violence, Lefebvre argues, is an integral aspect of what he calls the "abstract space" of capitalist domination:

> The violence involved does not stem from some force intervening aside from rationality, outside or beyond it. Rather, it manifests itself from the moment any action introduces the rational into the real, from the outside, by means of tools which strike, slice and cut—and keep doing so until the purpose of their aggression is achieved. For space is also instrumental—indeed it is the most general of tools. The space of the countryside, as contemplated by the walker in search of the natural, was the outcome of a first violation of nature. (289)

This vision of the violence of "abstract" capitalist space is obviously relevant to the history of European and American imperialism as well as to the process through which certain groups in society are marginalized. In this context, Lefebvre discusses the relationship between "vertical" and "horizontal" space: "By and large . . . horizontal space symbolizes submission [and] vertical space power" (236).

Building on Lefebvre, Edward W. Soja, in a 1996 study, posits the existence of an affirming "thirdspace" in American urban spaces. Soja says that he hopes to "re-describe and help clarify what . . . Lefebvre was writing about in the thematic 'Plan' of *The Production of Space*": "a trialectics of spatiality, of spatial thinking, of the spatial imagination that echoes from

Lefebvre's interweaving incantation of three different kinds of spaces: the *perceived* space of materialized Spatial Practice; the *conceived* space he defined as Representations of Space; and the *lived* Spaces of Representation" (10). Soja then proceeds to reenvision and redefine Lefebvre's three essential spatial forms. He labels "the concrete materiality of spatial forms . . . things that can be empirically mapped" as "firstspace" and "ideas about space . . . thoughtful re-presentations of human spatiality in mental or cognitive terms" as "secondspace." He moves then to his central thesis of "thirdspace":

> In the late 1960s . . . an-Other form of spatial awareness began to emerge. I have chosen to call this new awareness Thirdspace and to initiate its evolving definition by describing it as a product of a "thirding" of the spatial imagination, the creation of another mode of thinking about space that draws upon the material and mental spaces of the traditional dualism but extends well beyond them in scope, substance, and meaning. Simultaneously real and imagined, and more (both and also . . .), the exploration of Thirdspace can be described and inscribed in journeys to "real-and-imagined" (or perhaps "realandimagined"?) places. (10–11)

Soja's vision of thirdspace as "realandimagined" grows out of Lefebvre's concept of representational spaces "embodying complex symbolisms" and linked to art. It clearly extends the concept of space beyond the physical and the mental to the metaphoric. In addition to Lefebvre's text, a central inspiration for Soja's thirdspace is Borges's short story "The Aleph."

Soja believes that thirdspace is most easily found at the borders of urban cultures, and he seems to be envisioning borders in a fairly broad sense—for example, borders of neighborhoods, borders between races and genders, borders between heterosexuality and homosexuality. His argument posits that whatever is least fixed and least ordered is most likely to germinate the new and the affirmative. Certainly, thirdspace, in his argument, seems to imply the potential for the emergence of the redemptive and the revitalizing. Ted Clontz writes:

> With his conception of thirdspace, Soja hopes to present a model of thinking that breaks down binary conceptions of subject/object and center/periphery. . . . [I]t offers a way of discussing the status of human identities that captures a "radical subjectivity." . . . With [the con-

cept of radical subjectivity], Soja hopes to allow for a new mode of thinking that transcends the exclusionary and binary oppositions in such a way as to allow for the construction of spaces of resistance, both mental and physical. In these spaces, resistance for the marginalized in their varying incarnations can be constructed, and the various marginalized people(s) can form connections across binary us/other boundaries that allow for new spaces of resistance. (11–12)

Since in the ten texts to be discussed here the "radical" subjectivity of the characters in them has been infiltrated and co-opted either by debased mythologies or by the oppressive elements in the capitalistic culture or in American history or in all of these ways, this study posits a negative extension of Soja's concept of thirdspace that will be called "fourthspace" and will function as its third central organizing principle. Fourthspace assumes the existence of Soja's firstspace, secondspace, and thirdspace but projects another spatial dimension in which the liberation inherent in thirdspace has been co-opted and is no longer possible.

With one memorable exception, the characters in the ten texts examined here find no opportunities for (re)definition, for personal (re)creation in their existences on the borders of the cultural mainstream. Ironically, the male characters in Ellis's *American Psycho*, who live at the heart of capitalist power and thus realize no need for creative (re)definition, are in many ways the most culturally co-opted of all the characters in the ten novels. Living a dehumanizing existence based on commodification of the social Other, they nevertheless think they are liberated beings, in essence that they are the masters of the only universe they can see.

Systemic violence, depicted sometimes as the inevitable consequence of a male-dominated capitalism and sometimes as the expression of degraded mythologies, contributes to the varied forms of fourthspace found in these novels. Again with one exception, the margins, whether physical, mental, social, or cultural, offer no escape, no affirmation, no hope of redemption. These texts reflect, then, a level of pessimism that goes even beyond that customarily associated with literary naturalism. Whereas traditional naturalistic fiction presents a world so determined by external forces that no escape from them is conceivable, these contemporary texts, after positing the existence of a wide variety of marginal spaces, proceed to delineate these spaces as permeated by violence. In these novels, violence is a menacing force tied to excess, existing at the margins of physical, mental, and social space threatening to erupt in the "real worlds" of the text and transform these worlds into grotesque, surreal spaces. Sometimes in these texts violence becomes so excessive, so pervasive, as to become, in itself, a space that annihilates physical, mental, and social spaces. Thus a promise of redemption can be found in only one of the novels to be discussed here. The mythological dimensions in them are inherently repressive; ritual violence leads to repression, not transcendence.

In fact, Borges's vision of the Aleph fits, in some crucial ways, more comfortably with the concept of a negative fourthspace than with Soja's affirmative thirdspace. It is true that the discoverer of the Aleph in Borges's story, Carlos Argentino, describes it as something that, because it contains infinity and thus all possibility, is inherently redemptive; Argentino is enraptured with the potential for perpetual renewal that it represents: "If all the places of the world are within the Aleph, there too will be all stars, all lamps, all sources of light" (127). But as is customary for Borges, the narrative structure of "The Aleph" is modeled on the image of a labyrinth, with the result that the story's thematic implications are labyrinthine as well, perpetually receding from the reader's grasp. "Borges," the narrator of the tale, admits first to disliking Argentino, then to viewing him as a madman, and finally to being intensely jealous of him. When "Borges" views the Aleph he also perceives it as containing infinite possibility and all imaginable space and experience, but in sharp contrast to Argentino, he places at least equal emphasis on the negative as well as the positive aspects of his vision. He, for instance, sees "a woman in Inverness whom I shall never forget, saw her violent hair, her haughty body, saw a cancer in her breast" (130). In the story's conclusion, "Borges" rejects Argentino's vision as a "*false* Aleph" and postulates another Aleph, one that he has only read about, as the authentic container of infinity. The reader cannot determine if this rejection is an honest one on the narrator's part or merely a result of dislike and jealousy for a rival.

Soja's reading of "The Aleph," as informative and vital as it is to this study, is a limited one. To develop his vision of an affirmative and redemptive thirdspace, Soja largely accepts Argentino's Aleph as the "real" one; in effect, he focuses on the striking external appearance of the unforgettable woman in Inverness while ignoring "the cancer in her breast." The cancer will inevitably corrupt and doom her beauty—death is certainly one of the limitless possibilities of Borges's Aleph and, in fact, the one he stresses at the story's conclusion. The cancer within, the deadly reality lurking within a potential or only apparent image of redemption, is an appropriate metaphor for fourth-space.

Girard's vision of a sacred violence emerged from his study of cultures in which the power of purifying rituals was controlled by males (the rituals were generally conducted by male "priests"), and the phallocentric nature of modern capitalism has been discussed by Lefebvre, Jacques Lacan, Julia Kristeva, and others. It is appropriate, then, that a constant in the ten novels discussed here is a focus on masculine violence, either in ritualized forms or in random, isolated occurrences. In McCarthy's two Appalachian narratives and in the small-town novels of Banks, Nordan, and Allison, regional xeno-phobia adds a dimension to the repressive fourthspace that they explore, with racism a contributing factor in *Wolf Whistle*. On the extra-geographic level, violence relates to space in the ten novels in essentially two ways: first, through Bataille's kind of excess, it sometimes emerges as a space in itself that transcends the physical spaces described in the texts; second, at a less extreme level, violence contaminates implied thirdspace, severely limiting its potential for new freedom and liberation, and thus produces co-opted fourthspaces.

2

Discovering Fourthspace in Appalachia

Cormac McCarthy's *Outer Dark* and *Child of God*

Few American novelists have so thoroughly explored the various and complex ramifications of violence as Cormac McCarthy. Sustained critical attention was late in coming to McCarthy, and, especially in recent years, it has focused on his western novels: the anti-Western *Blood Meridian; or, The Evening Redness in the West* (1985) and the Border trilogy, *All the Pretty Horses* (1992), *The Crossing* (1994), and *Cities of the Plain* (1998). Certainly this attention is deserved. No text so thoroughly deconstructs the myth of a heroic American West as *Blood Meridian,* with its constantly accelerating body count; it demonstrates that Anglo domination of the North American continent was made possible by illiterate and violent men acting outside any established legal system. Thus the subtitle with its implication of a frontier that, even while vanishing, leaves behind its blood-soaked legacy. The Border trilogy—especially the first two volumes, *All the Pretty Horses* and *The Crossing*—represents a much more lyrical and forgiving modernist evocation of the frontier myth. *All the Pretty Horses* first brought McCarthy significant popular recognition and thereby inspired the re-publication of his neglected earlier novels.

In these texts, all set in Tennessee or in some less identifiable realm of Appalachia, McCarthy had been exploring the phenomenon of violence for two decades. The ambitious *Suttree* (1979) is set in a relatively contemporary Knoxville and is largely realistic in narrative approach. In contrast, *Outer Dark* (1968), while unmistakably set in rural Appalachia, seems to transcend precise definitions of space or time. While the setting of *Child of God* (1973) is identified as Sevier County, Tennessee, sometime around the mid-twentieth century, the text evokes a comparable sense of unreality. What

Vereen M. Bell says about *Outer Dark* is, to some degree, true of both novels: "The topography is vague, dreamlike, and surreal in a way that imposes an unwholesome, deranged aspect upon the entire scene" (33). In both texts, physical and social space are, at times, obliterated. While both short novels explore a desperation born of degrading poverty and stultifying ignorance, and can thus be seen as exposés of the disabling effects of systemic oppression, this is nevertheless only one of the levels on which the two texts are intended to function.

The elusive nature of space in the two texts is witnessed in three perceptive but contrasting critical discussions. In *Cormac McCarthy*, Robert L. Jarrett discusses the problems in attempting to approach the fictional landscape in McCarthy's Appalachian novels from familiar historical and literary sources. He notes that, in sharp contrast to the fiction of William Faulkner, a writer with whom McCarthy is often compared, McCarthy's novels, and especially *Outer Dark*, seem almost untouched by nineteenth-century southern history, specifically by "the antebellum South, the Confederacy, and Reconstruction." If there were a single identifiable county in McCarthy's Appalachia, it would defy the talents of any mapmaker. While McCarthy does not completely ignore race, it is far from being the overwhelming issue that it is in Faulkner's Yoknapatawpha County (Jarrett 24–25). In part, Jarrett attributes the seeming absence of history in McCarthy's fictional landscape to Appalachia's geographical and cultural isolation from the rest of the South; because slavery was never profitable in eastern Tennessee, he points out, the plantation system never flourished there. In addition, Appalachia has historically existed in political isolation from the rest of the South (24–27).

Brian Evenson and Gary M. Ciuba approach McCarthy's world from considerably more abstract critical perspectives. Evenson discusses the central characters in both the Appalachian and the western novels in a poststructuralist context defined by Gilles Deleuze and Felix Guattari in their analysis of "nomadology in *A Thousand Plateaus*" (Evenson 42). Dividing McCarthy's protagonists into two categories, "wanderers" and "nomads," Evenson places the three dark, murderous outlaws from *Outer Dark* and Lester Ballard from *Child of God* in the second category. Citing Deleuze and Guattari, Evenson writes that the defining characteristic of the nomad is a search for "smooth spaces," that is, open spaces free from limiting, regulating forces: "Such a topography can be actual or it can be the metaphorical equivalent: a moral or ethical open ground. The nomad's existence is a series of movements which explore the limitless, open possibilities of the smooth space" (42). McCarthy's complex aesthetic in *Outer Dark* and *Child of God* projects landscapes or spaces that fuse the "actual," the "metaphorical," *and* the "psychological" to create something that is simultaneously all of these and none of them.

This imagined landscape can perhaps be described as a kind of fourth-space, existing in a dimension somewhat similar to, but ultimately extremely unlike, Edward W. Soja's thirdspace. The fourthspace that distinguishes the world of *Outer Dark* and *Child of God* merges the material, the metaphoric or linguistic, and the psychological or subconscious, and only the darkest forms of freedom, the most horrific possibilities, result from the merger. Ultimately, nothing is transcended in McCarthy; no one is given the opportunity to explore spiritually affirming "borders" of existence.

The three grim outlaws of *Outer Dark* and the necrophilic murderer Lester Ballard act in a perverted realm of "smooth space." They perform acts of evil characterized by sheer excess, and McCarthy's two novels are, in part, explorations of such excess. On this level, they can usefully be read in the context of comments by Georges Bataille on work, reason, excess, and violence. Bataille posits an inherent duality in human beings that he defines through the binaries of work, a realm dominated by reason and secured through taboos, and excess, a realm of violent transgression of taboo: "One cannot fail to observe mankind's double nature throughout its career. There are two extremes. At one end, existence is basically orderly and decent. Work, concern for the children, kindness and honesty rule men's [the gender-specific language is in this case appropriate] dealings with their fellows. At the other, violence rages pitilessly. In certain circumstances the same men practise pillage and arson, murder, violence and torture. Excess contrasts with reason" (186).

McCarthy's fiction has always been focused on the second half of this duality; the excessive violence that dominates his fiction is thus an essential element in his aesthetic. The characters who inhabit the worlds of *Outer Dark* and *Child of God* are either exiles from the realm of work and reason or nomadic wanderers who have never even known it. The kind of "smooth space" they explore exists on several levels, all distinguished by the kind of extreme freedom that Bataille associates with excess; the violence in McCarthy's fiction must be senseless, is often unmotivated, and above all is supremely irrational.

McCarthy's art is thus intended to disturb by revealing a world from which the protective taboos that characterize what Bataille identifies as the realm of work have been torn away. For Bataille, this kind of intentionally disturbing art is essential for revealing the full dimension of human beings, for probing into a level of the natural so extreme that it may become unnatural: "Man has built up the rational world by his own efforts, but there remains within him an undercurrent of violence. Nature herself is violent, and however reasonable we may grow we may be mastered anew by a violence no longer that of nature but of a rational being who tries to obey but who succumbs to stirrings within himself that he cannot bring to heel" (40).

In this context, excess is an essential human characteristic, and one with which artists have long been fascinated. At times McCarthy's nomads seem almost bloodless embodiments of such excess, and as Evenson points out, they are inevitably at war with "civilized" human spaces. When they encounter a settled space, violence inevitably results; the nomad's quest for smooth space can only be pursued outside the boundaries of settlements. Evenson argues that McCarthy's ability to dramatize the violent confrontations of nomads with settled spaces is "precisely the appeal of McCarthy's greatest fictions" (43).

In an essay that should be read in conjunction with Evenson's (both are included in a collection of McCarthy criticism entitled *Sacred Violence*), Ciuba interprets *Child of God* through René Girard's theories concerning violence and sacrifice. In this context, he provides an interpretation of the relationship between the title of the novel and its protagonist, the murderous Lester Ballard:

> Lester Ballard is the child of an ancient tradition of sacred violence. René Girard contends that the sacred of primitive religion rose out of the salutary transcendence of violence by violence. At the founding moment of culture, humankind overcame internecine strife by focusing its mutual hostilities on slaying one of its own. The violence that once threatened to destroy the community became the violence that graciously delivered it. . . . Since the sacrifice transformed an accursed outcast into the redeemer of a fractious community, the godhead assumed both the maleficent and beneficent aspects of violence. The transgressor became the savior; the most heinous was also the Child of God. (77–78)

Thus, Lester Ballard becomes both sacrifice and sacrificer in an Appalachian community historically defined by violent injustice and oppression. It is as if a plague has been let loose upon the land, and Lester redeems it through the excess of his own transgressions. "Like some violent voluptuary in the religion of Georges Bataille," writes Ciuba, "he makes transgression the very sign of its transcendence" (78). Girard offers a further gloss on this paradoxical concept: "From the purely religious point of view, the surrogate victim . . . inevitably appears as a being who submits to violence without provoking a reprisal; a supernatural being who sows violence to reap peace; a mysterious savior who visits affliction on mankind in order subsequently to restore it to good health" (86).

Lester does not perfectly fit Girard's description. He submits to his initial displacement from the community only after he is knocked unconscious and forcibly removed from what was first his father's and then his own farm while it and the things on it are being auctioned off. Thus Lester's victimization is, to some degree, systemic; he is the product of decades of poverty and ignorance. Moreover, he exists in a world in which religious faith, to the degree that it exists at all, has been debased to a malevolent doctrine offering no genuine redemptive promise. While his crimes are certainly excessive in nature and execution, no one in the communal world of the novel would view him as a supernatural being. The sheer savagery of his acts serves to reinforce his undeniable humanness. He embodies the violent side of Bataille's concept of human duality; certainly work is as foreign to his being as excess is natural to it.

After he is forced off his farm, Lester gradually evolves into a representative of Evenson's nomad, living on the edge of cultivated space. In the course of the novel he is transformed from a communal outcast to a mysterious nomadic presence that periodically assaults the settlement. In an early scene, he is falsely accused of rape and, while being interrogated in the sheriff's office, pronounces what amounts to his judgment on the community: "you sons of bitches. . . . Goddamn all of ye" (52). Periodically the novel shifts into a communal narrative voice, which at one point summarizes the disgraceful history of the Ballard family, concluding on a note of perverse pride: "I'll say one thing about Lester though. You can trace em back to Adam if you want and goddamn if he don't outstrip em all" (81). It is significant that this judgment ties Lester's origins firmly to the first *human* sinner rather than seeking a supernatural explanation for his actions. In distinct contrast, the "grim triune" from *Outer Dark,* while always appearing in human form, seems something other than human.

Even more than *Child of God*—in fact, more than any other McCarthy novels—*Outer Dark* seems to take place in some ambiguous physical-social space devoid of history.[1] In part, this almost surreal setting can be understood as exemplifying Jarrett's description of Appalachia as a space on the periphery of the South and its history and traditions. In the opening of the novel, its two central characters, Culla and Rinthy Holme, brother and sister, are so isolated as to barely know that any larger community exists. This isolation is, moreover, not strictly spatial; Culla and Rinthy are victimized by a profound ignorance that is not simply a matter of literacy. It is as if they have somehow been untouched by any sustaining cultural values or accepted social customs. At one point Rinthy says, "They ain't a soul in this world but what is a stranger to me" (29). The brother and sister appear parentless and, except for each other, cut off from any family; the only reference to their background comes when Rinthy tells a family that takes her in and feeds her, "I bet I ain't eat two pones of lightbread in my life. I was raised hard" (60). Certainly, she seems never to have known anything approximating kindness or gentleness.

On one metaphoric level, Culla and Rinthy are re-creations of Adam and Eve, doomed to commit anew the unpardonable sin that threatens to exile them from human or divine mercy, to make them wanderers through a grotesquely fallen world. Thus their last name is cruelly ironic—they have never really known anything approximating "home" or even a safe space. Isolated from virtually everyone else, they almost doom each other. Before the novel opens, they have committed incest; the reader is introduced to them as the baby is about to be born. Culla delivers the baby himself after refusing to go in search of a midwife, since he wants to keep their sin secret. After delivering the child, he makes an ominous prophecy: "I don't look for it to live" (15).

Culla does not kill the child, though. Instead, he takes the infant and leaves it to die in some neighboring woods. McCarthy's description of Culla's misfortunes while carrying out his secret and desperate mission is, one assumes, deliberately excessive. After Culla stumbles and falls to the ground, he "lay there with his cheek to the earth. And as he lay there a far crack of lightning went bluely down the sky and bequeathed him an embryonic bird's first fissured vision of the world and transpiring instant and outrageous from dark to dark a final view of the grotto and the shapeless white plasm struggling upon the rich and incunabular moss like a lank swamp hare" (17).

While this kind of McCarthy prose has been condemned as excessive and imitative of Faulkner, in this case it serves a legitimate purpose. The quick shift to the "fissured vision" of the "embryonic bird" evokes a timeless, primal space underlying the mimetic Appalachian setting. Incest (however it is defined) is, of course, one of the oldest of human taboos, Girard believes, because, like murder, it assaults communal order in the most profound of ways. By destroying culturally accepted distinctions, it bequeaths chaos: "Incestuous propagation leads to formless duplications, sinister repetitions, a dark mixture of unnamable things" (Girard 75). Carrying his child, the result of "incestuous propagation," Culla has ventured into this "dark mixture of unnamable things" as much as, if not more than, he has entered forested material space. McCarthy seems to have emphasized Culla and Rinthy's cultural and social isolation partly in order to emphasize the extreme and primal nature of their resultant guilt.

Culla compounds his guilt by telling Rinthy that the baby is dead. When she demands to see where it is buried, he takes her into the woods where he has left the infant. Once there, they discover that the infant has been taken, either alive or dead, by a tinker who had intruded upon their isolation and tried to sell Culla a book of amateurish pornographic drawings. One remembers folkloric associations of tinkers with Satan, and this tinker seems to possess supernatural insight into the lives of the isolated brother and sister. The tinker is, in fact, the first of several prophet figures, usually demented to some degree, in the novel. The tinker's theft of the child forces Culla and Rinthy out of their isolated worlds as they separately seek to find the lost child, and McCarthy's linguistic excess merges with the psychological guilt of Culla and the maternal need of Rinthy to produce the debased fourth-space in which the novel takes place.

In their quests, both discover grotesquely fallen worlds, haunted by poverty, ignorance, and sheer malice. Bell describes *Outer Dark* as being "as brutally nihilistic as any serious novel written in this century in this nihilistic country" (34). Refuting Bell, Edwin T. Arnold asserts that a redemptive moral center underlies *Outer Dark* and all of McCarthy's fiction, including *Blood Meridian* with its unrelenting evocations of social, rather than strictly individual, acts of violence: "While I recognize and appreciate the postmodern celebration of McCarthy's exuberant violence, his astonishing approximation of chaos, his grand evocation of the mystery of the world, there is also evident in his work a profound belief in the need for moral order, a conviction that is essentially religious. There is, in addition, always the possibility of grace and redemption even in the darkest of his tales, although that redemption may require more of his characters than they are ultimately willing to give" (46).

Nihilism and something like religious affirmation are at war throughout McCarthy's novel. In this context, it is significant that the space through which Rinthy travels is more conventionally mimetic and more accepting than the dark and deadly landscape Culla encounters. Arnold perceptively analyzes Culla's descent into something that seems a great deal like both Christian and Sartrean imaginings of hell as resulting from a failure of courage, an attempt to flee from sin. That Culla's journey is at least as much a psychological and a spiritual experience as an actual exploration of mimetic space is foreshadowed by a horrific nightmare that opens the novel and haunts him for the remainder of the text:

> There was a prophet standing in the square with arms upheld in exhortation to the beggared multitude gathered there. A delegation of human ruin who attended him with blind eyes upturned and puckered stumps and leprous sores. . . . It grew cold and more black and silent and some began to cry out and some despaired but the sun did not return. Now the dreamer grew fearful. Voices were being raised against him. He was caught up in the crowd and the stink of their rags filled his nostrils. They grew seething and more mutinous and he tried to hide among them but they knew him even in that pit of hopeless dark and fell upon him with howls of outrage. (6)

Now Culla has been transformed into something closer to a Cain than an Adam figure. He has been banished and set apart from the rest of humanity. This introductory nightmare functions as a metaphoric introduction of the remainder of the novel. The pornography-selling tinker was merely the first of the ominous prophets Culla will encounter as he travels among "the beggared multitude." To some degree, the emphasis on the stinking "rags" of "the human ruin" evokes the more real or mimetic landscape of soul-killing poverty through which he will travel. It also alludes to the sinfulness and viciousness in which Culla finds human beings clothed and to his own sin, already that of incest and soon to be of child abandonment as well. Like Hawthorne's Young Goodman Brown, Culla undertakes a journey in which physical space, psychological guilt, and spiritual despair merge so completely as to become indistinguishable.

Shortly after the scenes of birth and abandonment, the novel depicts an incident that reoccurs in different forms throughout McCarthy's fiction. On a Sunday, Culla goes to the nearest store to buy some food for the weakened Rinthy. Inevitably he finds the store closed and hears a voice calling down at him "from an upper window": "We still christians here" (26). As indicated by the deliberate withholding of the uppercase C from "christians," the scene constitutes, on one level, condemnation of a southern Christian fundamentalism that denies support to those who exist outside it. Such "faith," McCarthy seems to imply, is divorced from any meaningful association with Christ; it merely looks down on and condemns those in physical or spiritual need. In this and comparable McCarthy scenes, God seems not so much absent as harsh and vindictive, as if looking down from an elevated space upon a desperately flawed humanity. Still, the most severe judgment on Culla comes from within; he believes that he has so violated established rules of human behavior as to stand in judgment outside the possibility of forgiveness. Most of all, it is Culla who withholds forgiveness from Culla.[2]

Once Culla undertakes his search for the stolen child, comparable judgments meet him at every turn.[3] Sometimes they seem innocent enough on the surface, as when a "squire" for whom he briefly works lectures him that "I hope you've not got a family. It's a sacred thing, a family. A sacred obligation" (47). Inevitably, Culla hears this pronouncement in the context of his sins of incest and child abandonment and cannot deny that he has, in fact, violated "a sacred obligation." Here as elsewhere in the text, outsiders—some of whom, like the squire, look down upon him from perspectives of social class or legal power—are, in some mysterious way, aware of his transgressions. Such judges exist on two levels, that of mimesis and psychological projection. The squire is a representative of class and economic superiority, of what Henri Lefebvre describes as the "power" of vertical space and the "submission" of horizontal space, as is made manifest in the squire's initial meeting with Culla in which the squire looks at the desperate young man "as he would anything for sale" (42). The squire's dominant position in the socioeconomic hierarchy is based on the power to objectify others, to treat them as commodities that can be used and then discarded. His power is transitory, however, as he ultimately runs into the three nomadic killers who coldly and senselessly murder him. But he is also an emblematic figure who embodies Culla's self-condemnation.

After the doomed squire, the next "judge" Culla encounters is an old man from whom he begs a drink of water. Twice, the old man tells Culla that he "wouldn't turn Satan away for a drink" (117). Like the squire, the old man appears to possess some mysterious knowledge of the primal nature of Culla's sins. Moreover, he turns out to be a snake hunter given to telling grotesque stories about victims of snakebite, and inside his cabin he has the skin of a monstrous rattlesnake tacked above his fireplace: "He was eight foot seven inches and had seventeen rattles. Big in the middle to where ye couldn't get your hands around him" (122). The scene recalls traditional associations of serpents with death and evil ranging from Genesis to Satan's magical staff in "Young Goodman Brown"; on a Freudian level, the phallic overtones of the monstrous snake recall Culla's intercourse with Rinthy. Later a man who has lost his entire family to cholera charges Culla with being a plague carrier, to which Culla responds not at all honestly, "Ain't nobody plagued" (138). Like that of Oedipus, Culla's incest seems to have let loose a plague on the countryside. One also recalls Camus's division in *The Plague* of human beings into the categories of plague carriers and plague fighters.

Near the end of the novel, Culla comes close to being executed in a black comic "(mis)reading" of an incident recounted in the New Testament book of Mark. He abruptly finds himself in the midst of a herd of hogs driven by men "gaunt and fever-eyed with incredible rag costumes and wild hair" (213). After some wildly absurd discussion between Culla and one of the drovers about "unclean" hogs, split hooves, and Jews ("What's a jew? That's one of them old-timey people from in the bible"), the drover concludes: "A hog is a hog. Pure and simple. And that's about all ye can say about him. And smart, don't think they ain't. Smart as the devil. And don't be fooled by one that ain't got nairy clove foot cause he's devilish too." Culla can only concur with such immaculate logic: "I guess hogs is hogs" (216). This exchange is a reminder of what the bleak central vision of *Outer Dark* can lead the reader to forget—there is wonderful black comedy in the novel, most of which has roots in southern and old southwestern folklore.

The mood of the scene quickly takes a more serious turn when the hogs inexplicably begin stampeding off the edge of a cliff into a river and the desperate drovers are transformed into beings barely recognizable as human: "[The swineherds] had begun to assume satanic looks with their staves and wild eyes as if they were . . . disciples of darkness got among these charges to herd them to their doom" (218). In the stampede, the younger brother of the drover with whom Culla had been talking is driven over the cliff to his death in the river below. Nevertheless, the scene undergoes another daring mood shift when Culla resumes conversation with the surviving drovers:

[One of the drovers]: That beats everything I ever seen.

[Culla]: That's pitiful about your brother.

[The drover]: I don't know what all I'm goin to tell mama. Herded off
a bluff with a parcel of hogs. I don't know how I'm going to tell her
that.

[Culla]: You could tell her he was drunk.

[The drover]: Tell her he got shot or somethin.

[Culla]: You wouldn't need to tell her he went to his reward with a herd
of hogs. (219)

Given the brutish behavior of most of the characters in the landscape
through which Culla travels, McCarthy seems to be saying that, should anyone somehow manage to receive "his reward," he will do so in the company
of a herd of hoggish human beings. It is not insignificant that Culla and the
drovers both assume that their mother would find lies about the deceased
man dying drunk or as a result of human violence more acceptable than the
truth.

In the biblical text that McCarthy is intentionally "(mis)reading" (Mark
5:1–17), a man with an "unclean spirit" whose "name is Legion; for we are
many" asks Christ to save him. In response, Christ sends the legion of "de-
mons" out of the man and into a herd of two thousand swine, who then rush
off "a steep place into the sea" and drown. Frightened by such power, those
who have witnessed the miracle promptly beg Christ to leave the region. The
savior is immediately rejected and symbolically banished. In this context, it
is not surprising that, with no evidence whatsoever, the surviving drovers
decide that Culla mysteriously caused the hogs to stampede, and another of
Culla's "judges," fittingly in this context the most deranged of all, abruptly
enters the text: "A parson or what looked like one was laboring over the crest
of the hill and coming toward them with one hand raised in blessing, greet-
ing, fending flies. He was dressed in a dusty frockcoat and carried a walking
stick and he wore a pair of octagonal glasses on the one pane of which the
late sun shone while a watery eye peered from the naked wire aperture of
the other" (221). McCarthy's absurdist humor continues to be in evidence as
the "parson" almost condemns Culla first to being lynched and then to being
thrown off the cliff into the river with the hogs by asserting that such acts
of retribution would be wrong: "Boys I believe he's plumb eat up with the
devil in him. But don't hang him. . . . Don't flang him off the bluff, boys, the
preacher said. I believe ye'd be better to hang him as that" (223).

After some deliberation, the drovers decide that hanging Culla would be the best course, and the preacher offers to baptize him first. When the outraged Culla refuses such a mode of salvation, the minister comments: "I guess a feller mires up so deep in sin after a while he don't want to hear nothin about grace and salvation. Not even a feller about to be hanged." To this speculation, one of the drovers adds this gloss: "It ain't no use, Reverend. He's too mean to be saved" (225). Of course, in this particular instance Culla is innocent, and not surprisingly, the reverend is later revealed to be a charlatan. Like the early scene at the store, this episode parodies a judgmental religious fundamentalism. Culla is, however, still in flight from the sins that drove him out into the world, and until he acknowledges them he is unworthy of salvation, not because he is "too mean" but because, as Arnold points out, he is too cowardly.

Yet such judges as these, as potentially deadly as they are, pale in comparison with the grim triune whom Culla encounters twice in the novel. The first occasion occurs after Culla has almost been drowned on a ferryboat; in this scene, the rampaging river that swallows up everyone on the ferry but Culla is no bad substitute for the river Styx. It is not then surprising that Culla, after crossing the river of death, encounters the three outlaws. It is in McCarthy's evocation of these three nightmarish figures, who exist on both mimetic and metaphoric levels, that the text's fourthspace is most overtly dramatized. At one point they are described as emerging upon the landscape out of nowhere, "*armed with crude agrarian weapons,* spade and brushhook . . . parodic figures transposed live and intact and violent out of a proletarian mural *and set mobile upon the empty fields, advancing against the twilight*" (35). They are grotesque parodies of the naturalistic figures created by Thomas Hart Benton in his American murals. Now as re-created by McCarthy, they threaten violent assault on an agrarian economic system that exploits and objectifies the small farmers of Appalachia, and thus their cold murder of the squire constitutes, on one level, retaliation against an exploitative social order. Described as coming across a field "attended by a constant circus of grasshoppers" (51) in the scene in which they murder the squire, they seem personifications of some delayed and apocalyptic judgment, this time recalling the plagues unleashed on Egypt in the Old Testament story of the clash between Moses and the pharoah.

On another level, they can also be understood as "psychic avengers," projections of Culla's guilt over his sins of incest and child abandonment.[4] In this context, they demonstrate the degree to which the fourthspace of *Outer*

Dark, in contrast to Soja's concept of a liberating thirdspace resulting from a merger of material space and cerebral recognition of the material, is frightening and restrictive. When Culla stumbles upon their camp, they, like several of the other "judges" in the text, appear to know about his past and recent experiences. Their unnamed leader, for instance, insists three times that Culla is the now drowned ferryman, thereby forcing the young man to deny three times that he is metaphorically the ferryman to hell.[5] While Culla may not correspond to Charon, he did set the progress of his secular damnation in motion through his sinful actions involving the lost child and thus transports himself into an earthly hell. Culla, feeling that he is in the presence of some not-quite-human force, tries to look into the eyes of the leader with unsettling results: "In the upslant of light [the leader's] beard shone and his mouth was red, and his eyes were shadowed lunettes with nothing there at all" (171).

In a preview of the novel's denouement, the satanic presence then insists that Culla partake of some almost inedible and never identified meat that the trio is cooking. Subsequently an ominous discussion of names ensues. Indicating one of the other two men, the leader and spokesman of the deadly trio says: "That'n ain't got a name. . . . He wanted me to give him one but I wouldn't do it. He don't need nary. You ever seen a man with no name afore?" (174).[6] The leader is identifying himself as the namegiver who possesses the power to withhold or bestow identity upon others and has thus assumed Culla's role as an Adam figure. He then proceeds to tease Culla with the mystery of his own name: "I expect they's lots would like to know that" (173–74). In part, the leader is playing a role derived from such popular-culture genres as the Western of the unnamed and thus doubly terrifying villain. More significantly, he is identifying himself with some force too powerful to be named, an Old Testament god of vengeance.[7]

With Culla and his transgressions clearly in mind, the leader next observes that "some things is best not named." Because it so threatens the social order, incest has traditionally been a sin too fundamentally unsettling to be acknowledged. The reference to things best left unnamed seems intended as a reminder to Culla of the infant he has abandoned and thereby caused to be abducted by the peddler. In this context, he later mocks Culla in a speech that appears to refer to his nameless companion but actually seems intended to evoke the child: "I wouldn't name him because if you cain't name somethin you cain't claim it. You cain't talk about it even. You cain't say what it is"

(177). The words are apparently a reminder to Culla that he has forfeited any right to the child, and they also reveal an awareness that the young man's concern for the lost infant is pretended. Certainly in contrast to Rinthy's, Culla's search is, at best, half hearted. Reinforcing his satanic role, the leader comments, "I like to keep the fire up. . . . They might be somebody coming" (175). He is thus identifying himself as the guardian of the fires of hell, as the enforcer of eternal punishment, perpetually on the lookout for sinners like Culla.

The multileveled nature of the trio's identity becomes manifest in this scene. On a strictly mimetic level, they are a savage gang of roving outlaws who assault the community out of sheer malevolence. But the several metaphoric levels on which they exist are more important. They are simultaneously "proletarian" warriors and agents of a vengeful god. In this context, it is significant that they execute the peddler after taking the infant from him. Their chosen mode of execution is lynching, an act that evokes the history of southern violence and injustice as well as the fate that Culla almost experiences at the hands of the charlatan minister and the simple-minded drovers. Moreover, they are projections of Culla's subconscious guilt, representatives of his sin and self-condemnation, a self-judgment that, as Arnold observes, he is too cowardly to acknowledge publicly. But they also embody a capacity for excessive evil that places them outside human comprehension. It is as if they are committed to violating all behavioral taboos, as if they are engaged in a prolonged assault on the order that is essential to preserving human community. Besides the several horrendous murders of which they are guilty, they unearth the dead, stealing the clothes of corpses and leaving them in positions that mock homosexual embrace. Girard points out that social taboos emerge out of a need to maintain order and that the ultimate threat to such order is death. Through their grave-robbing, the grim triune make this threat overt. It is hardly irrelevant that Culla is accused of the violation of the corpses, since in the course of the novel he is accused of virtually everything else. He has, in fact, violated those taboos that the three outlaws, existing outside any communal structure that includes women, have no opportunity to violate.

The full metaphoric role of the trio is not revealed until their last, climactic encounter with Culla. When he comes upon them this time, the child, now hideously disfigured, is with them: "It had a healed burn all down one side of it and the skin was papery and wrinkled like an old man's. It was naked and half coated with dust so that it seemed lightly furred and when it turned to look up at him [Culla] . . . saw one eyeless and angry red socket like a stokehole to a brain in flames" (231).

Perhaps not fully human themselves, the three have dehumanized the child, transforming it into something monstrous. Moreover, the leader continues the harsh questioning of Culla that he began in the earlier scene, again seeming possessed of some kind of supernatural insight. He knows, for instance, that the tinker stole a child from Culla and asserts that the child was Culla's as the result of an incestuous act. Twice, in what Arnold sees as the young man's culminating moment of cowardice, Culla denies the accusation and any responsibility for the child: "He ain't nothin to me" (235).

Subsequently, in an action that echoes Girard's description of the ritual sacrifice of the scapegoat in *Violence and the Sacred,* the leader holds the mutilated child over a burning fire and slits its throat with a knife. In committing incest, Culla violated one of the most basic of cultural taboos and thus instigated a sacrificial crisis that profoundly threatens the social order. As Girard explains, the sacrifice of an innocent is necessary to restore the order that Culla's acts of incest and child abandonment have endangered. Girard further specifies that, in order to prevent a destructive cycle of retributive violence, the victim should be powerless, with no ties to the individual whose violations of taboo have brought on the crisis. Above all, such cyclical violence is to be avoided:

> Vengeance professes to be an act of reprisal, and every reprisal calls for another reprisal. The crime to which the vengeance addresses itself is never an unprecedented offense; in almost every case it has been committed in revenge for some prior crime. Vengeance, then, is an interminable, infinitely repetitive process. Every time it turns up in some part of the community, it threatens to involve the whole social body. There is the risk that the act of vengeance will initiate a chain reaction whose consequences will quickly prove fatal to any society of modest size. The multiplication of reprisals instantaneously puts the very existence of society in jeopardy, and that is why it is universally proscribed. (14–15)

The leader's sacrifice of the unnamed child both clarifies and complicates the role of the grim triune as agents of retribution. Obviously, the infant, the very product of Culla's sin, is not an arbitrarily chosen victim with no connection to the original violation of taboo. It could, though, hardly be more powerless, since it has been abandoned and remains nameless. The leader slits its throat only after Culla again denies responsibility for it. In the several brutal murders they commit, the triune seem to be agents of retributive vengeance, punishers of unnamed crimes, devoted above all to putting the communal order at risk. An example of McCarthy's calculated narrative excess is evident in the remainder of this grim scene: "The child made no sound. It hung there with its one eye glazing over like a wet stone and the black blood pumping down its naked belly. The mute one knelt forward. He was drooling and making little whimpering noises in his throat. He knelt with his hands outstretched and his nostrils rimpled delicately. [The leader] handed him the child and he seized it up, looked once at Holme with witness eyes, and buried his moaning face in its throat" (236).

The mute one is the one from whom the leader has withheld a name, just as Culla has left his own child nameless. Now as punishment he is forced to witness its bloody sacrifice. The child, however monstrous it has become in the hands of the three, remains an innocent, and the mute's act of drinking its blood is a parody of Christian communion. Any doubt the reader might have that the strange meat which Culla was forced to eat in his earlier encounter with the trio was human flesh is now removed. Unwilling to confront his guilt, he has nevertheless been forced to partake of "the body" and, fully unrepentant, he can hardly chew it. All of this is not, of course, an endorsement of cannibalism. It represents McCarthy's vision that human beings are god, and god is human beings. The excess in this scene seems intended as testimony that any human action one can imagine, however diabolical, has almost certainly been already committed. In this context, it is perhaps worthwhile to see McCarthy as a post-Holocaust writer, since the Nazis exceeded any previously known boundaries of evil and thus threatened to make the word itself meaningless. Nevertheless, as the largely benevolent experiences of Rinthy, who is searching for her lost child and trying to negate Culla's sin, indicate, god's grace has not vanished from the world.

In one scene, the denuded and grotesquely arranged corpses that the triune has unearthed are brought into a town on the back of a wagon. Seeing them, an unidentified man says to Culla: "I hate knowin they is such people, don't you?" (88). One assumes that he does not mean the grotesquely displayed corpses but rather people who could do such things to the dead. One aspect of McCarthy's aesthetic is a determination to force upon the reader the awareness that, in fact, such people exist in the world. But in the context of the novel's fourthspace, actions like the triune's murders take on added di-

mensions. In part, they personify Culla's willingness to commit incest, abandon his child, and then repeatedly deny that the child is his, as well as
embodying Culla's self-condemnation for such actions. Excess in style and
details of plot are essential parts of the linguistic dimension of the text's
fourthspace. They contribute to its merger of a grotesquely detailed mimesis,
its metaphoric and sociological implications, and its surrealistic feeling as a
projection of Culla's subconscious. The space Culla enters is more complex
and thus ultimately more inescapable than the forest into which Goodman
Brown ventures. Because they exist completely outside the community (unless they are in fact projections of communal sin and guilt), the grim triune
is only privileged to move freely in an extended smooth space.

Child of God is a more clearly mimetic novel. Its geographical setting is identified as mid-twentieth-century Sevier County, Tennessee, and its fourthspace is thus less complex and—somewhat paradoxically, given the content
of the novel—less intimidating. Culla and the grim triune of *Outer Dark*
coalesce in the figure of Lester Ballard, who, hideous though his actions are,
remains recognizably human throughout the novel. Thus one dimension of
the fourthspace of *Outer Dark* is inevitably absent: Lester as recognizable
human being cannot be a projection of Lester's own subconscious guilt. Psychology, especially abnormal psychology, is a concern of *Child of God*, though
in a subtle manner. As several critics point out, the narration rarely intrudes
on Lester's consciousness; he is seen almost exclusively from a narrative distance, from outside. It is then difficult to know what, if any, degree of guilt
Lester feels as a result of his horrific actions. A severely curtailed psychological dimension is part of the fourthspace of the novel. Mimetic and metaphoric dimensions are extensively developed in the novel.

Evenson sees Lester Ballard as being "a nearly unadulterated nomad" (43).
This definition is appropriate, but it is important not to overlook the factors
that underlie the qualification. Evenson correctly observes that throughout
most of the novel, "Ballard lives absolutely on the fringe, his dependence on
society reduced to a minimum. Like the movie *Badlands, Child of God* por-
trays directionless violence, an amorality which refuses to apologize for itself, which denies judgment" (44). Lester is forced onto "the fringe" by the
suicide of his father and the resulting auction of his home and the false
charge of rape; he makes attempts, however halfhearted and doomed they
may be, to rejoin the community before his final descent into mad and senseless violence; and at the end he voluntarily submits himself to society's judg-

ment. Edwin Arnold points out that "what Lester wants is permanence, even (or especially) the permanence of death, but what he experiences in his life is change in the form of desertion and denial and loss. He expects to be abandoned" (56).

Lester is forced to retreat to society's fringe after the auction because he has literally nowhere else to go; after existing in virtual isolation since his father's suicide, he no longer knows, if he ever did, how to function in human society. He is then almost fated to occupy the kind of smooth space Evenson describes. Imprisoned because of the false charge of rape, Lester meets a black prisoner whose past and future foreshadow Lester's own. The African American's crime, in its sheer excess of brutality, previews the extremes of perversion that Lester will soon explore: he has beheaded a man with a pocketknife. Moreover, he feels no remorse for what he did ("all the trouble I ever was in was caused by gettin caught" [53]), and his self-definition is appropriate for Lester as well: "I'm a fugitive from the ways of the world. I'd be a fugitive from my mind if I had me some snow" (53). Still a kind of innocent at this point, Lester doesn't know anything about "snow" or any other narcotics. But he will soon become a fugitive from his own mind; he will evolve into the very prototype of excess that constitutes the binary opposite of reason in Bataille's paradigm. McCarthy sometimes employs a kind of after-the-fact communal narration to describe Lester, and one early such passage describes a propensity for sudden and frightening acts of violence.

Still, before committing acts that make his exile from the human community complete and irrevocable, Lester makes failed attempts to rejoin at least its outer limits. In fact, he once makes an overture for something approaching mainstream acceptance by abruptly entering a country church, but his presence merely serves to shock the preacher and the congregation, which he inadvertently further outrages: "Ballard had a cold and snuffled loudly through the service but nobody expected he would stop if God himself looked askance so no one looked" (32). Lester is condemned partly because of his family's history of poverty and lawlessness, and in this context he ironically attains a kind of stature in the community by entering its folklore. He is defined as being the most sinful member of two sinful families, the Ballards and the human race; the communal voice concludes a summary of the Ballard family with this: "I'll say one thing about Lester though. You can trace em back to Adam if you want and goddamn if he didn't outstrip them all" (81). This pronouncement is crucial to the judgment the text is making concerning the human capacity for evil—as shocked and disgusted as they are by his actions, the community feels a degree of genuine pride in having produced the sinner of sinners. In Hawthorne's dark forest, Satan tells Young Goodman Brown that "evil is the nature of mankind" and then welcomes the once innocent Puritan to the witches' sabbath, the "communion of your race." The community's pride in Lester's violent assault on the communal order indicates at least that evil is a strong part of human nature.

Not surprisingly, Lester is rejected by women throughout the novel. He attempts a grotesque courtship with a young woman who has a mentally retarded child. Having captured a live robin, he brings it to the child as a present, telling the woman that he has something for her, to which she replies: "You ain't got nothin I want" (77). When the child chews the legs off the living bird, Lester offers an explanation for the disgusting act: "He wanted it to where it couldn't run off" (79). McCarthy may well be venturing too obviously into the territory of William Faulkner and Flannery O'Connor in this scene, yet the episode of the young woman, the ghoulish child, and the robin is relevant to the rest of the text. Beginning with his father's suicide, people have been running away from Lester for some time. Moreover, the rejection by the young woman, as understandable as it is, effectively summarizes the communal response to Lester, who truly has nothing that anyone wants.

Comparable in its evocation of the deliberately repulsive is McCarthy's description of a deranged "dumpkeeper" and his family of nine daughters, each of which is "named out of an old medical dictionary gleaned from the rubbish he picked": "These gangling progeny with black hair hanging from their armpits now sat idle and wide-eyed day after day in chairs and crates about the little yard cleared out of the tips while their harried dam called them one by one to help with chores and one by one they shrugged or blinked with sluggard lids. Urethra, Cerebella, Hernia Sue" (26). Almost inevitably, the dumpkeeper discovers one of the daughters having sex in the woods and, after chasing the unknown young man away, tries to force himself on her. While such Erskine Caldwell–like misogyny and stereotyping of "poor white trash" is objectionable, the scene is thematically relevant to McCarthy's narrative strategy. *Child of God* is devoted to exploring the boundary between the human and the animal, the spiritual and the material, the rational and the excessive. McCarthy is deliberately assaulting the reader; his aesthetic is inherently transgressive in nature. Moreover, the "community" of the dumpkeeper's family, which exists outside any moral or ethical values, is the only one in which Lester is truly welcome; the family represents a transitional stage in Lester's descent into a horrific and multileveled smooth space.

The misogynistic overtones of the textual moments involving the woman, her monstrous child, and the robin and the dumpkeeper and his daughters pale in comparison to what is still to come. From an exile with some yearning still to be a part of the social order, Lester degenerates into a ghoulish figure so consumed by madness as to be scarcely recognizable as human. He becomes a murderer of women who collects the corpses of his victims in order to have sex with them. Moreover, he begins to dress in the clothing of the dead women and wears a literal fright wig "fashioned whole" from the scalp of one of his victims.

Nevertheless, as Edwin Arnold, John Lang, and Dianne C. Luce have argued, McCarthy goes to considerable lengths to prevent readers from misunderstanding Lester as an inhuman monster. Arnold points out that the first third of McCarthy's text is devoted to the stages of Lester's exile from society, and Lang analyzes the ways in which the condemning communal voice ironically creates compassion for Lester. Lang further comments that "ultimately, *Child of God* testifies not to the anomalous outrages committed by Lester Ballard but to the potential of violence inherent in all human beings. Lester's actions are often shocking, but they are not, unfortunately, unique" (94). In describing Lester before he begins his murderous rampage, Luce offers the most perceptive analysis of the role of sexuality in the novel: "Ballard's predicament is dramatized in terms of his human needs not only for a home and shelter but also for sexual contact. Considered peculiar, he finds it nearly impossible to approach the women he knows. They rebuff him not because they are chaste, nor because they are less crude than he, but because he is in some way marked as a pariah. As his parents and the law have dispossessed him of what he considers his by right, so the women he approaches deny him both sexual outlet and intimacy" (125). Of course, dead women cannot reject Lester; nor can they resist whatever he does to them. As Evenson points out, Lester "does not ask, as most of us would, what is the proper thing that should be done with a dead body, but rather what *can* be done with a dead body. For Ballard, a woman's dead body is a smooth space, open to myriad possibilities" (44).

None of this, of course, really resolves the issue of the novel's misogyny. In *Child of God,* McCarthy is intent upon exploring the extremes to which male appropriation and objectification of the female can be taken. If there is a more profound way to objectify a woman (or, for that matter, anyone) than killing her, it would be by sexually desecrating her corpse. It is important to remember that *Child of God* is an exercise in excess, in the outer limits of violation of the body and the spirit, and that it is set in a rural southern culture in which women have traditionally been objectified. Evenson is correct in seeing the dead bodies of women as representing a cumulative smooth space for Lester, but they are only one such space for McCarthy's "part-time ghoul" (174). The ultimate smooth space for Lester is madness, an insane discarding of any restrictions on or limitations to his murderous needs. Perhaps the defining aspect of his kind of madness is its seeming unawareness of all boundaries, not only those separating him from other people and even from nature itself but also those that separate the living from the dead. In his madness, McCarthy's protagonist is free to explore fully Bataille's dimension of excess, of the total renunciation of reason and order. His dressing in the clothes of his female victims and even constructing a wig out of the scalp of one of them can be understood in the context of a smooth space originating in his insane need to appropriate the bodies of his victims even more completely than by sexually violating them. Lester, in fact, wants to merge his body with theirs until what is left is a pure physicality from which all boundaries have been removed.

It is in this context that McCarthy's title is intended to be provocative, potentially even offensive, but ultimately inclusive of all forms of human behavior. In *Madness and Civilization: A History of Insanity in the Age of Reason,* Michel Foucault valorizes the madness that underlies some of the most memorable products of Western art:

> For Sade as for Goya, unreason continues to watch by night; but in this vigil it joins with fresh powers. The non-being it once was now becomes the power to annihilate. Through Sade and Goya, the Western world received the possibility of transcending its reason in violence, and of recovering tragic experience beyond the promises of dialectic. After Sade and Goya, and since them, unreason has belonged to whatever is decisive, for the modern world, in any work of art; that is, whatever any work of art contains that is both murderous and constraining. (136)

Foucault believes that an essential element of the aesthetic power of the art of unreason comes from the fact that society attempts to deny and repress the vision that sustains it. McCarthy can certainly be placed in this tradition; his work is rooted in a dimension of murderous unreason that is nevertheless undeniably human. In the fourthspace of *Child of God*, this dimension becomes increasingly dominant as the text progresses, often submerging the mimetic to such an extent that Appalachia as a place is almost forgotten. Truly, Lester and all he represents might emerge anywhere. Lester exists initially on the boundary between reason and unreason, but for a time he finds his own kind of liberation in crossing over into madness.

Lang writes that "Lester's crimes would not place him beyond a human continuum on which we find John Wayne Gacy, Ted Bundy, and Jeffrey Dahmer" (93), and indeed an underlying concern of McCarthy's aesthetic is to show that human beings are capable of any act that one can imagine, however violent it may be. Thus McCarthy is careful not to make Lester seem as abstract and metaphoric as he does the grim triune of *Outer Dark*, even though Lester's crimes differ from theirs only in being more clearly rooted in sexuality. Bell emphasizes the complex implications inherent in McCarthy's insistence that such crimes do not place Lester beyond the possibility of grace and redemption: "This is at once strange and not strange, for if Lester is in a state of grace—if such grace were in fact possible—this seems to be precisely and incomprehensibly what true grace would be like" (68).

In part, grace is possible for Lester because, despite the horrific nature of his crimes, he exists as a naturalistic victim and a sacrificial scapegoat. From the beginning of the novel, when his life is auctioned away and he is knocked unconscious, Lester is depicted as being controlled by external forces, some of them systemic and others fundamental and permanent. As one of Evenson's nomads, however reluctantly he joins their ranks, Lester necessarily exists outside the protection of the social order. In this context, it is not surprising that the loyal sheriff, significantly named Fate, declares himself Lester's merciless judge early in the novel. It is as if Fate knows that his antagonist will inevitably assault the social order he is charged with protecting, prophesying early in the novel that Lester will become a murderer. Moreover, like Culla and Rinthy Holme, Lester is also the victim of long-standing economic oppression and profound cultural ignorance.

At one point, McCarthy even goes to elaborate lengths during which he initially appears to shift the narrative perspective away from Lester to establish a historical context for his protagonist. A flood threatens to submerge the town and in fact most of Sevier County, after which Sheriff Fate joins some communal volunteers in rescue boats.[8] They begin to reminisce about local history and especially rival vigilante groups known as the White Caps and the Bluebills, both prototypes of the Ku Klux Klan. About the White Caps, one old man says: "They was a bunch of lowlife thieves and cowards and murderers. The only thing they ever done was to whip women and rob old people. And murder people in their beds at night" (165).[9] This discussion soon evokes memories of a legendary sheriff named Tom Davis who managed to subdue the White Caps. Paradoxically, but in the world of Cormac McCarthy inevitably, Davis eradicated violence only to celebrate it. The old man remembers a communal lynching of two White Caps that took on all the aspects of a carnival: "People had started in to town the evenin before. Slept in their wagons, a lot of em. Rolled out blankets on the courthouse lawn. . . . Women sellin sandwiches in the street. . . . [Davis] brung em from the jail, had two preachers with em and had their wives on their arms and all. Just like they was goin to church. All of em got up there on the scaffold and they sung and everybody fell in singin with em" (167). One remembers that the auction of Lester's farm also turned into a carnival. In Sevier County, violence has always been as close as the courthouse lawn, and the boundary between reason and the excess of unreason has always been an illusion. Thus Lester is merely the historic culmination of the communal legacy of violence. He is the naturalistic victim of historic, as well as economic, forces.

But Lester's victimization goes even deeper. Nature itself seems to have willed his destruction, a fact that Lester vaguely comprehends. Early in the novel he sees a pack of hunting dogs catch and destroy a wild boar and is fascinated by the bloody, choreographed violence unfolding before him: "Ballard watched this ballet tilt and swirl and churn mud up through the snow and watched the lovely blood welter there in its holograph of battle, spray burst from a ruptured lung, the dark heart's blood, pinwheel and pirouette, until shots rang and all was done" (69). Lester will become both boar and hound, the hunted and the merciless hunter fascinated with "the dark heart's blood" of his female victims. What is most significant here is that the hunters (the godlike producers of the ballet) remain out of sight, as such controlling powers must in literary naturalism.

The text directly challenges the reader on the second page, describing Lester as "a child of God much like yourself perhaps" (4). McCarthy's narrative strategy here is clear: the reader, at this point not really knowing Lester and certainly not having encountered him as murderer and necrophiliac, is not likely to resist such identification. *Child of God* demands that McCarthy's implied reader, at the novel's end, still accepts Lester as a human being different from other human beings only in the extremity of an isolation brought on by his descent into the realm of madness, by his insistence upon the discovery of the ultimate smooth space, by his assault on the boundaries between his own need for gratification and the bodies of others.

The early reference to Lester as "a child of god much like yourself perhaps" is superseded in the novel by a later and more confrontational passage, which is interestingly one of the few places in *Child of God* where McCarthy indulges in the kind of stylistic excess that characterizes *Outer Dark*. In it, Lester attempts to cross a flooded river by riding a crate filled with an "odd miscellany" consisting of "men's and ladies' clothes, [and] the three enormous stuffed toys" (155). When the crate is swept out from under him, he is near drowning until he is able to grab a log that has come close to smashing into him. The external narrative perspective then isolates him in the midst of the raging river: "Ballard was lost in a pandemonium of noises, the rifle aloft in one arm now like some demented hero or bedraggled parody of a patriotic poster come aswamp" (156).[10] Having isolated Lester in a cinematic manner,[11] the text now adopts a dialogical mode from which to issue its strongest challenge for the reader to view Lester as a "child of god": "He could not swim, but how would you drown him? His wrath seemed to buoy him up. Some halt in the way of things seems to work here. See him. You could say that he's sustained by his fellow men like you. Has peopled the shore with them calling to him. A race that gives suck to the maimed and the crazed, that wants their wrong blood in its history and will have it. . . . How is he then borne up? Or rather, why will not these waters take him?" (156). "Fellow men like you" belong to a human race that gives birth "to the maimed and the crazed"; the legacy of such beings is both monstrous and definitively human. Through this dialogical approach, McCarthy is insisting that the reader acknowledge a shared humanness with "the maimed and the crazed."

Whether or not the reader is willing to drown Lester, the human community of the text understandably demands that his prolonged assault of taboos central to the social order must be stopped. It also needs to sacrifice him as an embodiment of sacred violence gone mad; in the words of Ciuba: "Ballard eliminates the difference between the pious regard for sacred violence and the desire to arrogate such heavenly fury for his own power. . . . Like some violent voluptuary in the religion of Georges Bataille, he makes transgression the very sign of his transcendence. . . . The savage Lester is godlike precisely because he seems most ungodly" (78). Lester's rampage is the result of the sacrificial crisis evoked by the legacy of the White Caps and other such agents of Appalachian violence, and he must be stopped in order to avoid another cycle of reciprocal violence.

Having abandoned himself completely to smooth space, Lester has issued the most fundamental of challenges to the striated space of the community. His madness, which removes all boundaries from his insatiable demands, simultaneously liberates him and sets in motion his inevitable destruction. Lester becomes so much a part of the open space outside the community that he can almost merge himself with the landscape at will. Still, his narrow escape brings home to him the communal hatred, and this epiphany dismays him. He has a chance unspoken encounter with a young boy on a school bus that evokes a recognition in Lester of the sheer madness of his actions and of a time when he was not the communal outcast that he has become. It is as if he confronts suddenly the image of his own human innocence, of the same need for belonging that inspired his visit to the carnival. Now his smooth space has been compromised, and his insane assault on taboos and boundaries must end.

He thus presents himself at the county hospital, telling a startled night nurse that he belongs there. Ironically, he is never indicted for his crimes but is sent instead to the state hospital at Knoxville, where he is "placed in a cage next door but one to a demented gentleman who used to open folk's skulls and eat the brains inside with a spoon" (193).[12] It is as if the community's frenzied need for a scapegoat has simply played itself out, as if the moment for retributive sacrifice has passed. Finally, in 1965, Lester dies of pneumonia, after which his body is shipped to the medical school at Memphis, where an autopsy inevitably yields no insights into his behavior.

Child of God is a less complex novel than *Outer Dark*, eschewing the stylistic excess that characterizes the earlier novel, substituting for it excess of violent incidents. By denying himself narrative access to Lester's consciousness, McCarthy forces the reader to impose his or her own understanding of abnormal psychology on the text. Unlike the grim triune of *Outer Dark*, Lester Ballard cannot be understood on a purely mythic level. During the rescue trip in the boat, a sheriff's deputy asks the old man, who assumes something close to an authorial voice in the scene, if people were "meaner" during the days of the White Caps than they are at present. The old man's answer is crucial to an understanding of *Child of God* as well as *Outer Dark:* "No, . . . I don't. I think people are the same from the day God first made one" (168). Incest, child abandonment, murder, and necrophilia have been human actions since the beginning. Thus, society is always faced with the potential of a sacramental crisis. Still, in McCarthy's world, human beings are children of god and thus never completely beyond the possibility of salvation unless, like Culla Holme, they flee from it through cowardice or, like Lester Ballard, descend so deeply into madness that they exile themselves from redemption. And even then, Lester can experience a sudden awareness of his humanness that will bring him back into the arms of the community. Only the grim triune of *Outer Dark*, who exist in a largely metaphorical dimension and are thus not truly human at all, are beyond redemption.

3
Russell Banks's *Affliction*
"All Those Solitary Dumb Angry Men"

In his book on Russell Banks, Robert Niemi says this about *Affliction:* "Banks assiduously pursues his vocation as postmodern naturalist by delineating the family, community, and regional (even topographical and climactic) structures that have worked together to shape [Wade Whitehouse's] character and fate" (151). Certainly the naturalistic dimensions of Banks's text are clear. The defining characteristic of naturalism is determinism, and it would be difficult to find a fictional character whose existence is more extensively, or more complexly, determined by forces beyond his comprehension than Banks's blue-collar protagonist. Frank Norris's doomed McTeague seems almost free by comparison. Moreover, Wade Whitehouse is for Banks a favorite character type: the exploited lower-middle-class male worker whose rage at his economic entrapment results in his making an already hopeless condition even worse for himself and virtually everyone associated with him. In fact, Banks has almost defined this kind of fundamentally well-meaning blue-collar victim, who, in a desperation rooted in the hopelessness of his socio-economic position and subsequently magnified by his own ineptitude, descends into criminal activity either without fully realizing it or by justifying it to himself through elaborate paranoid reasoning. Recently divorced for the second time from the same woman, Whitehouse, in Niemi's words, "lives in lonely, alcoholic squalor in a decrepit trailer park" (152). In this novel, as well as in his short-story collection *Trailerpark* (1981), Banks has laid claim to a lower-economic-class social space that unavoidably proclaims its desperate instability. People living in trailer-park space, like the destitute whites whose fictional representatives inhabit *Bastard Out of Carolina, Child of God,* and *Outer Dark,* are often the targets of middle-class jokes (there is, for instance, an online website called Classic Trailer Parks of Mississippi), in part because their homes are designed to be mobile and easily reclaimable. No matter how long they may have actually lived in a community, they are usually perceived as transient and thus peripheral. They are, in essence, relegated to the margins of physical as well as social space. Trailer-park space falls far short of being the kind of redemptive "thirdspace" described by Edward Soja, since living in this space connotes, at least to others, the opposite of choice, a socioeconomic dead end.

Niemi is further perceptive in his analysis of the multiple levels of deterministic control over Wade. He is certainly a victim of family, most obviously of his alcoholic and savagely cruel father, Glenn Whitehouse. Perhaps even more painful than the horrific physical abuse Glenn inflicts on his children, and especially on Wade, is his determined refusal to give them even the most minimal tokens of paternal acceptance. Glenn is, in fact, both a monster and a mystery—a man who, for reasons partly discoverable but primarily lost to the passage of time, is incapable of human feeling. Together, his monstrosity and his mysteriousness make him one of the most fascinating and complex figures in contemporary American fiction. He seems, to some degree, a post-Holocaust characterization, a fictional repository of the incomprehensible cruelty and murder of the historic event that reshaped our awareness of the extremes of human nature and conduct. He is also, like Cormac McCarthy's Lester Ballard, a grotesque inversion of the American frontier myth, an almost predatory male whom it is not at all difficult to imagine performing acts of genocide and other atrocities in the American West. Most importantly, he merges with the novel's very landscape. To "explain" Glenn, then, would be to "explain" the secrets of the text's New Hampshire setting, and it is impossible to explain, or even comprehend, either.

The mystery of Glenn is tied to the topography of the novel's isolated setting. Early in the text, Rolfe Whitehouse, Wade's brother and the novel's narrator, says that "there are . . . two crucially different climate zones . . . divided by an invisible line running across New Hampshire" and that "south of that unmapped line, the climate is characterized by weather typical of most of the northeastern industrial United States; north of it, the weather is typical of eastern Canada" (60–61). He further clarifies:

This has been the case since the autumn of the year of the first appearance of human beings in the region—late-arriving bands of Pleistocene hunters drifting south and east all the way from Asia be-

hind the herds of elk and woolly mammoths—and it remains true today, so that, not surprisingly, the lives of the people residing south of
that line from the beginning seem to have reflected the generosity and
temperance of the climate there, while those who have lived north of
it have reflected in their daily lives the astringency, the sheer malignity
and the dull extreme of the climate there. It is the difference, let us say,
between China and Mongolia, or between England and Scotland,
Michigan and Manitoba: people adapt, or they quickly die. Or they
move. (61)

It would seem difficult to find a more overt statement of environmental determinism than this. The personality and character of human beings, their
very nature, depends on which side of an invisible topographic line they live.
But there is considerably more involved here than the kind of environmental
determinism that one associates, for instance, with Stephen Crane. In Banks's
text, climate and topography merge with mythic history. Rolfe has a reason
for introducing "Pleistocene hunters" and "woolly mammoths" into his description of the New Hampshire climate. The chilling, inhuman brutality of
the region has roots in prehistory, in a mythic age of savage hunters and their
now vanished prey. And it is this same prehistory that contains the secret of
Glenn Whitehouse's cold sadism. Ironically, at the end of the novel, Wade
Whitehouse will be transformed into first "savage" and then "prey."

In a late passage, the text emphasizes the impossibility of discovering
the origin, and thus explaining the nature, of Glenn Whitehouse. Rolfe
introduces the narrative of his father's past with a question that is central to
the novel as a whole: "All those solitary dumb angry men, Wade and Pop
and his father and grandfather, had once been boys with intelligent eyes and
brightly innocent mouths, unafraid and loving creatures eager to please and
be pleased. What had turned them so quickly into the embittered brutes they
had become? Were they all beaten by their fathers; was it really that simple?"
(322). The text's implicit answer to Rolfe's question seems to be, "No, it isn't
at all that simple."

In fact, very little is simple, or even knowable, about Glenn's ancestral and
personal background. Rolfe tells us that his father "was orphaned at ten and
sent to live with an elderly aunt and uncle in Nova Scotia, and when he was
fourteen he had run away, following the reapers west across Canada, chasing
the harvest from the Maritimes to British Columbia" (322). Later he returned east, married (after first impregnating his future wife), and began to

work in Lawford, New Hampshire, paper mills. In this account of his father, Rolfe further emphasizes Glenn's position outside family history:

> When we were children and Pop . . . spoke of his father, it was as if he were speaking of a distant relative who had died before he was born, and when he spoke of his mother it was as if she were a figure in an almost forgotten dream. . . . So it was as if he had no parents, no past, no childhood, even. His father had not even a name—Pop's father's and mother's graves were in Sidney, Nova Scotia . . . they had been killed one winter night when a kerosene stove exploded and their house burned down. As for Pop's grandfather and grandmother, there was nothing; they were as lost in history as if they had lived and died ten thousand years ago. (322–23)

Moreover, although Glenn had siblings of an indeterminate number, he never made any attempt to find them, or even to learn what had happened to them. Thus, Rolfe, and consequently the reader, cannot know whether Glenn was beaten by his father. It is a not unlikely surmise that, as an orphaned child, following farm laborers literally across the country and back, he experienced a great deal of brutality of all kinds. But on a strictly personal level, Glenn is virtually without history, his story having been swallowed up by national history and mythology.

Yet on another level, history is a central subtext in *Affliction*. Banks is devoted to documenting American reality since the 1960s, that tragic decade dominated by the assassinations of charismatic and powerful political figures and a senseless and seemingly endless war. The Vietnam War dramatized the exploitative nature of American foreign policy and exposed the cultural assumptions that underlie American literary modernism as meaningless, or even worse, repressive. The war is an important subtext in *Affliction*—Elbourne and Charlie have, before the present tense of the novel, fled from Glenn's brutality to Vietnam only to die there; Wade also enlisted in the army, hoping to go to Vietnam as well, only to be frustrated by being sent to Korea instead. That his three oldest sons seek a refuge from Glenn in Vietnam emphasizes indirectly the savage abuse they suffer at his hands. Glenn seems, then, to personify the 1960s vision of an American paternalistic culture gone mad. His daughter, Lena, has undertaken her own desperate flight from him in "marriage with the Wonder Truck driver and obesity and charismatic Christianity and five squabbling children of her own" (96). In the present tense of the text, Lena, along with her husband, Clyde, and their "squabbling children," delight in proclaiming the damnation awaiting the rest of her immediate family. Glenn has so thoroughly terrified his children that they are in literal and metaphoric flight from him, until Wade, in an climactic act of insane desperation, kills him.

Central to the 1960s counterculture was a vision of the fathers destroying their children, either literally in the horrific bloodshed of Vietnam or figuratively by imposing upon them a soulless national culture devoted exclusively to materialistic values. Despite his relative poverty and his escape from the Vietnam War, Wade is a victim of such a culture. The small town in which he grew up under the cruel domination of his father and the destructive passivity of his mother is depicted as a cold, isolated, and ultimately endangered community. In an early passage, Rolfe, who has found sanctuary in the Boston suburbs, describes Lawford as an anachronistic community, an old paper-mill town from which the mills have disappeared, and in the text's closing pages he says that "the community, as such, no longer exists" (353). Since the closing of the mills, he says, "Lawford has existed mainly as someplace halfway between other places, a town people sometimes admit to having come from but where almost no one ever goes" (9). Those who remain in the town view themselves, and are viewed by others, as failures: "There are, of course, grown children who stay on in Lawford, and others who—after serving and being wounded in one of the wars or messing up a marriage elsewhere—come back to live in the old house and pump gas or style hair in town. Such children are regarded by their parents as failures; and they behave accordingly" (10). This passage encapsulates the trap in which Banks's blue-collar male characters usually find themselves: condemned by others as lost and inadequate, they drift into circumstances that do, in fact, destroy them. Wade is a prototype of such blue-collar losers; moreover, his dilemma is intensified by the fact that Glenn would condemn him even if he had somehow miraculously achieved success.

In the novel's present tense, Lawford survives primarily as a center for deer hunting—Massachusetts suburbanites invade it during hunting season and then quickly depart. When they go, they leave behind them a landscape drenched in blood. Rolfe describes the landscape surrounding Lawford during hunting season in imagery that echoes the horror of warfare: "Now and then the sound of gunfire from below drifted all the way up the long tangled side of the mountain, as if skirmishes were being fought there, isolated mopping-up actions and occasional sniper fire" (77). The space around Lawford serves as metonym for a Southeast Asia assaulted by American gunfire:

> There is a roar of gunfire, a second, a third, then wave after wave of killing noise, over and over, sweeping across the valleys and up the hills. Slugs, pellets, balls made of aluminum, lead, steel, rip into the body of the deer, crash through bone, penetrate and smash organs, rend muscle and sinew. Blood splashes into the air, across tree bark, stone, onto smooth white blankets of snow, where scarlet fades swiftly to pink . . . urine, entrails, blood, mucous spill from the animal's body: as heavy-booted hunters rush across the frozen snow-covered ground to claim the kill. (68–69)

The invading hunters exult in the kill, in the sheer gore of the slaughter of the deer, just as American soldiers in Vietnam came to exult in the "kill" of the Vietcong. Banks's underlying thesis here is that violence works like a narcotic, destroying the humanity of those who engage in it, and that a history of exultation in the kill has created an inescapable legacy of bloodshed in the landscape surrounding Lawford. At one point the text metaphorically treats the lust of the hunters as an "ancient" hunger: "In Lawford, in backyards, deer hung from makeshift gallows, in dark barns on meat hooks, in garages from winch chains or rope tied to beams; and behind fogged-over kitchen windows, hunters . . . ate hearty breakfasts, eggs and bacon, pancakes smeared with butter and covered with maple syrup, huge steaming mugs of coffee . . . their blood running, excited in ancient ways, proud and relieved and suddenly ravenous for food" (74–75).

The suburbanites are responding to the ancestral male impulse of the kill. For them, hunting and killing the deer represents more than simple recreation; the hunt has become a form of ritualized male violence rooted in an ancient and long-forgotten survival instinct. Natty Bumppo has been transformed into a middle-class Boston suburbanite. And the hunters require trophies, a demand that has produced surreal results: "[The hunters] knew a taxidermist over in Saugus who could stuff a whole deer, if you got it to him quickly enough, could mount it in a lifelike re-creation of the way it looked at the very instant you shot it, hind feet kicking the air, white tail flagged, eyes wide with terror and pain, and you could put it in your basement recreation room if you wanted to" (268). Separated from any meaningful role in nature, the suburbanites seek to destroy it through objectification—they need proof (for themselves primarily) that they have been faithful to the ancestral ritual of killing. Moreover, they want to capture and isolate in time and space the actual moment of the kill and thus celebrate the "terror and pain" of the game they have destroyed. The suburbanites' assault on the New Hampshire woods merges with the mythology of a landscape cursed since the prehistory of Pleistocene hunters and the novel's subtext of the Vietnam War to evoke a horrific fourthspace. The hunters engage in a debased sacrificial ritual and bequeath to their surroundings a plague of violence far removed from any mythic past. Unlike Rolfe's "Pleistocene hunters" and "woolly mammoths," they kill simply to assert phallic dominance over their prey.

Wade Whitehouse is far removed from the deer-hunting class. But, residing at the heart of the blood-soaked landscape, he is susceptible to infection from the plague of killing, and at the end of the novel he hunts and kills, not a deer, but a human being. In this context it is important to remember Wade's frustration over not having been sent to Vietnam by the army. Again, though, the text emphasizes that the American culture of male violence has roots that extend back into the very origins of the national experience. Thus the space surrounding Lawford functions in the novel as a microcosm for a nation literally born out of the violence of war and, more than once, preserved in the same way. Growing up in the freezing and claustrophobic landscape of mid-twentieth-century New Hampshire, Wade shares the myth of an open and heroic frontier that has long been central to the American consciousness. Ironically, he even dreams of finding protection against his father's savagery in popular-culture celebrations of frontier heroism.

The novel's first detailed account of Glenn savagely assaulting Wade is introduced by a deceptively reassuring description of Wade and his mother watching *Gunsmoke,* the Western television series that was enormously popular in the 1950s and early 1960s. Wade finds comfort and security in the program's frontier marshal hero, Matt Dillon. James Arness, the actor who portrayed Dillon, is described as "a tall loose-limbed man whose big lantern-jawed face comforted Wade somehow, although it was like no face he knew personally. . . . [E]ven so, Wade let himself dream over that large kindly strong face, wishing not that his father looked like U.S. Marshal Matt Dillon but that his father knew such a man, that's all, had a friend whose good-natured strength would quiet him down and at the same time cheer him up, make his father less turbulent and unpredictable, less dangerous" (99–100). The painful irony of this passage operates on several levels. Knowing his father's brutality intimately, Wade cannot, even in fantasy, transform Glenn into a heroic figure—the best he can do is dream of a benevolent older male figure who could somehow mitigate his father's brutality.[1] Moreover, the reader remembers, even if Wade forgets, that Matt Dillon is a fiction, an inherently contradictory prototype of the male hero, the western gunfighter who maintains peace and order by killing the "bad guys." Given the Vietnam subtext of the novel, it is difficult not to believe that Banks introduces Dillon and *Gunsmoke* into the text as popular-culture emblems of the American economic and military imperialism that would result in the nightmare of Vietnam. More than one military spokesman for that war seemed to be describing the United States as the embodiment of a western hero enforcing order by killing the "bad" Vietcong.

Finally, of course, Glenn Whitehouse did indeed have a frontier experience, the details of which he refuses to divulge but which one can guess were anything but benevolent and reassuring, and this aspect of his past is central to the climactic irony in this crucial scene. Glenn attacks Wade when his son, attempting to please his mother, refuses his sudden and loud command to turn off the television set. To Wade, his father's intrusive voice demanding silence seems to merge with the television space of *Gunsmoke:* "Wade thought for a second that Pop sounded like Marshal Dillon in Miss Kitty's bar daring a drunken gunfighter to reach for his gun" (100). In fact, though Glenn is much closer to being "a drunken gunfighter" than a heroic marshal, Wade continues to associate his father with Dillon and himself with one of Dillon's deserving victims, "a puny terrified punk," even during the worst moments of the beating. Wade's fantasy of finding protection from his father in western fantasy is invaded by the savage reality of Glenn Whitehouse and all that he represents. Victimized so horribly by his father, Wade will increasingly surrender to self-contempt, a feeling intensified by recurrent failures to defend either himself or his mother from abuse. There are simply too many forces aligned against him—a barbaric mythic history, his father's sadistic abuse, (exacerbated by his mother's guilt-inducing codependency), the alienated and chilling community of Lawford and the frozen and blood-soaked space surrounding it, his two failed marriages with Lillian, his personal and emotional isolation, his failure to win the love of his young daughter, Jill, and all his job frustrations—and he finally succumbs to horrific violence. In fact, the final straw in Wade's psychological disintegration seems to be an awareness that he is after all no different from his father.

Wade's failure to be his mother's protector is unforgettably dramatized in what may be the novel's single most horrifying scene. In the present tense of the novel, Wade and his companion, Margie Fogg, discover that a drunk and unfeeling Glenn has allowed his wife literally to freeze to death when the furnace in that farmhouse breaks down and he doesn't even try to get help. After the discovery of Sally's body, when Margie asks Glenn if he is sorry, the brutal old man responds in a self-pitying manner: "Sad. Yes. Sad. I wish, I wish it was me in there instead of her. . . . That's what makes me sad. I'm the one should've froze to death." An outraged Maggie can only respond: "You are right." The symbolic overtones of Sally's death by freezing are crucial to the central meaning of Banks's novel—the "affliction" from which virtually everyone in the text (except Maggie) suffers is an emotional and spiritual coldness, a failure to reach out in a selfless way to others. Sally's death also establishes her as a victim of the chronotope in which she is trapped—a barren landscape dominated by extreme cold and marriage to a cruel and unfeeling husband, a merger of inhumane physical, social, and mental space. Inevitably, Wade has been tormented since childhood by guilt over his inability to protect her, and this guilt, while it contributes significantly to his destruction, emanates from what is perhaps his most redeeming characteristic.

In contrast to his brother Rolfe and his sister, Lena, Wade does not leave Lawford; he remains trapped in a dead-end job and a forbidding environment in part because he paradoxically loves Lawford and the surrounding area, but in part because of his desire and need to protect his mother. Wade is typical of Banks's blue-collar anti-heroes—he wants to be a decent, responsible man, but he feels that the array of forces with which he is in conflict make that impossible. At one point in the text he imagines sweeping away all such forces with one "wild bearish swing of his arm": "Then at last he could be a good father, husband, son and brother. He could become a good man. That was all he wanted, for God's sake. To be a good man. He imagined goodness as a state that gave a man power and clarity in every conscious moment of his daily life" (320). Of course, such a vision of "goodness" is simplistic and outdated—a Matt Dillon frontier morality increasingly incomprehensible in a post-1960s world; but, unlike his father and ultimately Rolfe, Wade does desire to be faithful to his concept of "goodness," however limited and even self-destructive it is.

But again in a manner typical of the Banks blue-collar protagonist, Wade is prevented from achieving this modest moral code, in part because he simply doesn't know how. Matt Dillon is a fiction and an increasingly dangerous one; Glenn Whitehouse is anything but a decent male role model. An interesting subtext in *Affliction* concerns the complex damage that destructive models of "masculine" behavior can inflict on young males. In *After the Lovedeath,* Lawrence Kramer offers a valuable analysis of the dangerous arbitrariness of distinctions between "the masculine" and "the feminine" and of the ways in which such an arbitrary and binary approach to identity can lead to misogyny and self-hatred in the male. Kramer argues first that "both the idea of avoiding feminization and the idea of reacting against internal(ized) femininity assume the presence of an intact core of preexisting masculinity" and that "no core of preexisting masculinity exists except as a position always occupied by someone other than the subject" (120). Adapting the ideas of Freud and Lacan, Kramer defines the socialization process as the necessary submission of the individual ego to "authority" and asserts that such submission is arbitrarily associated with "femininity": "Women are those who are chosen to personify this condition in the avowed space of social life, so that others, called men, can disavow it" (120). Abuse of the female becomes then a mode of indirect rebellion against "authority," which cannot otherwise be safely challenged. In this context, Wade's climactic acts of violence can be seen as desperate attempts to break free from a multilayered repressive "authority."

Interestingly, though, both of the targets of Wade's rebellion are male. Still, his final capitulation to violence results from his unintentionally striking his daughter, Jill, and causing her nose to bleed, an act instantly followed by the sudden appearance of Glenn, who looks "at Wade with a smile on his face like a devil" (338). Having failed so completely to protect his mother, Wade has now inflicted pain on his daughter; Glenn's sudden appearance reminds him that he has, however unwillingly, reenacted the Whitehouse legacy of abuse against children and females. In an especially brutal scene, frustration over this and all the other failures in his life explodes into his killing Glenn, perhaps in self-defense, and then disposing of his father's body in a fiery ritual. Having killed once, Wade is now both free enough and unbalanced enough to stalk and murder Jack Hewitt, a young man with whom he has become increasingly obsessed over the course of the novel. After Wade hits Jill, his already fragile faith in not being "made of what [his father] is made of" evaporates instantly—now that he feels no different from his father, he sees no reason to control his rage and violence and, in fact, directs them first at his father and now his doppelgänger. The killing of Glenn constitutes a form of indirect suicide, and Wade's subsequent burning of his father's body is a desperate attempt at a mythic kind of self-purification.

To a considerable extent, Wade's life can also be seen as a failed attempt to live up to an arbitrary image of "masculinity." He significantly does not dream of being a good person but rather of being a good *man*. And he sees goodness as constituting a route to "power and clarity," in large part because he, in his job and in his life, has virtually no power and has long ceased to see anything with true clarity. Wade is plagued by disturbing dreams throughout the novel; in one, he abruptly realizes

> That there are no women in his dreams and the girl babies are dolls. There must be something wrong with that. Men do not have babies, women do. But what about men?
>
> *What do men do?* he cries, and he woke up, tears streaming down his face in the darkness of his trailer. (137)

In this half-unconscious epiphany, Wade realizes, for a moment, the crippling inadequacy of his binary vision of the masculine and the feminine, but his experience and his situation do not allow him to pursue the implications of such a realization. Still, it is impossible to imagine Glenn Whitehouse or any of the novel's other male characters, with the significant exception of Rolfe, having comparable epiphanies. In addition, none of the other male characters, probably *including Rolfe,* would be as devastated by inadvertently striking his child as is Wade.

Rolfe is the novel's most enigmatic figure. Indeed, while narrating Wade's tragic story, Rolfe constructs an elaborate mask that conceals much of his own identity. He is something of a cerebral trickster who enjoys playing complex intellectual games with Wade and with the reader, and the games he plays with narration are central to the most common criticism of Banks's text. Reviewers of *Affliction* wondered how Rolfe could have the detailed knowledge of Wade's thought process that the narrative provides. Robert Niemi acknowledges that while this objection is probably impossible to answer with complete satisfaction, the negative consequences of eliminating Rolfe as narrator would more than outweigh any resulting gain in narrative plausibility: "Without his mediation, Wade's story would surely lose psychological and moral depth, because Wade's story is also Rolfe's" (161). To some extent, it is even more Rolfe's than it is Wade's.

In the course of the novel, Rolfe, a teacher and a very conscious intellectual, enunciates some of his motivations for telling Wade's story, while not uncommonly trying to disguise, or even deny, the most painful implications of what he is saying. In an epilogue, after quoting a newspaper account of the double murder committed by his brother, he approaches Wade's life as an abstract puzzle, the answer to which is simultaneously fascinating and finally undiscoverable: "You read [the newspaper account of the double murder] and move quickly on. . . . You forget it, because you do not understand it: you cannot understand how a man, a *normal* man, a man like you and me, could do such a terrible thing. He must not be like you and me. It is easier by far to understand diplomatic maneuvers in Jordan, natural calamities in the third world and the economics of addictive drugs than an isolated explosion of homicidal rage in a small American town" (354). Here, Rolfe at once faces and denies his most fundamental fear. In some ways, he is considerably more than "like" Wade. Banks, in *Affliction*, is making complex use of the doppelgänger motif—both Glenn Whitehouse and Jack Hewitt come to represent Wade's double, and Rolfe is painfully aware that Wade represents his own. Earlier in the text, he has made this symbolic connection with Wade overt more than once. In his concluding discussion of the newspaper account, he refuses to pursue the repercussions of such a frightening admission.

Wade and, by association, Rolfe himself must be "*normal*" men like everyone else. In fact, as children of Glenn Whitehouse, they never were, or never could be, that. Most of all, Rolfe would like to forget that he, too, shares his father's satanic blood, and one aim of his narrative is to scapegoat Wade. Girard's concept of the sacrificial crisis sheds light on what Rolfe is attempting to do with Wade. Rolfe hopes that his older brother has paid the price of a familial violence by sacrificing the most immediate source of that violence, their father. But as Banks has made clear, it can hardly be that easy—the source of Glenn's satanic violence cannot be traced, since his own family origins have been lost. Moreover, Glenn exists, on one level, as a metonymic representative of the blood-soaked landscape surrounding Lawford; and while Rolfe is, as he acknowledges in the opening pages of the text, a product of that same town and that same landscape, he paradoxically insists on his separation from it. But on another level of denial, Rolfe, in the epilogue, tries to retreat from such self-understanding by transforming Wade into an intellectual puzzle, a question of space. He tries to argue, in a context of prevailing urban and small-town stereotypes, that the central mystery represented by Wade's double murder is that it occurred in a small town. Like the well-read young man that he is, Rolfe is attempting to tell himself that violence is a peculiarity of crowded and isolating urban space, when he knows how inextricably linked the horror of Glenn Whitehouse is to the frozen and isolated New Hampshire landscape.

Much of Rolfe's narration is a complicated and doomed attempt to repress truth by telling it. In the opening pages of the text, he describes himself as fulfilling a kind of familial role in telling Wade's story: "I tell it for [the surviving family members] . . . as much as for myself. They want, through the telling, to regain him; I want only to be rid of him. His story is my ghost life, and I want to exorcise it" (2). Just as Wade literally kills his two doubles, Rolfe is attempting a symbolic murder of Wade, his own doppelgänger. Most of all, Rolfe is afraid that the murderous rage that infected his father and brother is latent within himself. Illogically, he personifies Wade as the embodiment of Glenn's savagery, hoping to "exorcise" Wade and thereby his own capacity for cruelty and violence by telling his brother's story. *Affliction* becomes then a kind of attempted murder through narration—Rolfe is trying to "tell" his brother out of existence; and in this context, it is significant that Wade is still alive and in hiding when the novel ends. Rolfe's attempted "murder" of Wade has failed—Wade, in fact, is now a more threatening force than ever, an invisible figure who may reappear at any place at any time. Thus, Rolfe has succeeded only momentarily in vanquishing his own rage and potential for violence.

Yet, Rolfe hardly needs to fear becoming another Wade—he is simply too emotionally cold to react to anything with rage or violence. To his credit, he understands that he is another kind of victim of his father, and specifically of Glenn's alcoholism: "[Wade] knew better than anyone else in the family that I had not drunk anything alcoholic since college and in fact had drunk almost not at all even then. We never discussed it, Wade and I, any more than we discussed his drinking, but I think we both knew that they were equal and opposite reactions to the same force" (225).

The teaching profession provides Rolfe sanctuary against excess of any kind; and, given his family legacy, he fears excess most. Georges Bataille would likely appreciate Banks's characterization of Rolfe as a man so frightened of emotional and physical excess that he virtually dehumanizes himself. Still, Rolfe remains, at least on some level, human and is therefore incapable of the total repression he seeks to attain. Thus, in the narration of Wade's story—in linguistic excess, as it were—he finds a safety valve. In fact, he finds this form of excess doubly safe—he is not the central character in his story and words; after all, *he* never killed anyone. But, in *Affliction*, Rolfe's words certainly become accomplices to murder.

Fully aware of the desperate situation in which Wade increasingly finds himself, Rolfe provides the missing elements in the structure of his brother's paranoia. However seriously he intends it, he elaborates a conspiracy theory to Wade that the older brother desperately adopts as the means of escape from the pain and humiliation of his life. The trigger for Rolfe's hypothesis and Wade's obsession is the accidental death of a hunter named Evan Twombley, for whom Jack Hewitt is serving as guide. On the sole evidence that Twombley, a labor official, was to be a future witness in a congressional investigation of ties between labor unions and organized crime, Rolfe, on the telephone, outlines to Wade a scenario in which Twombley's son-in-law, Mel Gordon, hired Jack Hewitt to kill Twombley in order to succeed to the union presidency himself. As assistant police chief, Wade is obligated at least to look at Twombley's murder. But as his brother, of all people, should have realized, Wade, especially in the context of Rolfe's conspiracy theory, cannot just look at the case; instead, he becomes obsessed with finding some redemptive meaning in it. Banks, in this episode, is exploring the appeal that conspiracy theories have held for Americans since the late 1960s—conspiracies, however widespread and malevolent, are preferable to chaos.

Rolfe's theory is especially attractive to Wade because, early in the novel, Mel Gordon defies and humiliates him as he, looking like "a demented scarecrow" (71), directs traffic in one of his duties as school crossing guard. Moreover, Gordon LaRiviere, master behind-the-scenes plotter in Lawford city government and Wade's boss in the several part-time positions he holds, prevents Wade from extracting any justice against Gordon. As much as anything else in the novel, Wade's relationship with, and personal response to, LaRiviere reveals the tenuous nature of his identity and of his grip on reality. Wade has long admired LaRiviere as master manipulator, seeing in his boss a mentor, a successful male role model, even while resenting the subservient role he plays in LaRiviere's web of enterprises. In contrast, LaRiviere's feelings toward his subordinate are quite basic and mirror his attitude toward most people: "In LaRiviere's world, you win and win big, or you lose and lose everything. Survival, mere survival, does not exist for him, except as a dismal loss, which is one of the several reasons he despised Wade" (119). After LaRiviere's support of Mel Gordon subsequent to the traffic violation, Wade can no longer remain oblivious to the contempt that his mentor feels for him.

Thus, Rolfe's hypothesis offers Wade a desperately needed substitute around which he can restructure his world. He is transformed into a contemporary Matt Dillon intent on exposing the ring of "bad guys" around La-Riviere and Gordon. How Jack Hewitt fits into all this is more complex and is, in fact, one of the least successful aspects of Banks's novel. For Wade, Hewitt seems to be a projection of himself at a younger age, in a time of hope and promise that in fact never existed. Hewitt is an athlete, as was Wade, and before sustaining an arm injury he was briefly in the Boston Red Sox organization. Wade envisions Jack as a hopeful, romantic reincarnation of his own nightmarish youth and adolescence and comes to hate the young man because he seems so carefree, so untroubled. It seems in part, then, that, in killing Jack, Wade is executing his own youth. Moreover, he does this after his disillusionment with LaRiviere, when he can no longer even fantasize any escape from his severely proscribed existence.

Just as revealing as Rolfe's irresponsibility—his dangerous complicity in describing such a hypothetical conspiracy to Wade when he knows that his brother is moving ever closer to some climactic violence—is the way he repudiates it in the text's concluding pages: "The evidence, all of it, was incontrovertible. What was not scientific was logical; and what was not logical was scientific. Just as the evidence that Jack Hewitt did not shoot Evan Twombley, not even by accident, is now seen by everyone as incontrovertible. Even by me. There was no motive, and Jack left no secret bank account, no stash of hundred-dollar bills: the links between Jack and Twombley, LaRiviere and Mel Gordon, existed only in Wade's wild imagining—and briefly, I admit, in mine as well" (351). In fact, they existed first in his. For Rolfe, the conspiracy theory is a supplemental narrative, a second story he can tell to distract himself from the unpleasant personal implications of Wade's story. (In reality there is a conspiracy going on, but it is much more prosaic in nature than either Wade or Rolfe would like: LaRiviere and Gordon are buying up all available property in Lawford in order to turn the town into a ski resort.) At any rate, it is not just his brother with whom Rolfe, as narrator, is playing games. He provides two versions of the Twombley death, in the first of which Jack Hewitt does murder the union official. This narrative trickery is one of the central reasons for criticism of Banks's handling of point of view in the novel.

As Niemi points out, reviewers were initially troubled by Banks's giving Rolfe seemingly unrestricted access to Wade's thoughts throughout most of the text only to abandon this narrative approach in the concluding, climactic section. Here Rolfe switches from being a virtually omniscient recorder of his brother's story to acting as an amateur detective seeking the details of his brother's killings of Glenn and Jack Hewitt from the few witnesses to Wade's last hours. He then admits that he can only provide a hypothetical account of Wade's final, decisive confrontation with their father. Significantly, in Rolfe's re-creation of Glenn's death, Wade initially acts out of self-defense, without premeditation. Thus, Rolfe allows Wade a degree of absolution. What certainly *is* premeditated is Wade's elaborate and ritualistic burning of his father's body, and in this regard external evidence seems to support Rolfe's version of what happened. It is as if Wade, finally liberated by killing his father in self-defense, then performs an act of sacrificial cleansing on Glenn's body. He has now attained a terrible kind of existential freedom: even though he willed neither act, he has hit his daughter and caused her to bleed and has killed the grim specter of his father. Thus, he is liberated to stalk and kill Jack Hewitt.

The limitations of the narrative mode that Rolfe adopts at the end of the text make sense in the context of his personality. After all, the material to be narrated here might be emotionally devastating if approached in an unmediated manner. Thus, Rolfe's final incarnation as amateur detective is his final means of distancing himself from his family's horrific story. By adopting the persona of an amateur sleuth, he sheds the burden of being a Whitehouse, his father's son and his brother's brother. The shift to Maggie's perspective in the funeral scene is a more troubling moment, unless this too is one of Rolfe's games with the reader, as if he were saying, "See, this rationally minded woman thinks I'm weird."

These games with narrative perspective seem to be the reason why Niemi labels *Affliction* as "*postmodernist* narration," exhibiting as it does a degree of "indeterminance," the constant deferring of meaning that calls attention to the "indeterminacy" of meaning. We do not finally know to what degree Rolfe *is* playing games with us; nor do we know the actual circumstances that resulted in Wade's killing Glenn and Jack Hewitt. Moreover, having Rolfe call attention to the conjectural nature of all this serves to emphasize the conjectural nature of all narration. Yet it is probably more profitable to discuss the novel in the context of what Robert Rebein has recently described as "a revitalization of realism" (17). Rebein writes that a contemporary realist such as Robert Stone "simply accepts the mimetic limitations of realism . . . as *obvious* . . . [in order] to build what Tom Wolfe insists will be a bigger, better realism" (19). He then succinctly summarizes his argument: "What stands out finally is that contemporary realist writers have *absorbed* postmodernism's most lasting contributions and gone on to forge a new realism that is more or less traditional in its handling of character, reportorial in its depiction of milieu and time, but is at the same time self-conscious about language and the limits of mimesis" (20).

And perhaps the accurate way to describe *Affliction* would be as an example of mythological naturalism. Wade Whitehouse is the victim of so many kinds of deterministic forces (Banks even has him suffering from an abscessed tooth until he pulls it himself with a pair of pliers) that, if taken entirely on a completely mimetic level, the novel would seem to be a sustained exercise in overkill (pun intended). Finally, though, his fate is most controlled by a kind of ritualized masculine violence that has merged with the weather and the very landscape of northern small-town New Hampshire. Rolfe fails in his final role as detective—the forces that molded Wade and, even more frighteningly, Glenn Whitehouse are inexplicable, lost somewhere back in the time when "late-arriving bands of Pleistocene hunters" invaded the frozen space surrounding Lawford, a space since soaked with the blood of countless deer and, at the end of *Affliction,* two human beings. It is as if Wade, in his pagan burning of Glenn's body, and Rolfe, in telling Wade's story, are attempting acts of ritual purification, as if they are seeking to end the sacrificial crisis that is plaguing the physical and psychological spaces in which they exist. If so, they both fail. Wade at the end has disappeared, an outcast trapped in his own madness, but his very invisibility enables him to further invade Rolfe's consciousness, to haunt his brother most likely until Rolfe's death. It is only fitting that *Affliction*'s opening scene takes place during Halloween.

Moreover, in its emotional sterility and fundamental dishonesty, Rolfe's narration becomes its own kind of fourthspace. His account of events seeks the margin between truth and invention for his own selfish motives. Not only does he want to analyze Wade out of existence, but he suggests to his brother the conspiracy theory that will lead inexorably to Wade's death, a theory in which he does not truly believe. In the unfeeling fourthspace of his narration, Rolfe seeks to escape his family, his past, his own spiritual barrenness, and any sense of responsibility for the events of the text.

4
Of Vultures, Eyeballs, and Parrots
Lewis Nordan's *Wolf Whistle*

Lewis Nordan's 1993 novel, *Wolf Whistle,* is a uniquely imaginative, even daring, re-creation of the notorious 1955 lynching of Emmett Till in Money, Mississippi. Till, a fourteen-year-old visitor to Mississippi from Chicago accused of making sexual advances toward a white woman, was kidnapped out of his great-uncle's house at night, then bludgeoned and shot before his body was thrown into the Tallahatchie River. Looking back at the lynching and its aftermath for *Time* magazine in 1999, Bebe Moore Campbell, who has written her own fictionalized account of the incident, observed:

> In 1955, Roy Bryant and J. W. Milam were declared not guilty by an all-white jury in less time than it takes to watch a movie. A month later, at the behest of a journalist who paid for the story, Milam felt enough public approbation to confess to the murder with impunity.
>
> Times have changed—but not completely. Though whites and blacks now monitor their attitudes about race, racial terrorism lives on. Killers who were never charged for their hate crimes roam free. From recent cases one might even be led to surmise that the Klan has given up white uniforms for blue ones. (35)

Campbell's comments encapsulate some of the difficulties inevitably faced by any writer attempting to transform the Till tragedy into meaningful fiction.[1]

Till's lynching was hardly a unique event in Mississippi, southern, and American history. That from 1876 until 1963 the perpetrators of such atrocities usually escaped punishment and even became local heroes is a painfully familiar story—after all, W. E. B. DuBois and other African-American

leaders struggled unsuccessfully for more than half a century to have lynching declared a federal crime and thus, at least potentially, punishable. The
historical ordinariness of the Till murder in itself creates problems for the
imaginative writer, and, paradoxically, the savage injustice of such ordinariness only compounds the problem. Moreover, the brutal violence that was
from the beginning an integral part of racial relations in America, and especially in the South and even more especially in Mississippi, has been re-
corded and explored by such writers as William Faulkner, Richard Wright,
and Eudora Welty. Thus it is no longer sufficient for the contemporary writer
to merely document that violence and injustice, or even to witness it as
Dorothy Allison does child abuse in *Bastard Out of Carolina.* If child abuse
remains something of an unspoken secret in American life and literature,
racism has been, for some time, certainly one of the most frequently discussed and analyzed American problems. Yet precisely because such tensions
still simmer beneath a superficial social politeness, new and imaginative
forms of witnessing it are essential.

As a white adolescent in Itta Bena, Mississippi, a community nearby
Money, in the 1950s, Lewis Nordan could not have ignored the Till lynching
had he wanted to, and it is hardly surprising that his adult writing often
reflects the cultural and psychological scars that it left. Moreover, in his case
it seems to go deeper than a vague white guilt. A central question emerges
from *Wolf Whistle* and from all of Nordan's fiction (as well as from his 2000
memoir, *Boy with Loaded Gun*): As the product of a geographical space in
which horror and injustice were undeniably commonplace and as someone
who, to a degree anyway, even loved that space, to what extent am I the
reflection of that horror and injustice? This question incorporates and transcends the Quentin Compson dilemma—existential consciousness will not
let Nordan simply love, hate, or deny his South. He can live with its memory
only by creatively plunging beneath its surface in order to discover and record
its mysteries.

The potential difficulty facing Nordan as a white southern writer in
choosing the Till murder as his subject matter can be illustrated by compar-
ing *Wolf Whistle* with Bebe Moore Campbell's 1992 novel, *Your Blues Ain't
Like Mine.* Moore feels free to explore the consequences of the Till murder
for the families of the white perpetrators and the black victim alike. She is,
moreover, quite successful in doing so; her investigation of the psychology of
the text's white characters (especially the subjugated wife of the primary
killer) is, in fact, even more incisive than her narration of the reactions of the

African-American relatives of the victim. In contrast, a white writer can only approach such a horrific racial murder with genuine apprehension; he or she must be constantly alert to the trap of unintentionally validating such brutal repression by the mere act of writing about it.[2]

Nordan, at first glance, would seem to add a further dimension to this complex narrative challenge by choosing to dramatize the Till tragedy from a perspective incorporating absurdist comedy and magic realism. His choice of an essentially comic mode might well seem insensitive in the context of the novel's dark subject matter. In an interview, Nordan says that his favorite fictional mode is irony and then emphasizes that irony and related forms of comedy are, for him, ports of entry into truly "serious" subject matter: "I [am] always writing from the same place, that is that deeply serious, melodramatic horror that's at the heart of my work. Something about me believes that comedy comes out of darkness and that all comedy is underpinned by loss" (Maher 118). While this statement of an aesthetic principle seems appropriate as a description of the work of Faulkner and other southern writers who document the tragic outrageousness of southern society from an assumed vantage point of outraged disbelief, Nordan's application of it is uniquely is own.

Perhaps nowhere in *Wolf Whistle* is this uniqueness better shown than in the description of a gang of buzzards that watches over the fictional town of Arrow Catcher, Mississippi:

> The locals called them swamp eagles, sometimes just eagles, though they were clearly buzzards. The birds were descendants and remnants of an ancient flock, attracted here long ago by the corpse-stench of a Civil War battle, when Balance Due [the poor white section of town] and the Belgian Congo [the African-American section] were only a big field, a significant Mississippi defeat. . . .
>
> These birds were a part of the glorious history of the South. They were written up, now and then, in local newspapers, and in newspapers all across the state of Mississippi. (68)

Clearly, irony is central to this passage. Northrop Frye's thesis in *Fables of Identity* that "the dialectic in myth that projects a paradise or heaven above our world and a hell or place of shades below it reappears in literature as the idealized world of pastoral and romance and the absurd, suffering, or frustrated world of irony and satire" (35) seems especially relevant here. Nordan's text clearly re-creates a Mississippi landscape of absurdity and suffering watched over by ancient buzzards.

The ironic mode of the novel is emphasized in its description of the buzzards who guard a battlefield, which was the scene of a "significant Mississippi defeat," as being "part of the glorious history of the South." Nordan is, in part, satirizing here the white southern fondness for living in a past that never existed, that is essentially the product of a debased, secular mythology. He depicts 1950s Arrow Catcher, and indeed the entire state of Mississippi, as being controlled by a myth (which is closer to being a fantasy) of the antebellum South as a heroic world where white supremacy was never questioned and African-American slaves were childlike beings who required white "protection," domination, and control. According to this debased myth, the Golden Age of the South was shattered and displaced by military defeat and northern invasion. Precisely because this pastoral ideal has been "lost," it occupies a central space in the psychology of the white inhabitants of the town and state. The legacy of the antebellum South, the text implies, was actually "a corpse-stench" that will not go away.

The text memorably summarizes the horror of the denied reality: "Some of the birds . . . were as ancient as the historical battle itself, older, ninety, a hundred years old, a few of them . . . had actually fed on the flesh and eyes and tongues and nutritious organ meat of Confederate troops, fallen, hungry, frightened boys before they were made buzzard bait by a mini-ball or cannon shot" (69). Of course, if the buzzards had fed on the flesh of the Confederate dead, logically they must have partaken of some dead Union soldiers as well. Rather than being parochial here, Nordan is concerned with demythologizing the Confederacy and the supposedly heroic values it was engaged in defending. But allegiance to the myth of a heroic South allows the white inhabitants of Arrow Catcher to ignore the stench—and, until the murder of Bobo, a fourteen-year-old black visitor from Chicago, indeed to ignore the ugly and disturbing realities that exist just below the quiet surface of the town. This capacity to ignore or revise reality is satirically emphasized in the text's account of the buzzards being commonly referred to in town as "swamp eagles" or "eagles"; hardly birds of heroic association, they are simply scavengers. The extent of the collective blindness to the reality of the white world that Nordan exposes is indicated by the vultures' elevation to the stature of folklore not just by the Arrow Catcher media but by "newspapers all across the state of Mississippi."

The most ancient of the buzzards have even been given names: "Vardaman and Bilbo and Hugh White and J. P. Coleman and Ross Barnett and other names of past and future governors and senators of the sovereign state of Mississippi" (69). These are the names of political figures who devoted themselves throughout the twentieth century to establishing and defending racism in Mississippi and who consequently perpetuated a corrupt political system based on enforced poverty and ignorance throughout the sovereign state. The buzzard named Ross Barnett, while "as good-natured and open-minded and as willing to share the riches of Mississippi as the next old buzzard" (72), possesses unusually good eyesight that gives him an advantage in the never-ending search for carrion that constitutes the vultures' lives.

Significantly, the vulture passage specifically mentions the sections of Arrow Catcher populated by poor whites and African Americans, the two groups most thoroughly exploited by this history. In prose that produces satiric effects through evocative language, Nordan delineates the sordid and debased reality underlying the myth over which the vultures hold protective watch:

[The younger vultures] possessed only blood-memories of the ancient feast, genetic egg-yolk longings for distant, unremembered culinary ecstasy and freedom from deprivation, and sat with hope in their bird hearts and nothing at all in their bird brains, for many years, decades really, a human lifetime and longer, above the homes of damaged rednecks and maniacs with pistols, on smelly lamp posts planted in stinking mud, whiling away all of their valuable, irretrievable daylight hours and years in the sad innocence of poultry-patience during this lean century since the glorious Festival of Dead Rebels long ago, and they were content for now with roadkill. (70)

Nordan's evocation of the vultures in *Wolf Whistle* must be one of the most remarkable passages in contemporary southern American fiction. It is, on one level, a tour de force of demythologization. Nordan seems intent on employing the crudest and most sordid images he can find to describe Mississippi's past and, by implication, its present. It is a state that survives on "blood-memories" of ancient slaughter and present "roadkill." Its inhabitants are "damaged rednecks" and "maniacs" obsessed with guns and violence. Nordan's unspoken assumption seems to be that such narrative excess is needed to explain or at least make plausible the murder of Bobo, his incarnation of Emmett Till, that lies at the center of the text.

Still, the bulk of the novel is devoted to humanizing Nordan's characters, most definitely including Solon Gregg, the demented poor white murderer of Bobo. Rather than being simply a stereotyped representative of southern racism or a one-dimensional product of class discrimination, Solon emerges as a sometimes amusing but ultimately horrifying human being. As with the novel as a whole, Nordan takes real risks with his characterization of Solon; the reader is often reduced to laughing at him but is never allowed to forget his human complexity or the menace he embodies. Even more than Allison in *Bastard Out of Carolina,* Nordan evokes the prototype of the poor white southerner as defined by Erskine Caldwell and other writers of the 1930s in order to reveal its inadequacy. Solon is simultaneously buffoon and killer, a kind of cultural innocent made lethal by desperation and ignorance. He is undeniably a product of southern racial and class hatred, but Nordan does not try to explain him away as only that.

In the novel, Solon is the unmistakable representative of Balance Due, a permanently debt-ridden and hopeless space. While the Vardamans and Bilbos and Barnetts were devoted to making certain that all the Balance Dues in Mississippi remained a cumulative exploited space, they knew that they could capture the political support of Balance Due inhabitants by invoking the specter of race. For these cynical politicians, the state's Solon Greggs were merely "roadkill." In the opening chapter, Nordan prepares the reader for Solon by having Alice Conroy, the novel's representative of an innocent humanism that is indestructible precisely because it is so unsophisticated in nature, lead her fourth graders on a field trip to Balance Due. Young Glenn Gregg has been hideously burned and lies near death, and Alice has decided that the boy's classmates should pay him a visit.

Alice, blessed with the gift of being oblivious to unpleasant reality, is undaunted by the ominous spectacle of Balance Due: "Filthy, violent men in shirtsleeves sat in doorways. They swaggered, they leered, they drank out of sacks, they worked in muddy yards on junker cars with White Knights bumper stickers. Bottle-trees clanked in the breeze. A hundred-year-old voodoo woman wearing a swastika stirred a cauldron above a fire in a yard nearby. A young man tried to convince a woman, a girl really, to let him shoot an apple off her head with a pistol" (7). Her class trip provides an indirect introduction to Solon Gregg. We learn in it that Glenn is in his present horrible condition as a result of trying to kill his father. Glenn had poured gasoline on Solon's bed, only to have it catch fire and consume him instead.

Having introduced Solon in this indirect manner, Nordan is now ready to bring him onto the scene. Solon appears at Arrow Catcher's central male homosocial space, Red's Goodlookin Bar and Gro., when Bobo seals his fate by visibly responding to Madame (Sally Anne) Montberclair, the female representative of the town's aristocracy. Nordan's craft is again on display in this subtly done scene. Without overtly appearing to do so, the text clarifies that it is the presence of Madame Montberclair, rather than any action of Bobo's, that threatens and outrages Solon. Her abrupt invasion of Red's, in fact, threatens all of the males present. This becomes especially true when she asks for Kotex. She is not only a foreign presence but one that foregrounds the secrets of female anatomy, a subject that the males for whom Red's is a kind of inviolable refuge pretend not to know about because it makes them uncomfortable: "Usually men bought Kotex. A man knew how to purchase a box of Kotex. A man would whisper a discreet word to Red—like, 'The Crimson Fairy's visiting my house today, podner, can you do a little something to help me out?'—and Red would slip him what he needed, like contraband to be smuggled away. This was the first time a woman had ever asked Red for such of a thing" (30). As far as violating taboos is concerned, Sally Anne Montberclair might just as well have suggested incest to the assembled males. Moreover, she adds to the outrage she has created by driving away with Bobo, who on a dare has made a sexual overture to Sally Anne, sitting in the front seat beside her. Thus, "the truth was out about Sally Anne Montberclair, she was modern" (29).

Such modernity makes Solon uncomfortable on two levels. Sally Anne's appearance at Red's is not only a gender invasion but a class assault as well. The Montberclairs do not come to Red's, and certainly if they did they would not ask for something so inappropriate. Even though historically and currently exploited by it, Solon has previously subscribed to the old southern mythology of heroic aristocratic males and pure aristocratic females, of benevolent landowners and loyal yeomen. In addition, he needs women like his wife, who appear clearly inferior to such aristocratic women, as sexual objects and targets of his emotional and physical abuse. Now, without warning, a supposedly pure aristocratic woman has appeared before him and forced attention on the secrets of her body—most of all, she has asserted her biological femaleness and thus shattered Solon's long-standing ideals. In fact, by openly asking for what she does, she, in his mind, descends to a level even beneath his wife. Moreover, Solon responds to Sally Anne sexually, as Bobo is accused of doing. His resulting self-hatred originates in two conflicting reactions: he desires a woman for whom he can only feel contempt because she has shattered his long-held ideals, but she nevertheless remains socially superior to him. Thus both he and Sally Anne deserve punishment. (Once again it is Victor Jory desiring sexual intercourse with Vivian Leigh, but this time feeling bad about it.)

But even this would not be enough. Sally Anne's behavior has brought the entire social order into question, and a sacrificial victim must be quickly identified. For Solon, Bobo's actions—indeed, his mere presence at Red's—provide an immediate answer to this need: African-American males, and especially young ones who "forget their place," long provided such an answer in Mississippi and throughout the South. Solon is a believer in yet another southern tradition—lynching. René Girard describes lynching as one the "forms of [collective] violence that break out spontaneously in countries threatened by crisis" (80). In the history of the American South, such moments of crisis have resulted from perceived threats to stability on several levels. Lynching was a distinctly male ritual, though often celebrated after the fact by women and children as well. Moreover, the victims were virtually always male, and some form of sexual torture and quite often castration preceded the actual murder of the victim. Just as importantly, the perpetrators of lynching were usually men of Solon's social class, the economically victimized inhabitants of numerous Balance Dues who felt their manhood threatened by an apparently hopeless and unending poverty. They could hardly challenge a system they barely understood and to which they had so committed their allegiance as to have adopted the mythology of "the Lost Cause," but they could always retaliate against African Americans, the more arbitrarily chosen the better. One remembers that lynching was defended by southern politicians and newspapers as a necessary institution for controlling the black population. Thus it became an integral part of a repressive social structure. Girard's mythological concept of violence and Redding's understanding of it as systemic in nature merge in Nordan's treatment of lynching. For men of whom Solon Gregg is a fictional representative, existence was a perpetual economic crisis in which those who profited from the social structure were sacrosanct, while random African Americans could always be identified for brutal and gory forms of sacrifice.

Sally Anne Montberclair, however, has violated the established social order, and Solon feels free to go to her husband, Dexter, and tell about her transgression with Bobo. After retreating to the Arrow Hotel, he strips himself naked, gets drunk, and decides that he has to kill someone. Initially he identifies himself as the logical victim. After all, besides having sexually responded to Sally Anne, he has been so inadequate a provider for his family that his son literally tried to burn him to death (burning alive rivaled hanging as a form of lynching). He even goes so far as to put the barrel of his pistol in his mouth until he decides that killing himself is not an adequate response to the collapse of his vision of social order. He then shifts the target to Glenn, his grotesquely burned son: "Seem like the least a daddy could do, after he caused so much trouble for the tyke. It'd be the one act of kindness Solon was ever responsible for" (106). He quickly decides to extend his generosity to include killing his wife and all of his children and *then* himself. There is a kind of grotesque logic in Solon's drunken thought process. He has failed to be an adequate provider for his family and has caused them untold suffering; thus, by killing them, he will alleviate their pain, and by killing himself he will assuage his guilt. He next has an intensely satisfying dream in which he envisions the corpses of his immediate family, plus that of his sister Juanita, who has married an African American whom Solon calls a "pimp." Juanita, his own sister, has violated the southern code in the most fundamental of ways and thus should be added to the list of the imminently dead.

Solon's generous plan to relieve the pain of his family and compensate for the guilt of his sister is sidetracked by another dream, however. In this one, he re-creates a moment in which Dexter Montberclair, while in the Korean War, fired blindly into some brush and killed eight people, "half . . . men in uniform, half . . . kids, old people" (114). In Solon's dream, this act of half-intended, senseless murder by the aristocratic Montberclair elevates him to heroic stature in the eyes of the men in his company. There are at least three possible ways in which to interpret the narrative complexity of this passage: Solon has somehow entered Montberclair's consciousness, a collective Arrow Catcher consciousness exists into which any of the townspeople may unpredictably enter, or the drunken Solon is projecting his repressed fantasies onto Montberclair and dreaming something that never happened. The incorporation of Korea into Nordan's novel seems somewhat intrusive, though thematically relevant; the implication seems to be that the American involvement in Korea was simply an extension of the kind of racism, cultural xenophobia, and capital exploitation that characterizes Nordan's Mississippi. In a manner comparable to the treatment of the U.S.-Vietnam interaction in Robert Stone's *Dog Soldiers,* the American experience in Korea has produced a nightmarish fourthspace in Mississippi defined by a senseless violence. The kind of racism that results in the murder of Bobo fuels much of this violence.

The culmination of Solon's dream seems to point toward the interpretation that Solon is subconsciously projecting his fantasies onto Montberclair. In the dream, he imagines the embittered aristocratic husband forcing the barrel of a pistol into Sally Anne's mouth. The phallic implications of all this seem clear, especially when one remembers Solon's having placed the barrel of a pistol in his own mouth before passing out. But even in fantasy Solon cannot imagine himself having sexual intercourse with Sally Anne, much less having her perform fellatio on him; while he does respond to her and wants to humiliate her, her social position makes her inaccessible even to his subconscious.

Solon is abruptly awakened by the voice of the real Dexter Montberclair, who has invaded his hotel room and offers him a thousand dollars to kidnap and kill Bobo. In the subsequent dialogue, the aristocratic landowner makes the murderous (il)logic of the southern class system quite explicit to Solon: "Decent whitefolks have always needed the likes of you . . . we need people like you to help keep our niggers in line . . . it gives you lower classes, you white-trash boys, some *raison d'etre*, wouldn't you say so?" (118).

Dexter is too dishonest to overtly acknowledge that he wants Bobo killed as revenge for Sally Anne's and Bobo's indiscretions, so he focuses on Solon's account of the young boy carrying a picture of a white woman in his billfold: "Do you see the arrogance involved here? He's got a wallet, in the first place, and now we find out about the picture?" (119). By owning a wallet, Bobo possesses an emblem of economic security and independence, which is for the aristocratic Montberclair possibly even more threatening than the charge of miscegenation. In fact, Dexter learns on the night of the kidnapping and murder that the picture is one of movie star Hedy Lamarr, and he is outraged both by Solon's having deliberately led him to believe that it is one of Sally Anne (which he must recover in order to avoid scandal and disgrace) and, somewhat irrationally, by Solon's not knowing who Hedy Lamarr is. Dexter, who counts on precisely this kind of xenophobic ignorance among the poor whites, has it suddenly backfire on him.

The account of Solon's murder of Bobo introduces the most creative and surprising of the narrative experiments contained in the text. One of Solon's shots hits Bobo in the eye and knocks the eye out of its socket, and the narrative focus abruptly shifts away from Solon to Bobo's detached eye, which allows the dead boy a cosmic and healing vision that no living character could conceivably have: "From the eye . . . the dead boy saw the world as if his seeing it were accompanied by an eternal music as . . . a cottonmouth hissing on a limb, the hymning of beehives, of a bird's nest, the bray of an iceman's mule, the cry of herons or mermaids in the swamp, and rain across wide water. In this music the demon eye saw . . . transformations, angels and devils, worlds invisible to him before death" (175). Thus only Bobo, the sacrificial victim, the martyred outsider, is allowed after death a vision of the tragic and magical beauty of the Mississippi landscape. The detached eye then watches Solon as he ties Bobo's body to a stolen gin fan before throwing it into the swamp.

Beneath the black water, Bobo's dark but redeeming vision continues: "He saw turtles and mussels and the earth of plantations sifted there from other states, another age, through a million ditches and on the feet of turkey vultures and blue herons and kingfishers. He saw schools of minnows and a trace of slave death from a century before. He saw baptizings and drownings" (180). This underwater vision echoes the text's account of the buzzards, Nordan's embodiments of the profiteers of southern class and race hatred. But in the drowned plantations it also presages the end of the oppressive southern class system: in the "trace of slave death," Bobo captures a lingering image of the legacy of that system of which his own body will be another trace. Finally, in a note reminiscent of T. S. Eliot, he envisions rituals of spiritual rebirth inextricably mixed with death by water.

This experiment in magic realism extends to other levels as well. Bobo enters the consciousness of the sleeping white boy, Sugar Mecklin, as "a mermaid, a bare-breasted creature combing her hair with a comb the color of bone" (183).[3] Thus alerted, Sugar joins his friend Sweet Austin to recover Bobo's body.[4] But entering Sugar's consciousness is a minor feat compared to what else the dead Bobo accomplishes. Most importantly, he enters the heart and mind of Alice Conroy, the text's image of a redemptive innocence. He even sees Alice seeing "his own dead body in a raindrop" (181). After this startling vision, she becomes more "black" and rebellious as the text progresses.

Earlier in the novel, Alice is a largely ludicrous figure, brooding over the end of a love affair with one of her married university professors and given to taking her fourth graders on wildly bizarre and inappropriate field trips, such as the visit to Glenn Gregg. She lives with her uncle Runt, his four children, and a frustrating parrot that refuses to repeat anything said to it. Still, her potential as a redemptive figure is indicated in an important flashback sequence organized around her past experience with, and attitude toward, magic. As a little girl, Alice was a rather typical child of American materialism who "didn't believe in magic," who in fact "didn't give it a thought" (154). Her potential for change is foreshadowed, though, by her love for her father, a man devoted to hunting and to exploring nature, and by her own response to the physical world of the Mississippi Delta. She responds to "deer in the morning, with tails like big white flags and antler rakes like rocking chairs for children . . . once she saw a brown bear, old man with a purple tongue, eating dewberries on the edge of the woods, careful to avoid the thorns of the wild and fragrant rose bushes entwined in the same fruit, in the same field" (157).

This passage is, in part, homage to Faulkner and "The Bear." Nordan is recognizing Faulkner as a literary forefather; more importantly, however, he shares Faulkner's vision of Mississippi as an Eden threatened by greed and a legacy of racist and class oppression. The innocent and unsophisticated Alice shares with Faulkner a reverence for the natural landscape of Mississippi, based on an affirmation of it as a world where magical experience is made possible by the mingling of human and animal life. As in Faulkner, Nordan's vision here is not simplistic anthropomorphism; in it, human beings are redeemed through communion with the nonhuman world. Her father becomes her guide in this new level of experience. When she says of the bear that "it's like an angel," her father responds, "It could kill us with scorn alone" (158). The natural world is magical, Alice learns, and she is thereby converted to a belief in magic as an alternate mode of existence. Still, even after the dead Bobo invades her adult consciousness through her vision of his body enclosed in a raindrop, she is frustrated by the seeming impracticality of her vision, assuming "the futility of magic to change anything of importance in the world" (159). The presumed irrelevance of magic in a world of violence and oppression dooms her faith in nature's ability to bring salvation.

For a time, Alice is dismayed by the potential of violence to despoil the new Eden and to corrupt the natural world. Yet her vision at the end is of a redemptive world of magic, of salvation through the natural world. She obtains this redemptive vision as a result of taking her fourth graders on the most controversial and daring of all her field trips, one even surpassing their visit to "the Prince of Darkness Funeral Parlor where they looked at a body" (225). She escorts them to the trial of Solon Gregg for the murder of Bobo. Significantly, Dexter Montberclair is not charged as an accomplice in the murder, even though Solon has left behind evidence that implicates both of them. Thus the aristocracy is left alone, the class system upheld. From the first, though, the presence of Alice and the white children at the trial violates the community's practice of racial segregation; they are seated in the front of the courtroom balcony, a space otherwise completely given over to African Americans. It is as if the legal community of Arrow Catcher is trying to hide their existence from the eyes of the white spectators at the trial.

Immediately upon entering the courthouse, Alice is overcome by the sheer whiteness of space inside: "She thought about Ahab and the whiteness of the Great Whale, the eternal evil verity of its metaphorical and blubbery self" (226). Looking down at Bobo's aunt and uncle isolated in the sea of whiteness that is the courtroom floor and thus made even more aware than they already are of their vulnerability, she is disgusted by the sheer, ugly injustice of it all: "All those white people down there! White! Even to Alice it looked like an abomination of some kind. White, white, bird dooky, white, it was sickening, a pestilence!" (226). Alice's revulsion at this sight awakens the presence of Bobo within her, and before she quite realizes what she is going to do, she shouts down to Bobo's uncle: "We are here. We colored people are behind you" (231). Of course, the white ocean in the courtroom is appalled by this, but Alice (or Alice-Bobo) is undismayed and begins waving frantically to catch the uncle's attention and thereby reassure him. Nordan next stretches his motif of redemption and salvation even further by having Alice's class wave, too. To convey the full significance of their action, the text enters the collective stream of consciousness of the children: "*We are suffering damage from this field trip into the heart of darkness and from our teacher that we may never recover from and we don't care because we love her and become visible to ourselves in her presence, and for reasons obscure we love you, too, old colored man, old colored woman, grieving souls, we suffer your loss, we fear for your life, we don't know what is going on at all*" (212).

Like much of *Wolf Whistle*, this spontaneous moment of identification of the schoolchildren with Bobo's uncle and aunt probably cannot stand much rational investigation (the novel is partly an experiment in magic realism, after all). Moreover, Alice's wards are only fourth graders, and there can be no guarantee that their epiphany of affirmation and redemption will survive their shaping by the racist world of Arrow Catcher. But the implication of some future redemption for Arrow Catcher is unmistakable. Bobo continues to fulfill his role as sacrificial victim of violence; his death foreshadows at least a momentary end to the legacy of senseless violence that threatens to engulf the community.

The level of risk inherent in Nordan's retelling of the Emmett Till story becomes unmistakably obvious in its account of the Solon Gregg trial. Absurdist comedy dominates much of it. The courtroom sergeant at arms, Peter Skeeter, "half Choctaw Indian," is sent to the balcony to admonish Alice and the children. One of the fourth graders is Peter's brother, Jeeter Skeeter, whom Peter challenges by asking why the young boy had yelled that he was colored. When Jeeter answers, "I *am* a colored person," Peter can only respond, "Well, not in the usual sense of the word" (235). Of course, whatever "the usual sense of the word" (presumably someone or something not white), Jeeter is closer to the truth than Peter. Nordan is satirizing the careless and pejorative use of the term *colored* in American, and especially southern, culture. Moreover, in giving the two brothers the names he does, he is coming very close to stereotypes of southern poor whites; but as is true in other ways, Nordan's clear acceptance of, even affection for, his fictional characters from this socioeconomic level allows him to get away with the near stereotyping. The exchange between Peter and Skeeter *is* amusing.

Even more amusing is the exchange between Peter and Alice's uncle Runt Conroy when the latter enters the courtroom with his recalcitrant parrot in hand. Peter, who values his job as sergeant at arms, momentarily tries to refuse the parrot admission: "If you was blind and needed the parrot to walk across the street with you, well . . . that'd be different." Never the strongest-willed of individuals, Peter surrenders to the absurdity of his own vision of a seeing-eye parrot: "It'd be kind of funny, though, wouldn't it, a blind man walking behind a parrot." Runt quickly understands that the way to overcome Peter's resistance to the courtroom admission of his parrot is to join in the game: "You'd have to walk kind of slow." Peter continues the joke he began: "You'd have to have a long leash" and then raises it to another level: "Blind children could go out for the arrow-catching team [a high school athletic team that does precisely what the term suggests] if they had a seeing-eye parrot. 'Arrow! Look out!'" (239). Inevitably, the sheer hilarity of all this so overcomes Peter that he forgets Runt and his pet and wanders away.

The parrot soon plays a memorable role in the trial's climactic moment. A clearly frightened but still determined Uncle is on the witness stand when the prosecutor, after trying for a last time to intimidate him, asks him to identify Bobo's kidnapper. At this moment, the parrot escapes Runt's lap and spectacularly takes flight throughout the courtroom, becoming the center of nearly everyone's attention. Only Uncle "failed to notice the wild and magical ascent of the African parrot, generations closer to their shared homeland than Uncle himself, brother to bright plumage and courageous heart" (250).

Watching from the balcony, Alice intuitively understands the significance of the parrot's unexpected flight: "The bird was the dead boy. It was Bobo—the magic of good and evil both" (254). Having invaded the consciousness of first Sugar Mecklin and then Alice, the spirit of Bobo has taken wing in the form of a creature native to Africa, the continent of his racial origin; and it promptly lights on the head of a stunned and outraged Solon Gregg, thus identifying his killer. So inspired, Uncle points at Solon and says in response to the prosecutor's question: "Thar he" (256); and Alice's heart responds, "*Thar he. Thar she blows*" (256). Not only Solon but the violent and racist society that produced him have been exposed.

Besides Alice and her fourth graders at the trial, the text dramatizes other hints of a possible redemption for the community of Arrow Catcher. After the discovery of Bobo's body by Sugar Mecklin and Sweet Austin, cruel jokes about the murdered young African American become common among the high school boys until one Smokey Viner, previously noted for his pro-clivity for head-butting inanimate objects and his ineptitude as an arrow catcher,[5] challenges them: "Y'all ought to be shamed of yourself, laughing about a boy got killed" (205). Later, when Smokey again demonstrates his courage, if no enhanced talent, in arrow-catching practice, the other boys are inspired by his example and "they saw hope. For themselves, for the Delta, for Mississippi, maybe the world" (210).[6] In addition, Runt Conroy begins to insist, albeit with mixed success, on being called by his given name, Cyrus; the parrot now repeats everything said to it.

Nordan knows, though, that such affirmation must be muted. Mississippi's history of violent racism and its still-intact economic system, based firmly on inequality and oppression, will not go away so easily. Solon is acquitted, and Alice Conroy, during his trial, thinks of Mississippi as "the sorriest state in the nation" (225). Finally, Smokey Viner is only one visionary young voice; quite a different kind of young male virtually takes over Red's Good-lookin Bar and Gro. Cyrus (née Runt) is especially bothered by the "new boys": "They were foul-mouthed and unruly and unpredictable and wild, and maybe dangerous. . . . These boys didn't seem to have been affected at all by the murder or the trial. It was unsettling to be around people who lived where this thing has happened and for them to seem not to have noticed. There was a little too much of Solon Gregg in every one of these young boys, young men, for Runt's taste" (260–61).

The 1960s would see the murders in Mississippi of civil rights leader Medgar Evers (1963) and the three young civil rights workers James Chaney,

Andrew Goodman, and Michael Schwerner (1964); real-life equivalents of the "new boys" at Red's probably were unaffected by those tragic events as well, if they did not actively cheer them. Evers's killer escaped punishment for three decades, even though, as with Solon Gregg, virtually everyone in the community knew of his involvement.[7]

To treat the Emmett Till case with the mixture of magic realism and absurdist humor that distinguishes *Wolf Whistle* is politically and artistically daring, especially for a white writer like Nordan.[8] It is doubly essential, then, that any affirmation in the novel be muted; it becomes a matter not just of realism but of racial sensitivity. Nordan must make it clear that he is not letting Mississippi off the hook. His success in doing so while still affirming the terrible and magical beauty of the landscape of the Delta results in a text that, while very different from Campbell's *Your Blues Ain't Like Mine*, is, in its own way, just as powerful.

5

The Myth of the Boatright Men

Dorothy Allison's *Bastard Out of Carolina*

The horribly abused though ultimately triumphant protagonist of Dorothy Allison's *Bastard Out of Carolina*, Ruth Anne Boatright, nicknamed Bone, is *literally* born of accidental violence. Anney Boatright, unmarried and eight months pregnant with Bone, is asleep in the backseat of a car driven by her brother-in-law when it smashes into the "slow-moving car" in front of it. Even though "she flew right over [the front-seat passengers'] heads, through the windshield, and over the car they hit" (2), Anney recovers completely from the accident after being unconscious for three days, during which time Ruth Anne is born and named by her grandmother and one of her aunts. Because Anney's mother and sister cannot write legibly and have never "bothered to discuss how Anney would be spelled," the child's name is spelled "three different ways" on the hospital form (2–3). But the worst humiliation comes when, for different reasons, neither woman reveals the name of the father, and the infant Ruth Anne is "certified a bastard by the state of South Carolina" (3). Getting the denigrating label removed from her daughter's birth certificate becomes a mission for Anney, one in which she succeeds only at the end of the novel when Ruth Anne is thirteen years old. Ruth Anne is nicknamed "Bone" because of her uncle Earle's comment that she is "no bigger than a knucklebone" (2), after which a young cousin pulls back her blanket "to see 'the bone'" (2).

This absurdist opening scene nicely encapsulates several of the novel's central thematic concerns. The Boatrights are called by others and refer to themselves as "poor whites," and *Bastard Out of Carolina* has been critically evaluated as a "poor white" novel. For instance, David Reynolds sees Allison's fiction as continuing in a subgenre of "white trash fiction" inspired by Erskine Caldwell and the Nelson Algren of *A Walk on the Wild Side* (1956). Reynolds's essay is especially valuable for its analysis of the term *white trash*. He sees it as tied to an American stereotype that, because it is based on an assumption of genetic inferiority, "assuages any guilt over economic inequality": "American society is not at fault if these low-others are genetically predisposed to be white trash" (360). Reynolds also makes a valuable distinction between the terms *white trash* and *poor white:* "Whereas 'poor' implies a solely economic designation, 'trash' is more general, implying debasement in all categories whether economic, sexual, moral, or intellectual" (365). In an introduction to the 2002 Penguin Plume paperback edition of her collection of short stories, *Trash*, Allison adds her own variation to this distinction: "There was this concept of the 'good' poor, and that fantasy had little to do with the everyday lives my family had survived. The good poor were hardworking, ragged but clean, and intrinsically honorable. We were the bad poor. We were men who drank and couldn't keep a job; women, invariably pregnant before marriage, who quickly became worn, fat, and old from working too many hours and bearing too many children; and children with runny noses, watery eyes, and the wrong attitudes" (vii).

At various moments in Allison's novel, members of the Boatright family, knowing that they are widely viewed as white trash, assume different postures toward the label—sometimes denying it, sometimes passively accepting it, and sometimes adopting it as a symbol of familial and class pride. The deterministic aspects of all three approaches are clear. Whether they deny the term or surrender to it or try to adopt it and transform its connotations, the Boatrights are allowing themselves to be defined externally in a context of societal stereotypes. *Bastard Out of Carolina* is, to a large extent, a naturalistic study in external and internal marginalization. One would be hard pressed to find a more striking illustration of external marginalization than Bone's state-issued birth certificate officially defining her as existing outside the realm of respectability. That despite their poverty and outsider status the Boatright family never completely surrenders to internal marginalization is indicated by Anney's long and finally successful struggle to remove the state-imposed stigma that hangs over her daughter from birth.

Nevertheless, as the opening scene demonstrates, the Boatrights contribute to the negative stereotypes that define and limit them. Bone has this to say about the cause of the accident: "My aunt Alma insists to this day that what happened was in no way Uncle Travis's fault, but I *know* that the first time I ever saw Uncle Travis sober was when I was seventeen and they had just removed half his stomach along with his liver. I cannot imagine that he hadn't been drinking. There's no question in my mind but that they had *all* been drinking, except Mama, who never could drink, and certainly not when she was pregnant" (2). For generations, alcoholism has plagued the Boatright family, but what has been even more devastating than the disease has been their reaction to it. Poverty contributes to their drinking, of course—in part they drink to forget, and the debilitating effects of drinking inevitably make escape from their poverty even more difficult than it already is—but the intensity with which the Boatrights deny that alcoholism is a family problem is just as important. Allison depicts Anney and, by implication, Bone as representatives of a new kind of Boatright, as women who struggle for a liberating honesty. In this struggle, Anney will ultimately fail because of her economic dependency as a victimized female and because of her inability to resist the demands of her own sexuality. Bone, in contrast, despite a horrific childhood during which she suffers repeated sexual, physical, and emotional abuse from her stepfather, Daddy Glen, will triumph through the narration of her traumatic experiences. To succeed in this she will have to accept the bitter lesson that, in the last analysis, there is no one on whom she can depend, not even Anney.

The roots of the Boatright males' problem with alcoholism go considerably deeper than simple denial; drinking becomes part of a family myth that they are constantly in the process of creating and maintaining, a myth that the women in the family, even though they suffer additional victimization precisely because of it, proudly affirm. One of Bone's central purposes in constructing her bitter bildungsroman is to deconstruct the myth of the Boatright males. At one point in the text, Aunt Ruth, the aunt who helped name Bone, tells her niece about some of the more memorable exploits of the Boatright men. "She devoted two whole days" to telling Bone about Great-Uncle Haslam Boatright, "who had driven a truck over at the JC Penney mill until he shot his wife and her lover on a weekend visit to Atlanta" (126). "Best of all," she relates the episode of Uncle Beau and Uncle Earle trying to enlist in the army in order to fight in the Korean War and getting "thrown out of the recruiting office into the muddy street after the sergeant got their arrest records" (126). Of course Beau and Earle were drunk at the time and were subsequently arrested, and the rest of their adventure sounds like something out of the most grotesque frontier humor: "'Oh, come on, son,' Beau was supposed to have told that sergeant after punching out the deputy and chewing on the ear of some innocent fool who'd made the mistake of trying to help, 'You an't gonna find better soldier material anywhere in the country. Hell, you can see we already know how to fight'" (127). Lacking as they are in male role models who might affirm lasting and meaningful values, Beau and Earle do indeed know how to fight. Their behavior at the army recruitment office, along with Great-Uncle Haslam's revenge assault, highlights the centrality of violence to the unfolding myth of the Boatright males.

Ruth offers her interpretation of the implications of the recruitment office story. Agreeing that Beau and Earle were hardly army material, she says: "But they'd love the chance to shoot strangers, drive trucks, and work on engines. No different really from what they do now, except for the uniform. They love that story, though, never seem to pay no mind to the fact that the army didn't want no trash that has spent so much time in jail and hasn't even finished high school." To which Bone offers a typically blunt response: "They're drunks" (127).

Ruth's comment that Beau and Earle would "love the chance to shoot strangers" emphasizes the centrality of violence to the evolving myth of the Boatright males and to their cult of masculinity. Economically disadvantaged and socially marginalized as white trash, they search for self-validation in visions of killing, the power implicit in taking the lives of others redeeming the powerlessness of their own existence. The culture out of which the Boatrights evolve views power as an exclusively male privilege; lacking that power, the Boatright men feel symbolically castrated. Poverty and social alienation constitute assaults on their maleness, and they seek to redeem their lost manhood through a collective fantasy that is both self-defeating and dangerous to others. Of course, the fantasy, along with their alcoholism, becomes part of a vicious cycle that further entraps them. Constituting another way in which they refuse to confront reality, it intensifies their social ostracism and economic vulnerability. Moreover, the Boatright males most commonly harm themselves and the women, willingly or otherwise, with whom they are involved. Ruth's analysis also emphasizes the fundamental randomness of the violence they valorize. According to her, it is "strangers" whom they would love to shoot, not enemies. In fact, the Boatright men seem to have very little comprehension of the nature of their real enemies, namely, the exploitative socioeconomic system in which they are trapped and their own crippling concept of manhood. They fall into the trap of personification that often tempts the socially desperate—it is, after all, easier to imagine attacking individual human beings, however remote and distant they may be, than combating abstract systems or confronting the fallacies of ingrained beliefs. Lacking—in fact, disdaining—education as they do, the Boatright males are especially susceptible to this trap. Bone's two-word response to Ruth is in part indicative of her refusal to be complicit in the Boatright fantasy of masculinity. More completely than her mother ever can, Bone sees through and repudiates the customary self-deception of her family. But before breaking free of the familial valorization of a manhood based on violence against others, she is almost destroyed by it.

Of the texts that constitute the focus of this study, *Bastard Out of Carolina* is the most traditionally naturalistic. The opening scene establishes the deterministic forces against which Bone and her mother must struggle: sudden and senseless violence, social ostracism, the almost total acceptance of male domination that characterizes the Boatright family, and the habitual denial by family members of their own complicity with the forces that oppress them. The dominating myth in the text is a largely self-created and self-perpetuating example of bricolage—that of the heroic and intensely masculine Boatright men. Certainly, the myth is, to some degree, a doomed attempt to deny the powerlessness in which the family is trapped and thus a response to external forces. It is also a mimicking of mythic white southern male heroism rooted in the fantasy of "the Lost Cause" and in such illicit vigilante resistance to Reconstruction as the Ku Klux Klan. The vigilante legends especially valorized violent male resistance to unpopular laws. But it is significant that such mythologizing in Allison's text is of a diminished order. The Boatrights have virtually no sense of any community outside their family. Even if they demonstrate loyalty to the Confederate flag, they view most other southerners as strangers. Though it may have roots in a peculiarly southern version of Girard's sacrificial crisis, the myth of the Boatright men is, in the time of Allison's text, an isolated and consciously cultivated fantasy with no visible connection to any external communal crisis. Every bit as dangerous and self-destructive, it is more degraded as a myth than the vanished ancestral legacy of violence that gives birth to Glenn Whitehouse in Russell Banks's *Affliction*. Comparable to Rolfe's narration in *Affliction*, the Boatright myth constitutes a debased fourthspace that harms everyone trapped in it.

Like Glenn and Wade Whitehouse, Allison's male characters exemplify Lawrence Kramer's thesis concerning the dangers and limitations inherent in a strict binary separation of "the masculine" and "the feminine." Adapting ideas of both Freud and Lacan, Kramer believes that the male need to deny androgyny leads to anger, misogyny, and self-hatred. In order to repress the multiplicity of their humanness, he argues, males have traditionally assumed "an intact core of preexisting masculinity" that the socialization process inevitably represses. While submission to authority is essential to functioning within society, such submission is arbitrarily associated with the female and thus with weakness. Abuse of the female becomes, then, a mode of indirect rebellion against a vague, almost mythological authority that limits an imagined masculine freedom (120). Allison's text carries this concept a few steps further. In it, female children are viewed as being especially weak and submissive and are thus especially vulnerable to male rage. Moreover, the Boatrights are preternaturally aware of the family myth that, they believe, simultaneously directs and excuses their actions. In fact, the fantasized heroism of the Boatright men has become so restricted in application and so consciously created and perpetuated that it would hardly qualify as a myth in a structuralist analysis of the mythologizing process. The controlling consciousness of the Boatright men has become overwhelmingly incestuous; they proclaim loyalty to the family and only to the family, yet even in this severely limited approach they fail.

Ironically, those charged with verbalizing and perpetuating the Boatright legacy are its most immediate victims—the Boatright women. Storytelling is central to the Boatright family. It becomes their most important means of resistance to the social forces that largely control them, and most often it is the women who tell the stories. It is important to clarify here that Bone (and by implication Allison) cherishes this particular family legacy. Grandmother Boatright is something of an unofficial family griot who insists that her own grandfather was of Cherokee descent, a kind, though not sexually faithful, man. At other points in the text this Cherokee ancestry is questioned; nevertheless, what is significant is Grandmother Boatright's insistence on it. It is her way of further romanticizing the myth of Boatright male prowess. Most importantly, Bone appropriates the Cherokee ancestral myth as a basis of her own rebellious identity: "Every third family in Greenville might have a little Cherokee, but I had been born with a full head of black hair. I've got my great-granddaddy's blood in me, I told myself. I am night's own daughter, my great-granddaddy's warrior child" (207).

Storytelling, especially as it relates to the horror of Daddy Glen's unrelenting abuse of Bone and to *Bastard Out of Carolina*'s lesbian subtext, has been the inspiration for some of the most illuminating critical discussion of Allison's novel. In an extended Lacanian analysis of the novel, Lynda Hart discusses it in the context of "witnessing" and writes that "*Bastard Out of*

Carolina is one of the most courageous novels of our time, a time that Shoshana Feldman has described as the age of testimony, an age in which witnessing itself has become a major trauma" (170). Hart then applies the concepts of testimony and witnessing to the text after an initial clarification: "I begin with Feldman, not because I want to make the too easy and often heinous comparison between the Holocaust and any or all other traumatic events, but because the testimonial *as form* is often the complex, intimate medium for the expression of the incest survivor as well. And, indeed, the language of psychologists who have written about incest survivors and Feldman's articulation of the testimonial converge in often unexpected but immensely illuminating ways" (171). Hart's treatment of Allison's novel as a mode of witnessing incestuous abuse is helpful on two levels. First, it sheds light on the survivor guilt that haunts Bone throughout the text and becomes especially evident in Allison's narration of her masturbatory fantasies. Second, Hart is perceptive in her analysis of the phenomenon in which victims often remember traumatic events in ways that differ from the memories of other people. In order to survive, those caught in the midst of horrific repression and abuse unconsciously construct their own personal truths that are no less valid or important than more objective and documentary truth. This, Hart speculates, is as true of Bone as of virtually all survivors; she then argues that Allison's text lies outside clear and traditional definitions of genre and can most accurately be described as a "pseudotestimonial" (173).

Hart, like other critics of the novel (see, e.g., Cvetkovich), approaches it as a lesbian text. After a preliminary discussion of the novel in the context of an orality practiced by poor white southerners, Jillian Sandell, noting that Allison has assumed the label of "queer white trash," evaluates the novel as a transgressive critique of class and sexual oppression. Sandell stresses that Allison's class identification sometimes distances her from other lesbian critics and writers. Moreover, she notes that, especially in her treatment of Bone's masturbatory fantasies, Allison explores the links between sexual abuse and violence in ways that trouble even lesbian critics:

> Allison reclaims, therefore, the label "white trash" as a political strategy to expose class-based discrimination in the United States and to emphasize the structural, rather than volitional, nature of economic oppression. She calls herself "queer" to reclaim those aspects of her identity that have defined her as marginal among lesbians, and to emphasize the social (as well as sexual) aspects of such an identity. . . .

Allison writes that much of the hatred that has been directed at her sexual preference is really class hatred, and vice versa, which underscores the ways in which both her sexuality and her class status are constructed as falling outside the normative (and overlapping) moral orders of the middle-classes and the queer community. (215–16)

Sandell's insight that Allison proclaims her double marginalization as the core of her identity is perceptive—*Bastard Out of Carolina* is a text meant to assault repressive assumptions and practices no matter what their origins. Thus, for Bone and by implication Allison, the act of storytelling necessitates documenting in graphic detail the abuse she has suffered.[1] Only in this way can she expose complacent class assumptions and the nightmarish legacy of abuse of women and children. Only in this way can she achieve self-empowerment. Moreover, as Sandell observes, by writing from within the stereotypes of "poor white trash" and "queer," Allison hopes to reverse their negative connotations.[2]

Bone becomes, then, a very different kind of storyteller from the other Boatright women. She refuses to mythologize the males of the family; in her *story,* which is *Bastard Out of Carolina,* they are depicted as spoiled and dangerous adult children defiantly proud of their irresponsibility. All of this is not to deny the view of Sandell and others that *Bastard* assumes "the structural, rather than the volitional, nature of economic oppression" or the strong element of love in Bone's feelings toward her Boatright uncles, who finally do become, however ineffectually, her defenders against Daddy Glen. Allison is repudiating the assumption that "poor white" status is either biological or chosen. The Boatrights are trapped in a relentless and grinding poverty that, by the 1950s and 1960s in which the novel is set, has become an integral part of the socioeconomic structure in the American South. No war on poverty ever has significantly benefited them; nor will one. The destructive and self-destructive nature of the male Boatrights' response to their economic entrapment makes their situation doubly hopeless. They truly lack vision; they are unable and unwilling to see beyond their familial circle. *Bastard Out of Carolina* is a hegemonic study of the interrelationships of power and powerlessness. Poor and economically powerless, the Boatright men construct and perpetuate a myth of their heroic exploits, which are in fact violent and self-destructive and thus reinforce the dominant society's stereotypes about them. Intensely misogynistic, the myth assumes a view of women as inferior, as beings created to serve them and to celebrate their adventures. A circular irony is in effect here—the Boatright men proclaim women to be inferior and lacking in heroic stature, while the women, in order to protect the self-deception of their men, treat them like children. Until Bone, then, no one is forced to grow up and confront the multileveled reality of the Boatright entrapment, and Bone is ultimately able to do so only after seven horrible years of abuse have marginalized her from almost everyone.

Initially, Bone, like a good Boatright woman, idolizes her uncles, who in turn usually show her the same kindness that they do the other children in the family. As a child, Bone admires and envies the irresponsible behavior of her uncles: "Men could do anything, and everything they did, no matter how violent or mistaken, was viewed with humor and understanding. . . . What men did was just what men did. Some days I would grind my teeth, wishing I had been born a boy" (23). Bone initially buys into the Boatright binary of irresponsible masculine freedom and submissive feminine nurturing. Her uncle Earle is both the embodiment of Boatright maleness and Bone's favorite uncle: "He was known as Black Earle for three counties around. Mama said he was called Black Earle for that black black hair that fell over his eyes in a great soft curl, but Aunt Raylene said it was for his black, black heart" (24). "A good-looking man, soft-spoken and hardworking" (23), Earle was unabashedly unfaithful to his wife until she left him. He claims not to understand how his legendary infidelities could have hurt her—after all, as biologically grown-up children, Boatright men have always done, and are supposed to do, whatever they want. Aunt Ruth understands a great deal, and excuses a great deal, about Earle: "Earle's got the magic . . . [he] is just a magnet to women. Breaks their hearts and makes them like it. . . . All these youngsters playing at being something, imagining they can drive women wild with their narrow little hips and sweet baby smiles, they never gonna have the gift Earle has, don't even know enough to recognize it for what it is. A sad wounded man who genuinely likes women—that's what Earle is, a hurt little boy with just enough meanness to keep a woman interested" (24–25).

On the surface, Earle fits into an American popular-culture image of the sexually attractive and essentially lovable rogue who cares so much about all women that he finds it difficult to be loyal to any one of them—the film personae of Clark Gable and Robert Mitchum, for instance. He is moreover the contemporary prototype of the perhaps mythic Cherokee ancestor, the intimidating but gentle male of exotic origin who both is and is not part of the dominant white culture. But he is also a man who has been wounded by life and a "hurt little boy" who always expects to be forgiven for acts of behavior that hurt others. He rejects religion completely and believes the world to be "irredeemably corrupt" (147). Society as a whole proves to be less forgiving than Aunt Ruth and the other Boatright women; near the end of the novel Uncle Earle is in prison, a fact for which Bone, though considerably matured by her own brutal experience, still mourns: "He's been sent to the county farm for busting a man's jaw and breaking a window down at the Cracker Blue Café. Aunt Alma said he's gotten into more fights at the farm and a bunch of men had held him down and shaved off all his black hair. I tried to imagine him baldheaded" (198). The Samson overtones of all this are obvious: society has acted as a Delilah shearing the hair that symbolizes Earle's strength and assurance. Ultimately, this or a comparable fate was inevitable for Earle. It is difficult for anyone, and virtually impossible for anyone from Earle's social position, to act out of infantile irresponsibility forever. Males, moreover, are less likely to be charmed by Earle than women are. Significantly, Aunt Raylene, Bone's lesbian aunt, attributes his nickname to his "black black heart" rather than to his hair. Yet because of his undeniable appeal, because he tries to protect her, and probably most of all because she identifies with his persona of the romantic criminal in conflict with an oppressive capitalist system, Bone continues to care about him. Popular-culture prototypes again come into play here; for Bone, Earle is a kind of Humphrey Bogart, James Cagney, or John Garfield.

Even though she is still a child, Bone also engages in criminal activity. Ironically, she is apprehended and humiliated for a minor kind of violation but gets away with a much more serious act. She shoplifts four Tootsie Rolls—two for herself and two for her younger sister, Reese—from the local Woolworth's, only to be promptly caught by her mother. Intensely aware of being viewed as "poor white trash," Anney tells Bone about a cousin who steals compulsively and then takes her back to the Woolworth's store to return the remaining Tootsie Rolls and to pay for those already eaten. After Bone confesses her theft, the self-righteous manager humiliates her and, in order to keep her from "grow[ing] up to be a thief," bans her from the store. The episode is central to Allison's exploration of class distinctions in America and the humiliation that results from them. Although she has only taken a few cents' worth of merchandise, Bone is treated like a genuine criminal. Her banishment from Woolworth's symbolizes the banishment of the poor from the benefits of American capitalism, while paradoxically emphasizing their dependence on impersonal, large-scale consumer outlets.

Woolworth's and comparable stores were essential for the survival of small towns like the Greenville, South Carolina, of 1955 that is the setting of Allison's text, functioning as a social as well as financial center of the community, empowered to make and enforce their own brand of morality. The very smallness of these communities negated the protection of anonymity offered by urban department stores without providing to the poor any offsetting benefit or support. The manager of the store of course knew that Bone and Anney were Boatrights and thereby helpless in the face of whatever treatment he deemed appropriate for them; in yet another way, the legend of the Boatright men victimizes those closest to them. The association of the Boatrights with violence and criminality makes it easy for the Woolworth's manager to treat Bone, even though still a child, as a criminal.

As young as she is, Bone intuitively understands that a middle-class child who had taken a few pennies' worth of candy would not be scapegoated as she is. She is justifiably enraged: "I wanted to kick [the manager] or throw up on him or scream his name on the street. The longer he looked at me, the more I hated him. If I could have killed him with my stare, I would have. The look in his eyes told me that he knew what I was thinking" (97). Aware of her apparent powerlessness, Bone waits literally for years to exact a more meaningful revenge on the impersonal institution of Woolworth's instead of lashing out at its manager, who is after all only a company functionary. Along with her cousin Grey, Bone, while staying at Aunt Raylene's, retrieves a trawling chain from the polluted river that runs beside Raylene's house, and later the two use it to carry out a nighttime assault on Woolworth's.

Breaking into the store is difficult, demanding both physical strength and elaborate strategy, and it is Bone who undertakes the essential planning. Once inside the store, she and Grey smash glass counters and generally ransack the merchandise. Escaping, they run past "a little group of gray-faced men just down from the Texaco station, all of them looking so much like my uncles it made my throat hurt. I yelled at them as I ran, 'The goddam Woolworth's doors are wide open. It's wide open. The whole store's wide open'" (226). Having been banned from the store and thus from the materialist and social heart of the community and having defied the ban in a daring and illicit manner, Bone asserts her class loyalty. She would like all the "poor white trash," all the "gray-faced men" and women, to invade the sanctuary of a capitalist system that excludes them from its rewards while subjecting them to social disapprobation and ridicule. Ultimately, the Woolworth's assault is, of course, a futile, quixotic gesture, but it gratifies Bone, who has proven herself to be a true Boatright and a "warrior."

Bone, though, is largely powerless against her most deadly enemy, her stepfather, who is virtually a casebook example of a man so desperately insecure about his masculinity and indeed his human worth that he requires a scapegoat on whom to enact senseless cruelty. Indirectly, Anney's marriage to Daddy Glen Waddell, the failed son of a successful and judgmental father, proves to be another way in which Bone is victimized by the myth of the heroic Boatright males. Trapped in his own binary vision of masculinity, Glen, constantly aware of his economic and social failure in a family of successful males, seeks redemption by marrying the Boatright family legend: "He would marry Black Earle's baby sister, marry the whole Boatright legend, shame his daddy [who routinely shames him] and shock his brothers. He would carry a knife in his pocket and kill any man who dared to touch her. Yes, he thought to himself, oh yes" (13). Glen exemplifies Lawrence Kramer's male enraged by his inevitable submission to authority who views such submission as a feminine form of weakness. To overcome such weakness, he seeks to ally himself with strength but can find no valid outlets for such an alliance. Appearing to fill this vacuum of redemptive myths is the legend of the Boatright males, and especially of Black Earle Boatright. But no one would ever mistake Glen for a real Boatright: "People talked about Glen's temper and his hands. He didn't drink, didn't mess around, didn't even talk dirty, but the air around him seemed to hum with vibration and his hands were enormous" (35). More importantly, he lacks the positive qualities that the men of the family do possess, such as a capacity for loyalty or genuine concern for children. It should be noted that Glen's idealizing of the Boatright males parallels Bone's childhood response to them. Unlike Bone, however, Glen never attains the maturity essential to transcending such misplaced hero worship.

Intensely proud, Glen seems to have been singled out by fate for humiliation: "[His] feet were so fine that his boots had to be bought in the boy's department of the Sears, Roebuck, while his gloves could only be found in the tall men's specialty stores" (34). His notorious temper and "enormous" hands bode ill for someone, and Bone quickly becomes their particular target. Never certain of possessing anyone's love because of his pervasive self-hatred, Glen singles out Bone as his rival for Anney's love. He also wants a male child of his own to validate his worth and his masculinity and as a means of pushing Bone to the background. Moreover, Bone's very existence intensifies his seething internal rage at his own inadequacy and a world that constantly calls attention to it; after all, Bone was born as a result of Anney's having loved another man before she loved him. He must then harm her in profound and pervasive ways that assault and negate her intrinsic human worth. Thus he not only beats her so severely as to hospitalize her more than once but also sexually abuses her when she is six years old and then, in a horrific scene, rapes her when she is thirteen. He is intent on making her damaged goods, a violated child who will become an outcast woman. In his abuse of Bone, he is, of course, betraying his treasured alliance with the Boatrights and especially with his role model, Black Earle Boatright, in part because he knows that he is not, and never will be, a real Boatright male. Uncle Earle gets into drunken fights with other men, whereas Glen, while quite sober, assaults a child. In a desperate and pathetic manner, Glen is attempting to enter the degraded fourthspace of the Boatright family myth.

Adding to the horror of the act itself, he first sexually abuses Bone while waiting for Anney to give birth to their child. The assault occurs in the front seat of Glen's car, parked in the hospital lot with Reese sleeping in the backseat. Before abusing her, he defiantly proclaims to Bone: "I know she's worried. . . . She thinks if it's a girl, I won't love it. But it will be our baby, and if it's a girl, we can make another soon enough. I'll have my son. Anney and I will have our boy. I know it. I know" (46). The speech tells Bone that she is emphatically not Glen and her mother's child and that girls can only be loved reluctantly and until boys are born. Always aware of his unworthiness to be a Boatright, Glen is attempting to prove his manhood by fathering a male child and to create with Anney his own nuclear family that excludes her children with other men. But as symbolized by his abnormally large hands and small feet, Glen is far from being the favorite of the gods. The baby, in fact a boy, is born dead, and the complications of the birth leave Anney unable to have more children. Glen will never have his boy and will himself continue to be perversely infantile. He is doomed to be his own grotesque child, a violent, emotional infant torn between intense self-hatred and equally extreme self-love.

Inevitably, Glen's unrelenting physical, sexual, and emotional abuse affects Bone's sexuality. Allison dramatizes the damage to her protagonist's sexual identity primarily through extensive description of Bone's masturbatory fantasies, and it is this aspect of the text that has proven to be the most controversial, especially with lesbian readers. As several critics have observed, the masturbation scenes have nothing very much to do with love or even pleasure, but a great deal to do with violence and power. Lynda Hart, in the context of her reading the novel as a "pseudotestimonial," sees the realistic detail of the masturbation fantasies as an essential aspect of their redemptive power. The unflinching detail of the scenes conveys the degree to which Allison's protagonist is determined to witness all the horror that she has experienced.[3]

Fire, masochism, grotesque phallic symbolism, and voyeurism are the dominant motifs in the masturbation scenes. In the first, fire and masochism dominate, as Bone fantasizes "being tied up and put in a haystack" and "someone" setting fire to the dry straw: "I am not sure if I came when the fire reached me or after I had imagined escaping it. But I came" (63). Obviously the scene is partially rooted in the traditional imagery of sexual passion as a fire that consumes the individual self, and particularly in American popular-culture manifestations of that concept—for example, the Johnny Cash–June Carter song "Ring of Fire." But what is most important in Bone's fantasy are the variations on this central image. For instance, she imagines herself bound and in the control of "someone," just as she is in reality bound within her mother's marriage to Glen and her own awakening sexuality. Bone is, after all, the product of a fundamentalist culture that defines both masturbation and female sexual desire as unnatural. She also feels the psychological guilt common to abuse victims, as if she is the instigator of Glen's sexual and physical assaults; and her irrational guilt and her very real powerlessness prevent her, even in fantasy, from naming her assailant. Only through narrating her story will she overcome her pervasive guilt and vulnerability. In Hart's terms, she must "witness" the supplanting of her former violated self by a new self re-created through language. Moreover, at this early stage she is not at all certain that she will ultimately succeed in escaping from the trap of her own violated desire.

By the end of the novel, her feelings are focused on hatred of Glen and rage at his relentless abuse of her. Now she fantasizes fire consuming not only herself but the town of Greenville as well:

"I thought about fire, purifying, raging, sweeping through Green-ville and clearing the earth. . . .

"Fire," I whispered. "Burn it all." I rolled over, putting both my hands under me. I clamped my teeth and rocked, seeing the blaze in my head, haystacks burning and nowhere to run, people falling behind

and the flames coming on, my own body pinned down and the fire
roaring closer.

"Yes," I said. Yes. I rocked and rocked, and orgasmed on my hand to
the dream of fire. (253–54)

In contrast to the first fantasy, fire not only consumes her but purifies her as
well, just as the rage expressed in her narration defines and ultimately empowers her. She is still struggling to liberate her sexuality from Daddy Glen's
perverse control and from the degraded fourthspace of the Boatright family
myth, and her envisioning her body as still being "pinned down" with the
"fire roaring closer" is evidence that her liberation is not yet complete. Such
external male dominance of the sexuality of a female subject is indeed troubling, and not only to feminist critics; yet the realistic detail of the masturbation scenes, and indeed of the entire novel, is essential to Bone liberating
herself.

That she is on the way to doing so is emphasized in the new externaliza-
tion of her rage. In her fantasy, Greenville, the phallogocentric society that
empowers abusive men and silences victimized children, is consumed along
with herself. She dreams of an Old Testament kind of punishment for the
culture in which she is trapped. Obviously, sexuality is for her still tied inexplicably to power and violence; now at the end of the text, she can envision
others as the victims of violence. *Bastard Out of Carolina* is an inherently
transgressive narrative, designed to burn away an abusive paternalism by witnessing its violent abuses of power. Thus, Allison insists on defining herself
as a queer white trash writer; forced by poverty and male abuse to view herself as marginalized, she unapologetically proclaims her marginalization as
her identity.

Bone's anger and rebelliousness demand to be expressed in additional
ways. In one of the novel's few humorous moments, Bone becomes a very
popular baby-sitter because of her storytelling; her stories "were full of boys
and girls gruesomely raped and murdered, babies cooked in pots of boiling
beans, vampires and soldiers and long razor-sharp knives" (119). The violence that Glen has inflicted on her, and which she longs to return, is transferred into gothic storytelling; it is thus safely disguised but increasingly
open. In addition, she enjoys playing "mean sisters," a game that she and some
other young girls invent; in it, the girls pretend to be the mean sisters of
popular-culture male heroes. The game is symbolically important on more

than one textual level, most obviously the chauvinism of the popular culture that, at least to some degree, molds Bone. She yearns for "meanness," a quality she associates with toughness, and there were very few tough women in 1950s American films and television programs, in which the dominant female images were those of the dismayingly perky teenage girl and the loyal, stay-at-home wife. Father did indeed know best in the popular culture that Bone knows as a child, whereas her own stepfather jarringly embodies paternalistic exploitation and evil. "Mean sisters" originates in Bone's now quite conscious desire for violent phallic revenge against Daddy Glen: "I practiced sticking Aunt Alma's knife into the porch, and listened to the boys cursing in the backyard. . . . I was mean and vicious, and all I really wanted to be doing was sticking that knife in Daddy Glen" (213). It thus represents an intermediate stage in the construction of Bone's transgressive self; the word *bone* is slang for the penis, and she yearns to penetrate her stepfather's body with the kind of savage brutality that characterizes his assaults against her.

It is hardly surprising, then, that Bone masturbates to the trawling chain that she and her cousins find in the river that runs beside Aunt Raylene's house. Aunt Raylene, the only truly positive adult role model in the novel, tries to discourage Bone and her cousins from playing with the chain through a graphic description of its purpose. Scolding her nephew Grey directly, but also her other nephews and nieces who have transformed the chain with its multiple hooks into a toy, she screams, "You think this is a big old fishhook? Well, it ain't. It's for trawling, for dragging. You go down in the river and they'll use something like this to pull you up in chunks. Pull you loose from the junk in that deep mud. Pull you up in pieces, you hear me? Nasty slices of you, little boy, for your mama to cry over" (186). Aunt Raylene's speech encapsulates the entire text by evoking a drowned, fragmented self, a self violently ripped to pieces, an image that metaphorically reflects what Daddy Glen has done to Bone. Only by pulling herself, through the act of narration, "loose from that deep mud" in which she is stuck can Bone restore herself. Before the process of salvation is complete, however, Bone masturbates while pulling the chain "back and forth" between her legs; for her, the length of the chain and its grotesque hooks are representative of Glen's penis, the instrument of her physical and psychic violation. While masturbating with the chain, she recalls secretly reading a pornographic novel belonging to Glen that describes "women who pushed stuff up inside them" (193). In this context, it is worth remembering that *bone* is male slang for both the penis and sexual intercourse.

Voyeurism is the dominant element in another of Bone's masturbation fantasies. In it she imagines Daddy Glen beating her in front of a witness or witnesses:

> Someone had to watch—some girl I admired who barely knew I existed, some girl from church or down the street, or one of my cousins; or even somebody I had seen on television. Sometimes a whole group of them would be watching. They couldn't help or get away. In my imagination I was proud and defiant. I'd stare back at him with my teeth set, making no sound at all. . . . Those who watched admired me and hated him. . . . Those who watched me, loved me. It was as if I was being beaten for them. I was wonderful in their eyes. (112)

In this passage, Bone's subconscious is struggling to achieve two simultaneously interrelated and contradictory things. It is trying to allow Bone to escape her pain by objectifying herself and also to redeem herself by adopting the persona of a martyr. She imagines herself transformed into increasingly distant "selves," ranging from a girl whom she admires but who is virtually unaware of her existence, to a doubly unreal girl from television. Then, in a manner comparable to Charlotte Perkins Gilman in "The Yellow Wallpaper," Allison shows her already objectified self splitting into a multiplicity of selves ("a whole group of them"), and from these fragments of her self she receives love and admiration. She vicariously receives "their" beatings and is thereby transformed into an incarnation of the stoic (and usually male) hero of American popular culture.

Obviously, Bone cannot permanently retreat into masochistic sexual fantasies. Sensing the repression inherent in the myth of the Boatright males, she tries desperately to find salvation in religion, specifically in southern Christian fundamentalism and even more specifically in gospel music (one of the most fascinating aspects of *Bastard Out of Carolina* is its exploration of the gospel music subculture and especially of the close connections between gospel and "popular" music in the South). Ultimately, though, Bone is disillusioned by the hypocrisy, racism, and morbidity of the gospel scene, which itself becomes a kind of degraded fourthspace. It is interesting that the gospel music segment contains one of the novel's very few references to race relations, the tragic focus of so much southern culture. It is as if the Boatrights, in their insularity, are even immune from the dominant cultural obsession of their region. The members of the grotesque Pearl family are the novel's primary representatives of the gospel music culture, and the social outcast Shannon Pearl functions as Bone's doppelgänger until Shannon dies hideously in a freakish fire. Thus the fire of Bone's sexual fantasies metaphorically reaches out to destroy her double. The morbidity of southern popular culture in general is revealed in one of Anne's favorite songs, "The Sign on the Highway," a gruesome description of a fatal, bloody car accident caused by "Beer, Wine and Whiskey" (150). For Bone, southern religious fundamentalism thus becomes another dead end, a myth as hollow and crippling as that of the Boatright males.

Yet Bone's core identity survives Daddy Glen's abuse and her disillusionment with the Boatright men and with southern fundamentalism. What she almost does not survive is a stunning final betrayal by Anney. For some time, Anney wills herself into denial of what Glen is doing to her daughter, even after Bone is hospitalized early in the novel after one especially savage beating by her stepfather. She increasingly blames Bone for what is being done to her, an especially heartbreaking mode of denial not uncommon among women in her position. After Glen's horrifying final rape and assault of Bone, Anney is forced into a choice between her husband and her daughter, and she chooses Glen. By characterizing Anney as a new kind of Boatright woman possessing genuine strength and independence, the novel makes this choice seem even more inexplicable than it already would be. Anney, though, is vulnerable in more than one way. She is economically disadvantaged, a mother struggling to survive in a patriarchal social and economic structure with no real place to go if she should leave Glen; and she does, incomprehensible as it seems, love Glen. Sexual passion intensifies her socioeconomic entrapment.

Before abandoning Bone, Anney gives her two gifts. The first is very intentionally given—after trying and failing to do so several times, she acquires a new birth certificate for her daughter that omits the designation "Father: UNKNOWN" (309). Thus the official stigma of "bastard" is removed from Bone. In contrast, Anney is not truly aware of the implications of her other, and more important, gift. By leaving Bone with Aunt Raylene, the text's only lesbian adult character, she provides her daughter with a saving role model. Thus Aunt Raylene succeeds precisely where the degraded fourthspaces of the Boatright men and southern Christian fundamentalism have failed; she sustains Bone and liberates her from the horror of her existence. In keeping with its dominantly naturalistic mode, the text downplays Bone's survival. In fact, the text itself is the primary evidence that Bone has survived. She has borne witness to the fragmentation and reintegration of her self; she has survived by telling her story. By redirecting her sexuality into homosexuality and into narration, she largely transcends the naturalistic limitations of her stark position. Moreover, her narration exemplifies Henri Lefebvre's call for the emergence of a "women's space": "It is hard to resist the conclusion that it is time for the sterile space of men, founded on violence and misery, to give way to a women's space. It would thus fall to women to achieve appropriation, a responsibility that they would successfully fulfill—in sharp contrast to the inability of male or manly designs to embrace anything but joyless domination, renunciation—and death" (380).

Playing for Death

Don DeLillo's *End Zone*

In *Fighting for Life: Contest, Sexuality, and Consciousness,* Walter J. Ong describes masculinity as "a high-risk condition: all or nothing" and asserts that "femininity, by contrast, is stable: in many hundreds of species, especially among higher animals, almost all females have offspring, almost all males do not." Obviously, in reproductive activity the male's function is quickly over, and he subsequently becomes what Ong calls "the expendable sex" (56). Defining his book as a work of "'noobiology,' the study of the biological setting of mental activity" (11), Ong argues that at the human level this biologically rooted male expendability results in a profound insecurity that can only be alleviated through a totalizing "adversativeness" (15). Because human males, like the males of other higher animals, are biologically conditioned to feel that their gender identity is always incomplete and at risk, they are perpetually driven to affirm and validate it through combat, Ong argues. Instinctively, he writes, males tend to respond to other males either through complex modes of bonding in which antagonism is barely concealed or through controlled and ritualized forms of combat. Ong further posits a gendered response to environment itself: "Human males tend to feel an environment . . . as a kind of againstness, something to be fought with and altered. Environment is feminine, and women typically find they can rely on it as it is or comes to them" (77).[1]

In contrast to Ong's noobiological approach, Lawrence Kramer, building on the ideas of Nietzsche, Foucault, and Lacan, offers a cultural and psychological interpretation of male aggression. In Western culture, Kramer writes, "the possibility of sexual violence ripples in the air like rising heat, visible and invisible at the same time. . . . Both men and women alike are enjoined to construct heterosexual gender identities based on a mercurial love-hate relationship to whatever is understood as femininity" (1). He further argues that male constructions of identity are inevitably ambiguous in nature because of the inadequacy of the penis as substitute for the patriarchal phallus, with its associations of power and authority. Capitalist culture is inherently hierarchal, with lasting power and authority not only unobtainable for virtually everyone but essentially invisible as well; consequently, a profound insecurity haunts the male psyche. To compensate, Kramer argues, the male becomes the enforcer of culturally sanctioned violence and repression; males define masculinity as "radically unambivalent," and thus strong, and femininity as "radically ambivalent" (2), and thus weak. Because of the insecurity that they struggle to deny, males most of all hate and fear ambiguity and ambivalence, which they have associated with women and "unmanly" men.

Of course, such arbitrary and insecure gender roles are perennially challenged and constantly on the verge of collapse. In doomed attempts to reinforce them, males turn to language and male rituals and games centered around real or symbolic violence or both. No contemporary American writer is a more important or more inventive observer of such attempts than Don DeLillo. In his 1972 novel, *End Zone*, he depicts the inevitable failure of a desperate mingling of language and violent games to support the masculine identities of his characters. While *End Zone* often reads like a depiction of Ong's concept of masculine adversativeness carried to an absurdist extreme, it can also be legitimately be discussed in the context of Kramer's cultural perspective. In the novel, DeLillo is not concerned with determining whether male violence is rooted in biological or cultural causes but rather with constructing a narrative that reveals, often in a parodic manner, the destructive effects of violence on the male psyche. Fundamentally, he is concerned with the language of violence. His text, then, is deterministic in the most basic of ways. Language is, after all, the essential route to consciousness, and in the male, violence has appropriated language itself, thus blocking any meaningful introspection about the origins and consequences of violence. Gary Harkness, the narrator of *End Zone*, struggles throughout the novel for precisely this kind of insight, but he is defeated and left mentally and physically exhausted by the struggle. Thus, in a "men's studies approach to the novel," Donald L. Deardorff II argues that *End Zone* "reveals DeLillo's preoccupation with examining the relationship between American masculinity and men's use of language" (74).

The novel focuses on the members of a football team rather arbitrarily and ironically associated with Logos College, located in the west Texas desert. The actual game of football (and its esoteric language) is one kind of masculine violence in the text. From football, the dimensions of masculine violence extend to the linguistic dehumanization of women and the potential for violent assault against the landscape inherent in technology and climactically to nuclear warfare and its own specialized vocabulary. The pairing of the languages of football and nuclear war might well have been simultaneously trite and forced, but DeLillo's sheer inventiveness in pursuing the analogy makes it original and convincing.

As Deardorff points out, "violence is at the core of the identity of the young men in *End Zone*": "Every player DeLillo introduces is held hostage by morbid visions of mass destruction, nuclear war, genocide, and disturbing sexual fantasies. Gary Harkness, the novel's troubled anti-hero, admits that he is obsessed with nuclear disaster" (74). One should not underestimate the importance of sexual fantasy here. DeLillo's characters are very much the fictional children of Ernest Hemingway; they view sex as not even a necessarily "good" form of "destruction" and are obsessed with death, especially the mass destruction of human life. They are terrified of their own physical and emotional weakness, a terror which, in the manner described by Kramer, they transpose to the supposedly ambivalent bodies of women. At one point in the novel, Gary Harkness, the narrator and an intensely cerebral football player, and one of his teammates, Bobby Luke, see two young women "walking slowly across campus toward the women's dormitory" (54). In a flat, almost ritualistic manner, Bobby observes: "gash" (54). Gary does not respond, retreating instead into a sexual fantasy characterized by its anti-eroticism and perverse dehumanization of the imagined female sexual partner. He fantasizes himself "in a Mexico City hotel" with "a girl in a cotton dress on a bed with brass posts. A ceiling fan rubbing the moist air. Scent of slick magazines. She'd be poor born, the dumbest thing in Texas, a girl from a gulf town, movie-made, her voice an unlaundered drawl, fierce and coarse, fit for bad-tempered talking blues" (55). Gary needs to construct a sexual partner for whom it will be impossible to feel anything, whom he can regard as barely human, "the *dumbest* thing in Texas." Seconds later, he loses his grasp on the fantasy and is unable to get back to the same girl, now mentally envisioning "a different one . . . almost monumental in her measureless dimensions" who soon attains such gigantic shape that she become "the hotel itself, an incredible cake of mosaic stone" (55). For Gary, the image of a female body so large that it can contain himself and everyone else in the hotel becomes a "body of perfect knowledge, the flesh made word" (55).

Indeed, it is necessary to Gary and all the other young males in the novel that the flesh be made word. For them, responding to sexuality as simple pleasure is impossible; the female body is at once too desirable and too flawed. They must then verbally and imaginatively dehumanize the female body, must respond to it as the primal source of birth *and* death, of creation *and* destruction, of fulfillment *and* annihilation. Gary is pulled out of his multi-level fantasy by hearing Bobby say, in the same unfeeling voice that characterized his first observation, "pussy" (55). In this way, the flesh of two actual young women walking toward their dormitory and of the imagined women of Gary's fantasy is translated into word—in fact two words, common male terms intended to debase the female. On a linguistic level they are responding to the female body in a manner comparable to the perhaps actualized violence of Patrick Bateman in Bret Easton Ellis's *American Psycho*.

It should be said that, among other things, Gary's role as narrator of *End Zone* demonstrates his awareness of the dehumanization inherent in his and his teammates' responses to women. Gary functions on a level of parodic awareness that no Hemingway character ever approaches. DeLillo is a satirist of the cult of machismo that the creator of Frederick Henry and Nick Adams glorified. At one point in the novel, Gary, after a victorious game, exits the shower and encounters teammate "Lloyd Philpot, Jr., wearing a jockstrap and red socks" (154). Philpot informs Gary of a current rumor that "there might be a queer on the squad" (154). Gary's response to Philpot is quite calm and rational; he asks what evidence exists of a homosexual presence on the team. Still the alarmist, Philpot answers ominously: "There are guys walking around here naked right now. It could be any one of them" (155). Of course, Gary, having just showered, is nude himself and Philpot nearly so.

DeLillo essentially abandons the motif of a homosexual lurking on the squad after this scene because he has done all he needs to do with it. The anonymous homosexual that threatens Philpot and other players is, of course, their own androgyny. In the context of Lawrence's analysis of obsessive masculinity, they are terrified by the ambivalence of their own sexual responses and the limitations of their own bodies. One can hardly miss the humor of a Philpot, attired only in an athletic supporter and red socks, seeking out a naked Gary to discuss the threat of homosexual infiltration of the squad.

Though DeLillo does not emphasize the point, one can assume that a reason for Gary's calmness here is his intuitive understanding of the naturalness of androgyny as a form of sexual response. In contrast, Philpot wants, in a manner that René Girard would undoubtedly comprehend, to isolate a scapegoat for his own disturbing sexual feelings and for the imperfections of his own body. In fact, DeLillo has set up the potential for an incident of retributive violence here but wisely chooses not to pursue it, since his book is concerned with other matters. Significantly, despite his advanced level of sensitivity and awareness, Gary does not challenge Philpot's use of the word "queer." Again, as in the scene with Bobby Luke, the flesh must be named and simultaneously dehumanized. "Gash," "pussy," and "queer" all function as masculine terms for suppressing eroticism, with its potential for commitment and the surrender of a total "masculine" control.

Ong argues that such male "adversativeness" toward the female is biologically determined: "The basic ontogenetic insecurity of males, beginning in the womb amid the mother's threatening hormones, is matched by their phylogenetic insecurity. Males are expendable for the good of the species" (143). Thus they develop various agonistic behaviors, including various forms of combat, in a doomed attempt to affirm their self-importance. Moreover, their commitment to adversarial relationships and behaviors contributes to their contempt for the female they inherently fear.

Gary's advanced sensitivity is central to another key scene in the novel. After a particularly disastrous practice, Coach Emmett Creed, the novel's Ahab figure, suggests that the team hold a beer party with "no coaches, no females, no time limits" (99). The party, which begins mildly with random throwing of beer bottles, soon disintegrates, as Creed knew it would, into an orgy of violence and gross physical excess:

> There was a pissing contest with about twenty entries trying not for distance but for altitude—a broom held by two men being the crossbar as it were, the broom raised in stages as contestants dropped out and others progressed. *It was the most disgusting, ridiculous and adolescent night I had ever spent.* The floor of the lounge was covered with beer, urine and ketchup, and we kept slipping and falling and then getting up and getting casually knocked down again by somebody passing by. Clothes were torn and there was blood to be seen on a few grinning faces. . . . I watched my teammates slip and fall into the beer and get up sick and laughing. (100; my emphasis)

Gary's observer role in this scene, his awareness that it is a "disgusting, ridiculous and adolescent night," is typical of his comparatively mature and complex perceptions throughout the novel. He fully understands what Creed had in mind by suggesting the beer party—the coach wanted to set in motion an occasion, from which he could then absent himself, that would serve to remind his players of their sheer animalism, an occasion that he intends to translate into the mindless brutality necessary for success on the football field. Such awareness is an indication that Gary will ultimately not be able to subordinate himself to the team; he is too intelligent, too aware, to make a complete transformation into a disciple of the coach's creed of surrender of the individual intelligence and ego to the anonymous physicality of the team. Gary functions at too advanced a level of linguistic sophistication to surrender his identity.

Yet the extent of his rebellion is, from the first, proscribed. While ridiculing Creed's doctrine of transcendence through discipline and pain, he still partially subscribes to it. While on the sidelines during games, Gary engages in a nonstop mock color commentary. During one contest, a teammate named Jeff Elliott asks Gary how he is feeling and gets the following surprising response: "Look at the arc lights, the crowd. . . . Existence without anxiety. . . . Knowing your body. . . . Understanding the real needs of man. . . . The universe was born in violence. Stars die violently. Elements are created out of cosmic violence" (121). After Elliott reminds him that it is, after all, only a football game, Gary responds, "I'm just fooling around, Jeff. I'm not serious" (122). But as his growing obsession with the language of nuclear warfare indicates, Gary is quite "serious." Deardorff reads *End Zone* as a study of "the postmodern dilemma of American men; they can't use language to escape harmful masculine paradigms because the words they must use are the very building blocks of the history and traditions that ensnare them. To talk is to take part in those traditions and to facilitate one's own emotional demise" (74).

When one remembers that the chief characteristic of literary naturalism is its obsession with characters who lack free will because they are the victims, if not the puppets, of external forces, it is easy to read *End Zone* as an example of a postmodernist naturalism or, to use June Howard's term, "latter-day naturalism."[2] Gary and the other characters in *End Zone* are the victims of a complex system of determining influences that are cumulatively more overwhelming than anything imagined by Frank Norris or Jack London. One can at least postulate that, had they possessed the intellectual sophistication, Norris's McTeague and Stephen Crane's Maggie might have been able to comprehend the biological and environmental forces that overwhelm them. Theoretically at least, language was still *potentially* available to them as a means of accessing consciousness. But for Gary and the other members of the Logos College football team, language, in fact, masks their victimization by violence.[3]

Gary is a kind of quest anti-hero whose perennial search for some viable system of order is undercut by the inherent chaos of the universe and his own irresistible attraction to violence and disorder. His need for and resistance to a paradigm of order is translated into longing for a sustaining father figure against whom he inevitably must rebel. His quest has led him all the way from his home in Michigan to the west Texas desert. Before arriving at Logos College and before the present tense of the novel begins, Gary has held and surrendered football scholarships to Syracuse University, Penn State University, Michigan State University, and the University of Miami. His father virtually forced him into taking up football in the first place: "He had played football at Michigan State. He had ambitions on my behalf and more or less at my expense. This is the custom among men who failed to be heroes; their sons must prove that the seed was not impoverished" (17). Gary is virtually born into the Western tradition of the male hero who must testify to the vitality of the race through physical competition, struggle, and endurance.

Paradoxically, his father, while attempting to form him in the mold of heroic masculinity, provides Gary with an insight that serves as the basis for his rebellion against the concept of a redemptive heroism. The father posts a clichéd sign in his son's room:

WHEN THE GOING GETS TOUGH
THE TOUGH GET GOING. (17)

After three years of looking at this sign, Gary has a very different kind of epiphany than the one his father intended: "I began to perceive a certain beauty in it. . . . The words became pictures. It was a sinister thing to discover at such an age, that words can escape their meanings. A strange beauty that sign began to express" (17). Gary is well on his way to the postmodernist insight that words can not only escape their meanings but that they have no inherent meanings. Thus he will never be able to accept any substitute father for very long.

At Penn State, Gary feels that there is "something hugely Asian" about the autumn days, and after tripping "on the same staircase on three successive days" he decides that he will no longer attend football practices (19). When questioned by the freshman coach about his refusal, Gary explains that he knows all the plays and fears that "endless repetition [of them] might be spiritually disastrous" (19). Without quite being able to articulate it, Gary yearns to discover some transcendent truth outside empirical experience. From the first, he is seeking a viable alternative to Western rationalism without knowing where to begin searching. When the coach stresses that participation in practice is a part of "the oneness necessary for a winning team," Gary considers, but quickly rejects, the coach's position: "It was a good concept, oneness, but I suggested that, to me at least, it could not be truly attractive unless it meant oneness with God or the universe or some equally redoubtable super-phenomenon. What he meant by oneness was in fact elevenness or twenty-twoness." Not surprisingly, the coach retreats from such an abstract and sophisticated level of debate: "He told me that my attitude was all wrong. People don't go to football games to see pass patterns run by theologians" (19). Thus the reader knows from the first that Gary will ultimately fail to subordinate himself to the hierarchical structure of a football team.

Nevertheless, he keeps trying, essentially because he likes football. Most of all, he loves the mindless violence of the sport. Involved in the accidental death of an opponent during a freshman game at Michigan State, he once again quits the game and drops out of the university. The death or grievous wounding of an opponent followed by guilt on the part of the hero is a potentially trite plot device in a novel dealing with masculine combat, but it works here because death is the implicit result of the cult of male violence to which Gary is, despite everything, devoted.[4] Thus, when he receives the offer of another football scholarship from Emmett Creed and remote Logos College, he quickly accepts it: "I had discovered a very simple truth. My life meant nothing without football" (22).

Part of Gary's attraction to football is the pain that goes with the sport. At one point he describes his reaction to finding himself at the bottom of a pileup after a tackle: "I smelled the turf and waited for the bodies to unpile. My rib cage was beginning to ache, a sense of stickiness, of glue. I felt quite happy. Somebody's hand was the back of my neck and he put all his weight on it as he lifted himself up" (121). Considerably more than simple masochism is involved here, though that is a distinctive element in Gary's character. In part, his devotion to pain works as a form of atonement for failing to live up to his father's ambitions for him. It also recalls the broad span of male initiation rituals in which the acceptance of pain is a central ingredient. Like many other young males in America, Gary has bought into the masculine myth of the brave warrior who risks death and pain to protect the social order. Thus his attraction to pain complements his obsession with violence and becomes another of the naturalistic forces that control him; it thus intensifies the novel's naturalistic overtones.

Moreover, the force that subordinates and incorporates all the others is language, impossible to resist, since it functions on both the external and internal levels. It is only right that Gary winds up at Logos College. He is attracted to Logos in part by its remoteness, the sheer improbability of its existence. In fact, the college is an extremely arbitrary construct newly imposed on the west Texas desert. This arbitrariness is made manifest in an early interview given to Gary by Mrs. Tom Wade, the college president and widow of the school's founder. Mrs. Tom, as everyone calls her, recounts her late husband's vision: "My husband loved this place. . . . He built it out of nothing. He had an idea and he followed it through to the end. He believed in reason. He was a man of reason. He cherished the very word. Unfortunately he was mute. . . . All he could do was grunt. He made disgusting sounds. Spit used to collect at both corners of his mouth. It wasn't a real pretty sight" (7). Despite the strong degree of black humor implicit in this passage, its final implications are not amusing. Tom Wade, the mute lover of words and devotee of reason, functions in the novel primarily as an embodiment of the failure of Western rationalism, which, as manifested in European imperialism, world wars, and instances of widespread technological violence, including the Holocaust, has also not been "a real pretty sight."

Wade's choice of the desert as the location of his college is also ironically significant. He attempted to construct an institution of higher learning in the center of a geographical and cultural nothingness that still surrounds it on all sides. Logos College cannot subdue the barren and inhuman space onto which it has been grafted, just as Western rationalism failed to control and contain human violence and irrationality. The creation of Logos, in fact, epitomizes Gary's epiphany concerning the arbitrary nature of language and meaning—it would be hard to imagine a more unnatural space in which to implant reason and to celebrate language than the barren, thinly populated, and silent desert of west Texas. No wonder that Wade was reduced to grunting and making "disgusting sounds."

The desert functions, then, as metaphor for a landscape of irrationality, a vast nothingness. It is therefore not surprising that Gary is drawn to it from the first. The desert entices him with an illusory promise of the transcendent meaning that he so much desires. But he soon feels threatened by the very silence that initially attracts him: "Day after day my eyes scanned in all directions a stunned earth, unchangingly dull, a land silenced by its own beginnings in the roaring heat, born dead, flat stones burying the memory. . . . Perhaps silence is dispersed by familiar things; their antiquity is heard. . . . But now, in the vast burning west, the silences were menacing. I decided not to eat meat for a few weeks" (31). Gary's plan for dealing with the threatening silence of the desert is appropriately futile and irrational. His not eating meat will hardly subdue the silence.

In more than one way, this passage hints at the dark side of Gary's quest for a transcendent meaning through playing a violent game in the threatening silence of the desert. In the theory of Georges Bataille, violence is half of the essential human duality; in fact, he argues that "excess contrasts with reason" (186). Gary is attracted by both the work of football, a mask of reason, and by the excess of its violence. In DeLillo's novel, the game of football, the arbitrary construct of Logos College, the barren desert, and most importantly language itself merge and evoke a destructive fourthspace. Language in *End Zone* is even more debased than it is in *Affliction*. In Banks's novel, Rolfe is consciously playing escapist games with the language of his narration with deadly results. In the fourthspace of DeLillo's novel, language is inherently empty and thus susceptible to cynical manipulation that ultimately reduces it to a potentially deadly meaninglessness.

The function of an Emmett Creed is to create a language that emphasizes orderliness while encouraging his players to sacrifice their bodies to pain induced through violence. Ultimately, Gary will be overwhelmed by his inability to sustain this duality. He is simply too intelligent to compartmentalize the attractions of work and excess. In a climactic dialogue with Taft Robinson, a black athlete chosen by Creed to integrate Logos College because of his speed, Gary formulates a critical self-insight: "As an athlete I have serious lapses. I don't play football as much as drift in and out of cloud banks of action and noise. I'm not a one-hundred-percent-in-the-American-grain football player. I tend to draw back now and again in order to make minor discoveries that have no bearing on anything. I conduct spurious examinations. I bullshit myself" (234).

Gary is, in fact, "bullshit[ing]" himself in this speech. The discoveries he makes are not at all minor or spurious; they constitute the unfolding self-awareness that will, in the end, come close to destroying him. Still, he is partly accurate in what he says—he is not "a one-hundred-percent-in-the-American-grain" anything, not even (as much as he loves the game) football player. His search for meaning in silence and simplicity, from the first, draws him to the primal nothingness of death. His presence at Logos College, an institution without a history, conceived out of nothing and located in the midst of silence and death, is almost inevitable.

Those who run Logos College seem not nearly so troubled as Gary by realizations of unpleasant truths and contradictions. Believing it is possible to give Logos viability through football, they hire Creed to transform Logos into a collegiate power. Mrs. Tom's ambition to make Logos prominent by building it into a football power reads like an absurdist fictional example of Ong's theories concerning the prominence of athletics in American universities. Ong argues that the traditional agonistic structure of the university in America disintegrated after women entered it in large numbers: "None of the conspicuously agonistic structures had a place in early girls' schools. As females entered schools originally intended only for males . . . these things happened: (1) Latin was dropped, first as a means of instruction and then as a required subject; (2) the agonistic, thesis method of teaching was replaced by less combative methods; (3) written examinations were substituted for public oral disputations and examinations; and (4) of course, physical punishment was minimized or suppressed" (135–36). But of course the suppressed agonistic impulses had to find some outlet, and Ong argues that intercollegiate athletics have increasingly served that function. The vast importance placed on intercollegiate athletics, he points out, is relatively new: "Certainly, the spectacle of two institutions of higher learning battling it out on the football field before fifty thousand or more spectators would have nonplussed Erasmus. . . . Programmed contest has moved in academia from the classroom and the disputation hall to the athletic field" (153).

Logos College, as a new, arbitrarily conceived institution of higher learning, can devote itself to the adversativeness of football in relative innocence—it, after all, never knew the agonistic structures of the traditional university. Moreover, Gary, who in his moments of genuine insight would like to transcend all agonistic structures, still needs the violence and pain of football. Thus he is vulnerable to Creed's message of a new start in the west Texas desert—after leaving Michigan State, Miami, and Penn State, he has few options left: "Exile or outcast, distinctions tend to vanish when the temperature exceeds one hundred" (6).

Mrs. Tom's account of the Creed hiring and its background has further ominous overtones. To some degree here, DeLillo is, as in other novels, satirizing Texas as geographic space and cultural construct. In *Americana* (1971) and *Libra* (1988), the latter a fictionalized biography of Lee Harvey Oswald, DeLillo depicts Texas as the embodiment of American irrationality and violence. The assassination of President John F. Kennedy in Dallas was the primary inspiration for DeLillo's dark vision of Texas. Paul Civello writes that for the native New Yorker, DeLillo, Dallas, and the Kennedy assassination are symbolic "of the dark heart lying beneath America's image of itself" ("Don DeLillo" 18). Those who control Logos College are apparently not troubled by the inherent contradiction of an institution supposedly established as an oasis of reason seeking recognition through the violent and irrational sport of football. If they are troubled, they can count on being reassured by the messianic Creed.

DeLillo's description of Creed contains another of the novel's multileveled satiric dimensions. As the text describes it, Creed's background is that of a flawed American icon. Stories of his past have reached mythic proportions: "He had been born in Texas, in either a log cabin or a manger, depending on who was telling the story, on the banks of the Rio Grande in what is now Big Bend National Park. The sporting press liked to call him Big Bend" (9). At least according to Gary, Creed is not the only apparent incarnation of Lincoln at Logos College: "[Mrs. Tom] was the only woman I had ever seen who might accurately be described as Lincolnesque. Beyond appearance I had no firm idea of her reality; she was tall, black-browed, stark as a railroad spike" (6). The associations of Creed and Mrs. Tom with the Great Emancipator are intensely ironic—they do integrate Logos College, but only for the purpose of building a winning football team. Their personae are finally as deceptive as is language in DeLillo's text: their images hardly correspond to their inner realities, just as words bear only arbitrary associations with meaning. Further, Creed intuitively understands the vulnerability of language to cynical manipulation. The implicit allusion to the birth of Christ in the Creed language satirizes the religious reverence for football in Texas.

In fact, though, Creed has not always acted in a Christlike manner. Once the coach of nationally prominent college football programs, he virtually ended his career in a moment of irrational violence: "A second-string quarterback said or did something he didn't like and Creed broke his jaw. It became something of a national scandal and he went into obscurity for three years until Mrs. Tom beckoned him to West Texas" (10). In this notorious instance Creed acted more like Patton than Christ, and it is ironically appropriate that Mrs. Tom either ignores the violence in the man she chooses to make Logos College famous or comprehends that this is precisely the quality she needs in a football coach. Perhaps it is both, since, unlike Gary Harkness, Taft Robinson, and a third football player named Anatole Bloomberg, she is untroubled by inherent contradictions.[5]

At least most of the time, so is Creed. He has developed a philosophy of football that incorporates elements of militarism, traditional middle-class morality, fundamentalist religion, anti-intellectualism, patriotism, and a kind of popularized stoicism that is inherently schizophrenic. For instance, in a speech to the team he says: "Write home on a regular basis. Dress neatly. Be courteous. Articulate your problems. Do not drag-ass. Anything I have no use for, it's a football player who consistently drag-asses. Move swiftly from place to place, both on the field and in the corridors of buildings. Don't ever get too proud to pray" (11). Here DeLillo beautifully emphasizes the inherent contradictions in Creed's creed through the linguistic discrepancy between a slang term like "drag-ass" and the formalistic, even poetic, instruction to "move swiftly from place to place." Creed later tells Gary that he has "never seen a good football player who wanted to learn a foreign language" (199). He even has a philosophical justification for the pain and brutality of football: "Football is a complex of systems. . . . People stress the violence. That's the smallest part of it. Football is brutal only from a distance. In the middle of it there's a calm, a tranquillity. The players accept pain. There's a sense of order even at the end of a running play with bodies strewn everywhere. When the systems interlock, there's a satisfaction to the game that can't be duplicated. There's a harmony" (199).

Late in the novel, sensing that Gary's loyalty to him and commitment to the team is slipping, Creed implicitly offers to become Gary's surrogate father. He, of course, knows that this is how Gary has viewed him from the first. As shown in his indirect encouraging of the team's evening of descent into barbarism, Creed has a unique talent for psychological manipulation which he is quite ready to use. For Gary and the others, he even assumes godlike proportions: "He was the maker of plays, the name-giver. We were his chalk-scrawls. Something like that" (135). Creed's power is based in his understanding of language, his awareness that whoever knows how to control words can easily manipulate people. In this context, he is the perfect coach for Logos College.

Ultimately, though, Gary's intelligence and sensitivity render him unfit to be a Creed disciple. Even when responding to Creed, he is always aware of the coach's cynical agenda of manipulation. In addition, as foreshadowed in Gary's dialogue with the Penn State freshman coach, Creed's creed and football are finally incapable of providing Gary with the all-encompassing vision of truth through simplicity for which he is searching. Creed, like Logos College itself, is artificial, an alien being imposed on the primal silence of the west Texas desert, and Gary desperately needs to discover a theology as vast and arid as the desert itself. The violence of football, despite the reassurance through discipline and pain that it brings Gary, inevitably proves to be an inadequate substitute for the transcendent truth he seeks; death and the language of death come closer to providing him with answers. Gary's obsession began with a book, "an immense volume about the possibilities of nuclear war," a reading assigned in one of his courses at the University of Miami.

Just as he is always aware of the inherent complexities in his responses to football and Creed, Gary knows that his response to the book constitutes a simple and terrible problem:

> I enjoyed the book. I liked reading about the deaths of tens of millions of people. I liked dwelling on the destruction of great cities. Five to twenty million dead. Fifty to a hundred million dead. . . . People burned and unable to breathe. People being evacuated from doomed cities. People diseased and starving. . . . Pleasure in the contemplation of millions dead and dying. I became fascinated by words and phrases like thermal hurricane, overkill, circular error probability, post-attack environment, stark deterrence, dose-rate contours, kill-ratio, spasm war. . . . Old weapons vanished. Megatonnage soared. New concepts appeared—the rationality of irrationality. (20–21)

Understandably, Gary wonders whether his obsession with mass death and suffering indicates that he is going mad. In part, visions of a nuclear holocaust offer him the simple and terrible truth that he seeks; nuclear weapons have the potential to reduce everything to the vast silence of the desert. In addition, Gary is fascinated by the fact that an entire language of nuclear destruction has evolved. Obviously, he is not the only person thinking about the unthinkable. Just as he is always aware of the manipulations of Creed and the other coaches for whom he plays, he comprehends the degree to which the language of nuclear warfare is deliberately designed to hide the horror that it is ostensibly describing. How, after all, does one "overkill" someone or something?

Thomas LeClair, one of DeLillo's most perceptive critics, describes Gary as a character who represents the conflicting interpretive modes of logocentrism and deconstruction: "Gary Harkness, who thinks of himself as an 'exile,' oscillates between these two modes of interpretation, accepting and rebelling against logocentric values, playing games and searching for an end to them. Author DeLillo, fully conscious of how these two models work, keeps a useful, illustrative tension between them, understanding, as a writer, that he cannot help but propose a deciphering, that his text has a first and a last page, and that he cannot stand outside language" (110). Even a writer with DeLillo's essentially postmodernist vision, knowing that any relationship between words and meaning is an arbitrary construct, ultimately recognizes that words are all he has. While Logos is an arbitrary construct imposed on the desert of death and meaninglessness, it remains the only place where the writer can start. Moreover, LeClair is correct is seeing Gary as both rebel and conformist; the inherent struggle between these conflicting personas will, before the novel ends, come quite close to destroying him.

Gary increasingly comes to recognize that Creed will not serve him as surrogate father, as the male prophet of a saving simplicity, but he does not abandon his quest for such a figure. He turns to Logos College's ROTC commander, Major Staley, like Gary a new arrival in the west Texas desert. Gary and Staley meet in a motel room to discuss the language and the reality of nuclear warfare.[6] In the conversation, which quickly becomes something closer to a lecture, in fact something quite like one of Creed's speeches to the football team, Staley equates the bomb with God in its potential for unlimited power. His argument makes the bomb into something closer to an antigod, with limitless destruction replacing unlimited creativity. Without really intending to, he continues Gary's education in the arbitrariness of language, an education that began when Gary's father posted signs in his room. Staley communicates his vision of "humane" warfare: "I think what'll happen in the not-too-distant future is that we'll have humane wars. Each side agrees to use clean bombs. And each side agrees to limit the amount of megatons he uses. In other words we'll get together with them beforehand and there'll be an agreement that if the issue can't be settled, whatever the issue might be, then let's make certain we keep the war as relatively humane as possible" (81).

Staley's visions are, of course, quite mad. If "we" and "they" can't agree to avoid warfare in the first place, it seems unlikely that the two sides can reach an agreement on conducting a "clean" war. It constitutes an extreme version of Creed's gospel, with its uncritical mixture of middle-class puritanism (the weapons of death must be clean), combat as a game (Staley's two hypothetical warring nations will reach a prior agreement on the rules of combat; all that is missing are referees to enforce the rules), and militarism. Staley and Creed both preach doctrines that privilege the agonistic behaviors, the kind of masculine "adversativeness" that Ong describes. Later in the conversation, Staley makes the implicit gender bias in his vision overt in language that Ong would find quite familiar: "War is the ultimate realization of modern technology. For centuries men have tested themselves in war. War was the final test, the great experience, the privilege, the honor, the self-sacrifice or what have you, the absolutely ultimate determination of what kind of man you were" (83). Staley then proceeds to bemoan the deterioration of modern manhood, a deterioration for which technology compensates: "[Now] war brings out the best in technology" (85). For Staley, the masculinity of technology is a given.

Mark Osteen argues that the concept of nuclear destruction assumes religious proportions in *End Zone:* "Nuclear weapons . . . inspire both awe and dread, and remain mysteriously fascinating both because of their complex technology and because of their seemingly limitless power. The numinousness of nuclear weapons—their mystery and power—induces us to identify with their destructive force, and indeed finally to try to merge with their power by letting them rain down" (151). By emphasizing the limitless power of nuclear weapons and the potential totality of mass destruction, Staley initially provides Gary with a vision of the cosmic simplicity that he seeks. This vision of simplicity resulting from nuclear destruction, of the bomb as antigod delivering salvation through annihilation, is the most thoroughly debased of all the fourthspaces examined in this study.

But the same cerebral side of Gary that ultimately disqualifies him as a Creed disciple enables him to see the essential emptiness of Staley's vision. He points out the inadequacy of "words to express thirty million dead" and asserts that the words found in nuclear discourse fail to "explain," "clarify," or "express." "They're painkillers. Everything becomes abstract." Gary must inevitably reject Staley as surrogate father, just as he has rejected Creed. The central irony of Staley's presence in the novel is that, in trying to give Gary a more refined language for mass nuclear destruction than he already possesses, the major destroys Gary's religious response to mass death. Staley ultimately functions as the third of the father figures in the novel who have unwittingly revealed the sheer arbitrariness of language to Gary. Thus it is hardly surprising when, at the end of the novel, Gary suffers a physical collapse, undoubtedly rooted in emotion, so total that he has to be hospitalized. Once again he has failed to find a surrogate father and a vision of redemptive simplicity.

Gary, in fact, suffers from a paradoxical curse. He is so innately intelligent that he can see through all the false and destructive visions that he for a time explores, but he is also so locked into traditional and linguistic concepts of masculinity that he can never fully transcend them. While he can comprehend the arbitrary nature of such visions, and for that matter of language itself, he cannot escape them. Indeed, a dominant theme in DeLillo's fiction is the impossibility of escaping, of transcending language corrupted by masculine tradition and violence. Gary's dilemma anticipates the profound disillusionment experienced by Bill Grey, the writer-protagonist of DeLillo's 1991 novel *Mao II:* "and he was near the point where he wanted to eliminate things that no longer mattered, things that still mattered, all excess and all necessity, and why not begin with words" (160).

Drifting through Urantia

Greyhound Space in Denis Johnson's *Angels*

Denis Johnson's *Angels* opens with the female protagonist, Jamie Mays, board-ing a Greyhound bus and thereby entering into a space that will define, and severely proscribe, her existence. On the bus she meets Bill Houston, the dark angel who becomes her companion on a journey that will take her across a continent and back and, more crucially, into a harrowing confrontation with her very soul. Violence becomes a third companion in her nightmarish quest for validation and stability. The debased and littered public space as-signed to the economically disadvantaged, the spiritual dreams and visions of those condemned to economic and spiritual poverty, and a nightmarish fourthspace that emerges from the violent interaction of the first two consti-tute the dominant geography of Johnson's 1983 novel.[1] The novel's surrealis-tic levels of diction are enhanced by the constant eliding of boundaries among the three spaces. In addition, the text's central characters sometimes trespass into a postmodern middle- and upper-class space, in one climactic instance with deadly results.

The novel opens with these symbolic and vaguely ominous words: "In the Oakland Greyhound all the people were dwarfs" (3). In the American mythos it is the marginalized and the powerless who travel by bus, and in the reality of the American socioeconomic structure such people are indeed diminished. Fleeing from existence in a trailer park and a marriage to an unfaithful husband, Jamie, along with her two young daughters, boards the bus in Oakland with no destination in mind. She is vaguely in search of the something better that America promises, but instead she finds herself trapped in an extended and impoverished physical-social space. The world that she and Bill Houston encounter consists of bus stations, seedy motels,

trailer parks, run-down movie theaters, and grimy back streets. With its connotations of transience and constant motion, "Greyhound space" is an appropriate label for this world.

In Pittsburgh, Jamie and Bill stay briefly at the Hotel Magellan, "a rotten
hotel, peopled by escapees, with pocked, frayed carpeting and bedding that
smelled of sorrow" (16). There is a strong note of irony in this description,
since those who seek refuge in the Magellan are not truly escapees at all; the
vast majority of them will never escape the Greyhound space into which they
have wandered or in which they have been trapped from birth. In fact, a
central implication of *Angels* is that no one can escape Greyhound space.
Economic disadvantage, the systemic injustice of an oppressive capitalism,
lays the foundations of the trap, and the sheer hopelessness of surmounting
this oppressive system ultimately deadens the souls of those who cannot escape it. In the Hotel Magellan even sorrow is secondhand, something vaguely
sensed in the atmosphere rather than deeply felt on a personal level; sorrow
and violence are permanent conditions in this world. Clearly visible from
the hotel is the postmodern space of downtown Pittsburgh, "the Golden Triangle, where the great buildings appeared ready to take off from Earth" (16).
The soaring buildings in the heart of the city simultaneously tantalize and
mock the refugees who wander pointlessly through Greyhound space. Like
the name *Magellan*, they connote great adventure, a daring exploration that
will free human beings from earthly restraints. Inwardly, however, Jamie and
Bill fear that the great adventure is not for them, and this fear proves to be
prophetic. In Johnson's novel, airports and bank lobbies join Pittsburgh's
Golden Triangle as representations of the alien middle- and upper-class
American social space that Jamie and Bill observe from their impoverished
vantage point in Greyhound space. Jamie would probably settle for fantasies
of being an occasional tourist in Golden Triangle space, but Bill tries to force
himself into it, an action that is at once absurd and tragic for everyone involved.

Both characters understand that money is the only passport from Greyhound space to Golden Triangle space, but, never having had any, neither has
any realistic understanding of how to acquire it. Moreover, the capitalist system leaves them few, if any, real opportunities for social mobility. Space
functions in Johnson's novel as metaphor for class, and Jamie and Bill are
part of a perpetually drifting American lumpenproletariat. Thus the action
of the novel moves from Oakland to Pittsburgh and then from Pittsburgh to
Phoenix. Johnson's protagonists are descendants of John Steinbeck's Joads,

condemned to a perpetual and fruitless search for the promise of American opportunity, a promise that has become a cruel myth. They are the reincarnations of Dreiser's Carrie Meeber staring into the shop windows of affluence with no Drouet or Hurstwood anywhere around. They hold charter membership in the shadow America glimpsed by Thomas Pynchon's Oedipa Maas in *The Crying of Lot 49:* "Drifters she had listened to, Americans speaking their language carefully, scholarly, as if they were wandering in exile from somewhere else invisible yet congruent with the cheered land she lived in; and walkers along the roads at night, zooming in and out of your headlights without looking up, too far from any town to have a real destination" (135). They are the shadow Americans whom middle- and upper-class citizens have resolutely trained themselves not to see.

Jamie's tourist mentality and Bill's propensity to violence and destructive desperation concerning money are memorably foreshadowed in the novel's early scenes. In Pittsburgh, Jamie tries to convince Bill to take her to Philadelphia to see the Liberty Bell. Bill's response to her request is revealing on more than one level: "I would love to see the Washington Monument because it doesn't piss around. It's tall. One other thing is those four big statutes of faces carved out of a mountain. But they ain't neither of them in Pittsburgh *or* Philly. Only thing in this state's the Liberty Bell, and that's just a bell" (19). The phallic overtones of Bill's admiration for the Washington Monument are more than a little comic (for all its surreal violence, *Angels* is at times a masterful example of black humor). Still, this awe of a "tall" monument is indicative of the degree to which he feels emasculated in an America that has sentenced him to existence in Greyhound space. His alienation from the mainstream American culture is indicated by his not knowing Mount Rushmore's name or that the faces carved on it were presidents and major cultural icons. But he is, in fact, perceptive in his response to the Liberty Bell; for those of his class, it is "just a bell."

Bill's potential for violating, and even exploiting, Jamie is revealed in an early scene in which he takes her to a grimy, unnamed bar where he indicates a willingness to pimp for her until she refuses to cooperate. After the bar episode, Bill and Jamie board a Pittsburgh city bus, another manifestation of Greyhound space. They literally travel to the end of the bus line, where a guilty and drunken Bill tries to bribe the incredulous driver to take them to Philadelphia so that his "wife" can see the Liberty Bell. When the driver refuses because of bus company rules, Bill succinctly states a personal philosophy that can only lead him to destruction: "There has to be rules to make things run right, . . . *but.* If you got an idea about breaking the rules to make things run *better,* why goddamn it then a course there ain't a reason in the world not to break the rules" (25). Typically, Bill is simultaneously prescient and self-deluded. He comprehends that the rules constitute evidence of the systemic control that has sentenced him to Greyhound space. Certainly as far as those trapped in the lumpenproletariat are concerned, things could indeed be run better. For an instant he seems close to a comprehension of the injustice implicit in any exploitation of a human being, of the injustice he was willing to commit in pimping Jamie, but in his drunken condition he settles for the kind of self-defeating action that characterizes his behavior throughout the novel.

Outside on the way to the bar, Bill has expressed his ambition to see Waylon Jennings perform. Admiring Jennings's carefully crafted public persona, Bill would like to think of himself as a romantic "outlaw," a man who can thumb his nose at society's rules and be admired for it. Later in the novel, Bill and Jamie, now in Chicago, go to the Biograph theater to see Jamie's favorite movie, *Endless Love.* Outside the Biograph, they suddenly realize that they are "standing in the alley where John Dillinger had been killed" (62). The text's allusions to Jennings and Dillinger demonstrate Johnson's mastery of bricolage in evoking an American myth.[2] During the depression, Dillinger, in reality a sadistic criminal, became something of a folk hero by robbing the banks that collectively constituted a synecdoche of a corrupt and failed economic system. A few decades later, Waylon Jennings, along with Willie Nelson and others, appropriated the label "Outlaws" as metaphor for their devotion to a music and lifestyle that defied the "rules" of then-mainstream Nashville and of middle-class American society. They of course became quite wealthy by doing so, since their rebellion was an essentially symbolic one. A parallel exists between the debased myth of the Boatright brothers in *Bastard Out of Carolina* and the veneration of outlaws, including wealthy living ones and vicious dead ones, in *Angels.* Bill Houston will take his defiance beyond the merely symbolic and meet a fate closer to Dillinger's than to the success of "Waylon and Willie and the boys." One lesson of *Angels* is that the capitalist system will sometimes appropriate symbolic acts of rebellion as a means of reinforcing its hegemony. At one point Bill robs a small Chicago hardware store; afterward, while riding an El train, he luxuriates in his daring: "He realized that he was the greatest thief of all time" (41). Bill is so intoxicated by the robbery that, as he catches glimpses of the lower-middle-class homes rushing by outside, he feels that his rapidly moving, transient space is superior to the fragile stability that he observes: "He witnessed their checkered tablecloths and the backs of their heads and the images moving on their television screens like things trapped under ice. The train was warm, the light was right" (41). This sense of power, illusory as it is, will be a contributing factor in Bill's decision to risk a more daring robbery, this time in the very heart of Golden Triangle space.

In the novel's climactic scene, Bill, along with his brothers James and Burris and a ludicrous criminal "mastermind" named Dwight Snow, attempt to rob a Phoenix bank. The narration of the failed robbery is a tour de force that encapsulates the major spaces of the novel's complex and shifting geography. In it, the narration is initially centered on James Houston, probably the truest outlaw in the Houston family and seemingly the brother most prone to violence. In a detail that echoes Bill's phallic admiration of the Washington Monument, James is sexually aroused by the thrill and danger of violating Golden Triangle space and has an orgasm upon entering the bank. He speaks lovingly to the revolver that "touched his thigh like a loving finger" (119). Almost instantly, though, he is intimidated by the sheer spaciousness of the bank interior: "He hadn't been prepared, somehow, for the largeness of it all, for the insignificance of the people surrounding them, as if this great chamber with its outsized plants and tall, thin fountain of water had been constructed for a race of monsters" (119). In its surreal size, the bank interior functions in Johnson's text as a metonymic representation of a repressive capitalist system that dwarfs individual human beings, especially habitués of Greyhound space such as the Houston brothers.

The bank interior was constructed to exclude the Houston brothers and Dwight Snow, and they can attempt to penetrate it only through violence. Like the other manifestations of Golden Triangle space in the novel, it is designed to physically diminish and thus dehumanize those who enter it, causing all who enter to realize that it was created for a "race" other than any they have encountered. With its "outsized plants," it is intended to miniaturize nature itself, and it thus exemplifies the sterile postmodernism that increasingly characterizes middle- and upper-middle-class urban space in America. By deliberately remaining invisible, those who design and profit the most from such space come to seem monstrous and frightening beings; it is dangerous, even impossible, to challenge them. Johnson incorporates a wonderfully incongruous moment into the robbery scene. After the Houstons and Snow show their weapons and begin the actual robbery, one customer ignores them and continues to write in his checkbook, "refusing any connection with this mysterious and violent event" (121). It is as if the unreality of the bank interior encourages the unnamed customer to ignore the danger surrounding him. Moreover, the Houstons and Snow probably seem unreal to him in another way—they do not belong here in Golden Triangle space.

As the climactic moment of the robbery scene nears, the narrative point of view shifts away from Bill to his brother Burris, who watches the robbery from outside in the getaway car he has been assigned to drive. Abruptly, Burris witnesses, in a distorted manner, a bank guard, who "seemed taller than a natural man," draw a weapon and shoot James in the abdomen. At this point, violence replaces the dehumanizing bank interior as the defining unreality in the scene. Even to Burris, who helped plan the robbery and thus knew beforehand that his brothers were armed, violence when it suddenly erupts seems unreal. The bank guard appears to him as being other than "a natural man," and this in fact quite ordinary man employed to protect the system controlled by a "race of monsters" enrages and terrifies him by shooting his brother. Johnson's mastery of narrative technique is evidenced in what immediately results from Burris's terror and outrage. Burris, the youngest of the Houston brothers, a drug addict who manages to "shoot up" on the way to the robbery and who is from the beginning the weakest link in the planned robbery, leaps out of the runaway car and screams, *"Kill that man!"* Johnson then communicates the finality of violence with the following brief and definitive statement: "And Bill did."

This deliberately cold account of Bill's fatal shooting of the guard effectively summarizes the vision of violence implicit in Johnson's novel. It is a force that is always latent in *Angels*, awaiting only the requisite circumstances to explode into actuality. It functions metaphorically as a fourth Johnson brother and as a perennial part of the novel's geography. Earlier in the text, Bill is described as standing "at the edge of violence" (58), a territory he has explored more than once. Prior to the bank robbery scene, he has had one rule that he refuses to break even to avenge the rape of Jamie: in his criminal career, he has always stopped short of murder without being able to explain why. When he does kill someone, it is an almost instinctual act that carries him irrevocably into the territory of violence and dooms him to a painful and public death. It is also significant that the novel's climactic moment of violence occurs in Golden Triangle space rather than in Greyhound space. In the world of *Angels*, violence is everywhere and always imminent.

Almost immediately after the bank robbery scene, Johnson once again assumes the role of bricoleur to produce another narrative tour de force. A thoroughly demoralized Burris flees the getaway car, thus ensuring the apprehension and arrest of Bill, Dwight, and James (who is badly wounded). Banks seeks refuge in a run-down movie theater, an easily identifiable part of Greyhound space: "It was a sorrowful and ostentatious pre-war theater. Burris sensed rather than saw the pointless curtains dripping as if putrefied from the walls, as he waited at the turn of the aisle to trust his eyes. The seat he chose, in the very front row, shrieked as he sat down in it" (127). The theater is essentially secondhand space, bequeathed to the marginalized urban male after being rendered anachronistic by postmodern entertainment complexes. Inevitably, it shows reruns rather than newly released films.

Seeking only a hiding place, Burris is, for a time, hardly aware of the images being projected on the screen. When he does look up, he sees "two men [fighting] with knives in a western barroom" (128). The film commodifies violence specifically in the context of the American myth of a heroic, male-dominated West. At first Burris is distanced from it by his awareness of an essential distortion at its very center: "Wearing long trenchcoats, carrying shotguns and rifles, men on horses rode along a dirt road, passed into a forest, and made for a cabin in the clearing. Burris wished he could engage himself in their story—a story of men with guns, exactly like his own, except that nobody going to the movies ever guessed the essential, gigantic truth of it, which was that these men would trade everything they had for one clear moment of peace" (128). Such dangerous innocence is of course fundamental to the myth of the American West, in which violence is exhilarating, a ritualized enactment of male freedom. Peace is mythologized as residing at the very heart of violence—the outlaw finds peace through destroying all obstacles, including once-human but now objectified ones, that interfere with his (of course, virtually always *his*) free motion and the gratification of his desires. Distraught, Burris retreats to the theater's filthy restroom. Inside he writes homophobic graffiti on the wall of the partition inside which he is overcome by a nausea induced by fear and self-loathing. Aware that he has failed his own masculine code by fleeing and leaving behind the getaway car, he pathetically tries to reassert his hopelessly compromised masculinity in a culturally sanctioned manner, anonymously attacking gay men.

After returning to his seat, Burris becomes increasingly involved in the film, which is a revisionist dramatization of the exploits of Jesse and Frank James. The film depicts the James brothers as initially unwilling outlaws who were "driven to desperate measures by their status as renegades following the Civil War" (130). The myth of the James brothers was for years a Hollywood staple, the basis of several highly entertaining films, including Henry King's *Jesse James* (1939), Fritz Lang's *Return of Frank James* (1940), and Philip Kaufman's *Great Northfield, Minnesota Raid* (1972). It is not surprising, then, that Burris feels he has already seen the film he finds himself watching. In its several incarnations, he undoubtedly has, more than once. Once again, Johnson is exploring the appeal of outlaws, transformed by a debased mythology, for the residents of Greyhound space.

Inside the run-down theater, Burris is most likely watching *The Great Northfield, Minnesota Raid,* since the screen is suddenly devoted to a rather graphic re-creation of the James brothers' ill-fated attempt to rob a bank in that town and their subsequent ambush by the armed citizens of the town. For Burris, these violent images cut too close to what he has just witnessed and to what he can reasonably assume happened to his brothers after he deserted them:

> As [the James gang] rode . . . into the town of Northfield, Minnesota, everything started to go wrong. The teller in the bank claimed he couldn't open the vault, and in a hypnotic moment of anger and chaos, somebody shot his face off for him; and the people of the town of Northfield, it now turned out, had arranged themselves everywhere— behind barrels, on the wooden roofs, under the water troughs—to ambush the brothers and their comrades as they stepped out of the doors of the bank. From one end of the street to the other, the men faced nothing but the firepower of hideous strangers. Burris had never seen anything more horrifying. (131)

The "hypnotic" murder of the cinematic bank teller echoes Bill's instinctual shooting of the bank guard, and Burris fled from an imagined "horrifying" assault against his brothers, Dwight Snow, and himself.

Despite his earlier perception of the film's unreal glamorization of violence, Burris shares a dangerous kind of innocence with the novel's other inhabitants of Greyhound space. Watching the re-creation of Northfield's bloody ambush of the James gang, he is baffled and troubled by the hatred of the fictional citizens of Northfield for the outlaws and quickly relates it to the bank guard who inexplicably shot James. Burris cannot comprehend that forced penetration of Golden Triangle space threatens the very foundation of the capitalist order or that violence, once threatened, can escape control and establish its own chaotic geography. The theater scene brilliantly deconstructs the myth of the heroic Western. In the unnamed film, the James brothers are initially innocent victims, then heroic rebels, and finally very real victims. At the end they are threatened by the violence that they seem to unleash themselves, though they are only mimicking on a relatively small scale the systemic violence that sustains the capitalist system. Moreover, the legend of the James brothers as romantic outlaws is undercut by the text's depiction of the Houston brothers as pathetic and incompetent bank robbers. Burris, after all, is inside the theater only because he deserted his companions.

Johnson depicts Phoenix as an increasingly postmodernist surface space still devoted to an unreal western mythology. It is hardly surprising that in such an milieu the Houston brothers blunder into self-destructive violence. Along with Dwight, James is first shown in the novel repossessing two automobiles and a motorcycle. James is sexually excited when the man from whom the vehicles are repossessed fires a gun at him as he speeds away in one of the cars; he has been involved in, and survived, the gunfight of his fantasies. Still, the act of repossession itself reinforces the capitalist system and becomes then a kind of legitimized theft. Repossession functions as a metaphor for Johnson's Phoenix—a schizophrenic culture that subscribes to the Wild West myth as long as it does not really threaten the rigid social structure of the community.

In fact, the Houston brothers are no more the James brothers than they are John Dillinger or Waylon Jennings. They are doomed and rather pathetic habitués of Greyhound space, the inescapable nature of which is underscored in three interrelated scenes involving Jamie Mays. In the first, Jamie, searching for Bill in Chicago, encounters Ned Higher-and-Higher, dressed in a ludicrous red suit, who pretends to know Bill and volunteers to help Jamie find him. He first takes her, appropriately enough, to the Greyhound bus station coffee shop, where he defines the real importance of Greyhound space: "Just about anywhere you go . . . the bus station is the *exact* center of town. In case of a nuclear attack, the bus station would be Ground Zero. . . . If we were here when World War Three started, a bomb would drop almost in this restaurant. . . . We'd be *atomized* and *radioactive.* It wouldn't feel like dying. We'd be turned into particles of light. This is the center of things" (48).

Ned's analysis, like much of the writing in *Angels,* works on multiple levels. It is, for example, one of a number of instances in the novel satirizing the scientific knowledge of the residents of Greyhound space. Ned's scientific vocabulary might have been derived from any number of science-fiction movies or television programs. Increasingly in *Angels* such pseudoscientific superstition assumes ominous proportions. More significantly, this discussion of Ground Zero identifies Johnson's novel as a post-Hiroshima, post-Holocaust text; it dramatizes the diminished view of the stature of human life since 1945. In addition, it has important implications for *Angels*'s controlling spatial trope. Greyhound space may well be at the center of urban geography, but the center has been deserted by the dominant capitalist system in favor of outlying suburban spaces. Thus the center remains significant only as the meeting ground of an essentially transient population. One remembers Bud Korpenning, John Dos Passos's doomed protagonist in the modernist classic *Manhattan Transfer* (1925), who continually tries to reach the center of things in New York City, not realizing that no center exists. In Johnson's more contemporary text, the center still exists but has been bequeathed to the economically powerless. Ned's speech functions on still another level: his reference to being "turned into particles of light" is integral to the novel's multileveled symbolism of physical and spiritual light and darkness.

Shortly, Ned's surface absurdity is transformed into something else entirely. He tricks Jamie into an apartment building where he and his brother-in-law assault and rape her in a prolonged and animalistic manner. The intensely sadistic nature of the assault is indicated by Ned's having to restrain his brother-in-law from attacking Jamie with a knife. The degradation of the rape initiates Jamie's descent into a drug- and alcohol-induced breakdown that culminates in her incarceration in the Arizona State Hospital. The various wings of the hospital are named after famous women, and Jamie's time in the institution is marked by a steady descent into increasingly repressive spaces. She begins, for instance, in the Mamie Eisenhower Wing (1950s Republican respectability), is transferred first to the Helen Keller Wing (the silenced woman), then to the Madame Curie Wing (popularized science again), next to the Joan of Arc Wing (the female martyr), and finally to the Mathilda Wing (which she identifies as the "Middle of Things"). Threatened with the Mathilda Wing, she remembers Ned's speech and is terrified. Her terror, it turns out, is prophetic, since her time in the Mathilda Wing is dominated by shock therapy and a succession of other degrading experiences and horrific nightmares. Ultimately, the line between experience and nightmare vanishes and a surreal fourthspace emerges. In one of the thirdspace experiences, she hears or imagines hearing the Mathilda Wing referred to as Ground Zero. Once again, for Jamie as for other denizens of Greyhound space, potentially redemptive thirdspace has been appropriated by the structure that encloses her and transformed into a menacing fourthspace.

Thus, three crucial scenes involving Jamie (the coffee-shop scene, the sadistic rape scene, and her surreal vision inside the Mathilda Wing) are linked by the concept of Greyhound space as Ground Zero, the center of a dehumanized emptiness in which the soul is assaulted and threatened by the knife of social repression. Ned Higher-and-Higher initiates a degradation of Jamie that carries her lower and lower toward mental and spiritual destruction. During one of the electric shock treatments she has another vision, this time of "the angel": "His body is steady and beautiful and hairless, the wings white, incinerating, and pure, but the head changes rapidly—the head of an eagle, a goat, an insect, a mouse, a sheep with spiraling horns that turn and lengthen almost imperceptibly—and the entire message had no words." Jamie asks the angel whether "it," apparently meaning death, will hurt, and she receives a frightening answer: "'Oh babe.' The angel starts to cry. 'You can't imagine,' he said" (157). Throughout *Angels*, the alienated and frightened central characters seek some kind of spiritual reassurance, some message that meaning exists in their world, but they are always frustrated. As with Jamie and the angel, the messages they do receive have no words but still signal that something ominous is impending.

Johnson's Greyhound space is descended from T. S. Eliot's "waste land," and Jamie, following a pattern in the novel, turns, in her quest for meaning and salvation, to false spiritualists, American incarnations of Eliot's Madame Sosostris, sometimes themselves becoming prophetesses of apocalypse.[3] The most memorable prophetess in *Angels* is Mrs. Houston, the sixty-nine-year-old mother of the Houston brothers, who carries denial of reality to a frightening extreme. A vaguely Protestant fundamentalist, she carries her Bible wherever she goes, hoping that it will protect her from the Mormons and Hispanics, who she believes threaten her. In the second scene in which she appears, she is significantly depicted inside a branch of the bank that her sons will later try to rob. Rather quickly made to feel that she has no business inside the bank, she leaves abruptly (68). Less dramatically than her sons will do, she has briefly invaded Golden Triangle space, only to be promptly expelled as someone alien to it. In desperation, she rushes to Rose's Cantina, which turns outs not to be a cantina at all but a run-down home for varying kinds of spiritualists. Inside she first consults Miss Sybil, "a Jewish lady from Queens, the outline of whose enormous breasts showed plainly through her sheer yellow blouse" (71).[4]

After receiving sufficient hints from Mrs. Johnson concerning what her "client" wants to know, Miss Sybil says that "the Evil" has Bill Johnson. Wanting desperately to retreat from a prophecy that she has largely instigated, Mrs. Johnson demands assurance from Miss Sybil that "the good" will "triumph" "in the end." But the prophetess is tired and rushed and delivers instead a quite accurate summary of the spiritual nature of Greyhound space: "It's easy to talk about the future being so good and all, because it never comes, dear. But all you gotta do is look around you for half a minute. Nobody's keeping it secret from us that we're all in the toilet. We're in the sewer. Forecast tomorrow is more of the same" (71).

Later in the novel, Mrs. Johnson, in an amazing confession, specifically links Bill's conception to apocryphal violence: "I was thirty-three years old before I ever bore a child. . . . I cried out in my heart to the Lord that I was a waste of a woman . . . and the Reverend John Miller laid his hand across my forehead on my birthday in 1945—in a holy church, I'm ashamed to tell you, that has since been turned into some kind of roller-rink. And one week after that laying on of hands, they dropped the biggest bomb ever on the Japanese" (97). This confession encapsulates the narrative complexity of Johnson's text. By emphasizing that, when she conceived Bill, she was the same age as the crucified Christ, Mrs. Houston intends to relate the concept of salvation either to herself or to Bill or to both. She is, in fact, something of a perverse and demented Madonna figure throughout the novel. Through her, Johnson stresses the intensely secular nature of his depiction of a fallen world, a world locked into a futile search for some redemptive meaning. What was once a church is now "some kind of roller-rink"—the secularization of Greyhound space continues unabated. Virtually from the beginning, Bill's life has been characterized by a destructive innocence about the world into which he has been born. He is a truly naturalistic character, the victim of environment, fate, and an oppressive social system. The post-Hiroshima, post-Holocaust dimension of Johnson's text is made manifest in Mrs. Houston's linking of Bill's conception with the dropping of "the biggest bomb ever." If she cannot be the mother of Christ, she will become the mother of violence; and she gives birth to three criminal sons who attempt a robbery that ends in the death of a bank guard.

The robbery ultimately becomes a passport allowing Mrs. Houston to enter Golden Triangle space in a more rewarding manner than her abortive venture inside the bank. At Bill's trial for murder, she is in her glory. In the courtroom she luxuriates in this alien space with its "distant ceiling and ominous judge's bench . . . originless florescent illumination . . . austere and holy Modern Airport décor and . . . posh hush of [its] carpets and central cooling" (160). For her, the production of Golden Triangle space as a kind of capitalist heaven is no longer threatening: "Though her kind of people were generally ignored . . . by those who built and staffed these magnificent rooms, everyone was forced to see now that it was really for her kind that these places had been built, after all—and now *you* are working for *us*. . . . The last shall be first. It made her ashamed to take very much pride in all of this tragedy, and yet the day seemed electric . . . because her boy was on page one" (161).

Her family has been recognized by the dominant society and even granted admission to one of its most rarified of spaces, a courtroom. Of course, what she is intentionally not seeing is that her intrusion into this "austere and holy" social space is doomed to be a short-term one and is only made possible by her son's act of violence, which will ultimately bring about his own death. In this way, Bill *is* sacrificed for her and becomes a kind of secular Christ figure in much the same way as Joe Christmas in Faulkner's *Light in August*. Her ecstasy is complete when she later enters a real airport, Phoenix's Sky Harbor, in order to put Jamie's two daughters on a plane to take them back to their father; when she finds herself on "an escalator that was drawing [her] up some seventy or eighty feet toward a gigantic mosaic Phoenix bird rising up out of its ashes, she understood what it would be like to stand before the doors of Heaven, and knew how small a thing was an earthly life" (168). The image of heaven as a commodified capitalist space seems to Mrs. Johnson all that could be desired. It is interesting to note that the text describes the old, abandoned Phoenix airport as having been "more like a bus station than a center of international flight" (168).

A prophetess possibly even more bizarre than Mrs. Johnson is Burris's "woman," Jeanine. For Jeanine the holy book is something called the *Urantia Book,* which details Lucifer's failed rebellion against "Christ Michael." According to the *Urantia Book,* "the one we call the Devil is named Caligastia. He was a prince . . . a deposed planetary prince of Urantia." Even though Lucifer's rebellion failed, "archrebels" roam throughout the Earth, which is actually Urantia, and "continue their deceptive and seductive efforts to confuse and mislead the minds of men and angels" (91). Like the novel's other prophetic visions, Jeanine's analysis of Urantia works on several levels. It is another of Johnson's satiric descriptions of the kind of surreal and debased wedding of popular science with a debased mythology that captures the imaginations of those in Greyhound space.[5] Further, it is revealing of the intense appeal that conspiracies, especially those involving UFOs, have held for marginalized Americans since the end of World War II. It is not insignificant that Burris is shooting up with heroin as Jeanine tells him about Urantia. More seriously, though, the "archrebels" of an oppressive socioeconomic system, through the manipulation of mass culture, have been quite successful in confusing the minds of the central characters in *Angels*. For them, Ground Zero functions as an appropriate name for mental and spiritual, as well as physical, space. Once released from the Arizona State Hospital and finally off drugs, Jamie realizes that she has been "fucked up" "in the area of religion" (199). It is thematically important that she describes religion as an area, just as she would a physical space.

Bill Houston, who alone takes the fall for the abortive bank robbery and the murder of the guard, comes to experience a sequence of spaces that correspond to the surreal wings of the Arizona State Hospital. A series of penal institutions become Ground Zero for him, an extended secret Greyhound space in which he progresses toward his most literal death. On the second day after his arrest, he awakens to find himself in a flooded cell located in a section of the prison reserved for "special captives isolated because they were believed capable of great violence" (137). His mother should feel gratified; the state has already tacitly recognized her as the mother of violence. The flood in Bill's prison cell recalls Eliot's admonition to the inhabitants of the waste land to fear "death by water."

The concluding section of the novel, with its narration of Bill's progress downward through levels of Ground Zero, reads like a secularized version of René Girard's "sacrificial crisis." In *Violence and the Sacred*, Girard discusses the extreme threat that violence represents for human societies:

> Once violence has penetrated a community it engages in an orgy of self-propagation. There appears to be no way of bringing the reprisals to a halt before the community has been annihilated.
>
> If there are really such events as sacrificial crises, some sort of braking mechanism, an automatic control that goes into effect before everything is destroyed, must be built into them. In the final stages of a sacrificial crisis the very viability of human society is put in question. (67)

Girard believes that in primitive societies, ritual sacrifices functioned as the "braking mechanism" that contained potential "epidemics" of violence. It is almost a cliché to refer to modern American society as being plagued by an "epidemic of violence," and *Angels* dramatizes the ways in which a postmodern capitalist society creates its own rituals as a mode of controlling violence. An essential difference between the contemporary culture depicted by Johnson and the "primitive cultures" discussed by Girard is the substitution of the secular for the sacred.

Girard further argues that sacrifice in human societies functions as a substitute for "reciprocal violence," which, with its seductive appeal to human beings and its potential for endlessness, threatens the very fabric of any social structure. Thus a scapegoat must be identified as the necessarily arbitrary embodiment of the epidemic that threatens the social order: "In destroying the surrogate victim, men believe that they are ridding themselves of some present ill. And indeed they *are*, for they are effectively doing away with those forms of violence that beguile the imagination and provoke emulation" (82). Since Bill undeniably shot and killed the bank guard, it might be difficult to see him as a sacrificial victim. Consequently, Johnson has to go to some lengths to establish this association.

James Houston (clearly the most instinctively violent of the Houston brothers), Burris, and Dwight Snow all escape significant punishment for the robbery through plea bargains and administrative oversights. In Johnson's novel, the legal system seems to make two arbitrary decisions from the first: it will direct its resources toward the punishment of only one of the bank robbers, and that one will be Bill. That Snow and James primarily planned the robbery seems irrelevant to the system, and Burris is too clearly pathetic to bother about. Two characters—Bill's court-appointed public defender, Samuel Fredericks (known as Freddy), and "the Death House three-to-eleven guard," Brian—serve as secular "priests" charged with overseeing Bill's sacrifice.

Bill's first meeting with Freddy sets the tone of their relationship. In it, Freddy informs Bill of his strategy for defending him: "We're going to convince [the jury] you're stupid and tragic, but basically a nice guy" (139). The odds against the success of such an approach are, of course, overwhelming. Freddy next describes the "deal" that the state is offering Bill: "You agree to plead guilty to first-degree murder, and they'll agree to do everything they can to execute you. The Assistant DA says it's almost like going free." When Bill asks if dying in the gas chamber will hurt, Freddy repeats the message that Jamie's "angel" from the Mathilda Wing relayed to her: "You can't imagine." The appearance of these three ominous words in these two contexts emphasizes the essential unity of the Ground Zero dimension of Greyhound space, as do Jamie's symbolic death in the Mathilda Wing and Bill's impending literal death in the gas chamber.

Bill is shown entering death row literally naked, having been stripped of the protective disguise of clothing in preparation for his imminent sacrifice. Soon, Brian, acting out of a perverse form of kindness, offers him a tour of the gas chamber. Once inside, Bill realizes the full extent of the state's appropriation of his privacy: "He wouldn't be allowed to wear a shirt, he'd be half naked before strangers—and now it came over him vividly that his death would be attended, observed, and monitored by people who couldn't appreciate how much he wanted to live. They would probably think, because he offered no resistance, that all of this was all right with him. But it wasn't. They just didn't know him. They were strangers" (175). As sacrificial victim, Bill must be objectified. Since he has been chosen to die as a means of controlling an epidemic of violence, his physical humanity must be displayed while his individuality is simultaneously denied. Nevertheless, it briefly seems that he will be saved through the substitution of another sacrificial victim in his place.

The person with the longest seniority on death row is Richard Clay Wilson, a convicted child murderer: "A sixteen-year-old dropout, a loner, a Southside denizen with nothing to recommend or condemn him, he'd been discovered with the hacked skeletons and dismembered bodies of four missing children, and his lawyers had thrown him to the wolves" (186–87). Despite being a child murderer, Wilson has come to be accepted, and even somewhat respected, by the other inmates of death row simply because of his having been trapped so long in a state between life and death. Bill feels the general ambivalence about Wilson: "It was Houston's duty as a human being to hate this monster, this psychotic mutant born out of the always tragic mingling of separate races [Bill echoes his mother's racism and intolerance]. But he was confused. He felt removed from the places where his ideas made sense. . . . There was a great project taking place here—he and Richard were going to be killed" (187). The "great project" taking place is the identification and subsequent sacrifice of a surrogate figure. That the execution will not be a form of reciprocal violence is indicated by the essential arbitrariness of the victim. Since it seems that either Wilson or Bill will do, the execution can have little to do with any specific crime; instead, the epidemic of crime needs to be halted and controlled.

The existence of Wilson becomes Freddy's last hope for Bill's salvation. Freddy has been around long enough to know that the state will not execute two prisoners in a short time span, and since Wilson is black and a murderer of children, he seems the likely choice as scapegoat. Wilson himself assumes this and tells Bill that he will not "go to Jesus": "I am an alien from another planet. I was not meant to be saved" (186). Brian believes that Wilson will be Bill's savior. He tells Bill that the child murderer "may not believe in Jesus, but that man is Jesus to you" (187) and advises Wilson that he is "dying for William H. Houston's sins" (188). Like the novel's other characters, Wilson is a resident of Greyhound space who is condemned to invisibility by the dominant society; in fact, his invisibility is double, since his blackness separates him from the white lumpenproletariat culture represented by the Houstons. Thus he feels like a being "from another planet."

But, with absolutely no explanation, the penal system abruptly decides to execute Bill instead. This decision leaves Freddy stunned and baffled, even though he understands the essential arbitrariness of public execution. In the novel's last major scene, groups of people spontaneously gather outside the prison as witnesses of the execution. The text emphasizes the absence of any representations of the judicial or legal establishment; instead, the witnesses, like the designated victim, are inhabitants of Greyhound space: "These people . . . who'd probably gone to the same school as William Houston, Jr., or been acquainted with one or more of his relatives or had the same parole officer—came here because they sensed that why they themselves had not been executed was inexplicable, a miracle" (203). Certainly any one of them might at any time be chosen as scapegoat. Thus the execution becomes a perverse ritual of communion in which social outcasts briefly bond before disappearing back into a social system that objectifies them.

At one point in the novel, Bill reflects on the separate "spaces" before and after his act of pulling the trigger and killing the bank guard and tries to understand how one space changed so abruptly and completely into the other. He is unable to do so, just as he is unable to comprehend the point of his random movement throughout Greyhound space outside prison and then through the levels of Ground Zero inside. Truly, all the central characters in *Angels* feel like "alien[s] from another planet," like archrebels wandering through Urantia.

The Return of John Smith

Sherman Alexie's *Indian Killer*

Sherman Alexie's *Indian Killer* falls closer to the naturalistic than to the mythological end of the continuum of violence proposed earlier, though not so close as *Bastard Out of Carolina*, *Dog Soldiers*, or *Angels*. Like *Angels, Indian Killer* has some strong affinities with a distinct naturalistic tradition in the American urban novel. Moreover, except for a few crucial departures, it is a mimetic novel; its plot is an often parodic variation of the detective novel, and a thinly disguised Rush Limbaugh is a major target of its satire. Still, a usually hidden but nevertheless pervasive supernaturalism underlies, or more precisely haunts, the text. Periodically, and crucially in the novel's brief ending, it intrudes on, and even submerges, the novel's dominant realism. In *Indian Killer* this supernaturalism emerges out of a history of death and ending and a mythology of death and re-creation. Central ingredients in Alexie's creation of a fourthspace in the novel are the history of white suppression and exile of the Native American, the subsequent near extinction of rich and diverse tribal cultures, and a myth of Indian retaliation, so long deferred as to be virtually forgotten.[1]

Set in Seattle, Washington, *Indian Killer*, while resolutely *not* solving its central mystery, depicts a set of major and minor characters who cumulatively cover the spectrum of social class in the urban Northwest. Included are a well-meaning but misguided middle-class white couple and the Native American son whom they adopt; a militant Indian college woman and her embittered cousin; a naive white detective story writer who appropriates "Indian culture"; and what Alexie describes as a new "urban tribe" of largely homeless Native Americans that is made up of "outcasts" from numerous tribes (38–39). In Alexie's text, Seattle becomes something of a microscopic representation of the history of white expansion into the American West, the subsequent emergence of a class structure paralleling Europe and the eastern United States, and the resultant displacement of Native American tribes.

In *The Lone Ranger and Tonto Fistfight in Heaven* (1993) and *Reservation Blues* (1995), Alexie brings his unique brand of absurdist humor to the development of comparable themes, but in *Indian Killer* he is (pun intended) deadly serious. The plot of *Indian Killer* is centered around two especially horrific murders of white men, the kidnapping of a young white boy, and retaliatory assaults against homeless Native Americans by white men. Girard's concept of sacrificial crisis offers rich possibilities for interpreting the text. In this case, the primal cause is known—it was the violent suppression of the First Nations by whites. In the twentieth century, the hereditary victims of this assault have seemingly been left helpless, condemned to exist as survivors of a vanquished and vanished culture forbidden to assimilate into the urban cultural mainstream.

They can only dream of what Girard describes as private (as opposed to public) revenge: "Public vengeance is the exclusive property of well-policed societies, and our society calls it the judicial system" (15). On the surface it might seem that Alexie's twentieth-century survivors of the violent nineteenth-century suppression of First Nation cultures, living as they do in a "well-policed" urban center, would have access to the "judicial center" and other avenues of "public vengeance," but Alexie's text, like other fiction by Native American writers, is devoted, in part, to demonstrating that they do not now have, and in fact have never had, such access. The judicial system, along with the U.S. government and military, have historically functioned as their oppressors, constructing, interpreting, and enforcing cynical treaty after cynical treaty designed to appropriate Native American land and culture. In *Indian Killer*, Alexie dramatizes various ways in which contemporary American culture continues this appropriation.

Consequently, the need for private vengeance has been suppressed, forced underground until it finally emerges in an epidemic of anger. *Indian Killer* illustrates Girard's vision of what happens when the need for public vengeance is denied: "Inevitably the moment comes when violence can only be countered by more violence. Whether we fail or succeed in our effort to subdue it, the real victor is always violence. The *mimetic* attributes of violence are extraordinary—sometimes direct and positive, at other times indirect and negative. The more men strive to curb their violent impulses, the more these impulses prosper. The very weapons used to combat violence are turned against their users. Violence is like a raging fire that feeds on the very objects intended to smother its flames" (31).

To illustrate a long and dangerously repressed need for Native American vengeance, Alexie adapts a bit of Native American history and mythology, the late-nineteenth-century phenomenon of Wovoka and the Ghost Dance. Inspired in part by Christian theology, Wovoka, a Nevada Paiute, was proclaimed as "the Indian Messiah." Angie Debo describes the essence of his prophecy, the ritual that he proposed to hasten its fulfillment, and the rapid spread of his cult:

> Christ had come to earth once, and the white people had killed him; now he had come to the Indians. God gave him a certain sacred paint and new words to sing with the Paiute dances, and if these were used in faith, the old ways and the dead Indians would return. The cult and its accompanying ceremonies, known to the whites as the "ghost dance," spread first to the Shoshonis and Bannocks, then to the Crows and across the mountains to the Northwest. . . . Now a new earth would move slowly from the northwest to cover [the land]; and on it would ride the Messiah, their resurrected relatives, and the wild life. It would push the white men into the sea or back to the place from whence they came. Even the date was set—the spring of 1891 when the grass should be an inch high. (289)

Two points need to be made about Wovoka and the Ghost Dance phenomenon: first, the cult specifically prohibited violence among Native Americans and did not advocate violence against whites, who were going to be driven into the sea by the ceremonies of the dance anyway; and second, the only violence it provoked was by the U.S. Army against Indians, most tragically the 1890 massacre at Wounded Knee.

In *Indian Killer*, Alexie employs the Wovoka story and prophecy as a largely understated subtext, the full implications of which are not made overt until the novel's eerie one-paragraph conclusion. In order to bring about this narrative indirection, he skillfully appropriates the conventions of the detective story, including the genre's historic links to urban fiction.[2] The text skillfully puts the reader in the position of a detective investigating leads concerning the identity of the killer or killers of the white adult men and the kidnapper of the white male child. Three primary suspects are at the center of the narrative focus of the novel, none of whom ultimately seems likely to be the "Indian killer," though all of them are associated with the "murder" of Native American cultures.[3]

The first of the three, John Smith, is a psychologically damaged Native American young man adopted by a Seattle white couple. Smith is simultaneously a frightening and a vulnerable figure, as the novel's surrealistic opening chapter, significantly entitled "Mythology," foreshadows. In this chapter, Smith fantasizes his birth on an Indian reservation. He imagines his mother as a fourteen-year-old Native American woman; but, never having been told the real circumstances of his birth, he is unable to evoke her identity in any more specific fashion: "John's mother is Navajo or Lakota. She is Apache or Seminole. She is Yakama or Spokane" (4). His fantasy is much more specific in other respects, however. In a detail that probably constitutes a "(mis)reading" of Hemingway's short story "Indian Camp," a white doctor is performing a cesarean delivery without anesthetic (Hemingway is a special target of Alexie's satire throughout the text). As in "Indian Camp," the operation is performed in a cramped, unsanitary space.

In describing the doctor, Alexie manages some stinging satire of historic white philanthropy toward Native Americans. The doctor, twenty-nine years old and from "Iowa or Illinois," where he had never seen an Indian, is forced to practice medicine on the reservation to repay a government-provided medical school scholarship. Nevertheless, he "has fallen in love with Indians. He thinks them impossibly funny and irreverent. During the hospital staff meetings, all of the Indians sit together and whisper behind their hands. . . . The white doctor often wishes he could sit with the Indians and whisper behind his hands. But he maintains a personable and professional distance" (5–6). John imagines the doctor's having been forced to treat the Indians and bearing such involuntary servitude by envisioning them as lovable children whose secret and humorous world he would abstractly like to invade. Barred from that, he has brutally invaded the body of John's mother: "The doctor's hands are deep inside John's mother . . . who is bleeding profusely where they have cut her to make room for John's head" (5). As in Hemingway's story, there are clear overtones of violent sexual penetration of the female Indian body by a white man.

Immediately after the delivery, the infant John is taken away from his mother and given to "a man in a white jumpsuit" who takes him up in a helicopter. In a daring narrative move, Alexie now extends the thematic application of John's fantasy: "Suddenly this is a war. . . . The helicopter gunman locks and loads, strafes the reservation with explosive shells. Indians hit the ground, drive their cars off roads, dive under flimsy kitchen tables. A few Indians . . . continue their slow walk down the reservation road, unperturbed by the gunfire. They have been through much worse" (6). The senseless assault on the reservation by the "helicopter gunman" evokes the white genocide of Native Americans as well as images of the Vietnam War with which John, growing up as an middle-class urban child, would have been most familiar. John is thus haunted by the history of U.S. imperialism, from nineteenth-century Manifest Destiny to Vietnam. In this context, his *literally* given name, John Smith, is symbolically important; he has the same white name as a legendary exploiter of Native American culture, and his Indian name—if he ever had one—is unknowable. John's identity has thus been appropriated, and his desire to create himself anew as Native American is doomed.

Still, he does try for such a healing re-creation. Later in the novel, John imagines a largely idyllic reservation life in which he has a loving, devoted mother. Mother and son live with an extended family of aunts, uncles, and grandparents (the father is significantly absent). In this idealized fantasy, his grandparents are teaching him the tribal language (knowing nothing of his background, he can get no more specific than this), he dances at his first powwow when he is four, and he experiences his first adolescent love affair with a beautiful young Indian girl named Dawn. The culture he evokes is one based on orality and storytelling: "His grandparents tell stories of the old times, before the white man came, when animals still talked. Coyote this, Coyote that. Raven flying around messing with everybody. Bear lumbering and rumbling across the grass" (48).[4]

Yet John imagines his reservation family passing time by playing Scrabble, and his evocations of family meals are right out of 1950s television situation comedies.[5] It is then too late even for John to re-create a true Indian self; his imagination has been co-opted and corrupted by the dominant white culture. Most of the time he is fully aware of this, and his resulting anger is a central part of what, for most of the novel, seems to be a latent capacity for murder as well as an integral part of the violent fourthspace of *Indian Killer.* In fact, John believes that, to redeem himself and his lost people, he must kill a white man. Realizing that his past has effectively been erased and that his people exist outside any hope of public vengeance, he focuses on private vengeance, dreaming of sacrificing a white scapegoat for the murder of his past and the cultural genocide of his people.

But John struggles unsuccessfully to identify precisely which white man to kill. Though initially certain that his victim must be a rich white man, he is unable to decide which particular one. Alexie brilliantly evokes the perverse logic of John's reasoning in this context: "Which white man had done the most harm to the world? Was it the richest white man? . . . But John could not convince himself that the richest man in the world deserved to die. . . . If he killed the richest white man in the world, then the second-richest white man would take his place. Nobody would even notice the difference. All the money would be switched from one account to another. . . . John could kill a thousand rich white men and not change a thing" (28). Despite his paranoia, John is quite perceptive in his analysis. It is impossible for him, as an isolated individual, to attack the white capitalist structure in any meaningful way. He is the victim of an imperialist history and an exploitative economic structure, thus as much a naturalistic victim of external forces as Richard Wright's Bigger Thomas. In fact, his situation is in some ways even more desperate than Bigger's—he has been removed from his native racial and ethnic culture. Moreover, the capitalistic system can survive the loss of any individual, even if he or she does occupy the highest position in it. John is correct, though, in identifying his target of private vengeance as male—historically, white males have been the imperialist oppressors of his people.

Similarly, John sees the futility in killing a poor white man, but not because he feels any more benevolent toward them: "John hated poor white men, but he knew killing them was a waste. They were already dead. They were zombies" (29). His hatred of the system that has destroyed his past and his people does not permit him to consider poor whites, also economic victims, as allies. John's anger is directed against racist, more than class, oppression; and, in fact, poor white men on the frontier were among the most brutal exploiters of his people as white Americans invaded the West. He is correct, though, in assuming that he could probably get away with killing one of the homeless white people, who would never be missed, who are ignored by the dominant culture as if they were dead.

John's murderous fantasies, at first glance, would seem to establish him as the likely killer of the bourgeois white victims in the novel, especially when the first of the murders is depicted in the very next chapter. Here Alexie uses the term "the killer" to describe the murderer and withholds all details about his identity, most significantly his race. For reasons other than proximity of the murder scene to John's paranoid fantasies, the narration skillfully leads the reader to assume for much of the novel that John is the killer. Though the white man is stabbed to death, the murder is described as being almost accidental in nature: "the killer had not necessarily meant for any of it to happen" (53). Still somewhat shocked by his own actions, the killer next decides that his victim's corpse must be treated in a ceremonially appropriate fashion. Thus he scalps the dead white man and only then truly becomes enraged:

> So much blood. . . . The blood was beautiful but not enough. One dead man was not enough. The killer was disappointed. Disappointment grew quickly into anger, then rage, and the killer brought the knife down into the white man's chest again and again. Still not satiated, the killer knew there was more work to do. The dead man's eyes were open and still, pupils dilated. With hands curved into talons, the killer tore the white man's eyes from his face and swallowed them whole. The killer then pulled two white owl feathers out of another pocket, and set them on the white man's chest. (54)

At first glance there seems to be a parallel between the killer's furious recognition that "one dead man was not enough" and John's epiphany that killing any one white man, no matter how rich the victim, is an insufficient response to past and present oppression. The details of scalping and the owl feathers might be white cultural evocations of Indianness, and John's Native American identity has, of course, been appropriated by that very culture. In some ways, the almost accidental nature of the murder inevitably recalls the indecisiveness rooted in John's psychological desperation. But precisely this indecisiveness signals that John cannot be the "Indian killer." Moreover, a second murder, this time of a middle-class white man who is followed by the killer after leaving a pornographic video store, seems calculated and deliberate, as the corpse is again scalped and owl feathers are left at the scene.

John tries too hard to return to some sense of a tribal self, and is too grieved at his failure to do so, to be the perpetrator of such a focused act of violence. Throughout the novel he is depicted too convincingly as naturalistic victim to be an agent of murder, though he does ultimately destroy himself after violently assaulting someone else. Much of John's paranoia results from his having been grafted, as an infant, onto an alien physical and social space in which he can never feel at peace. Not only is he taken from the reservation to live with a white couple, but he is taken to the city, the prototype of white capitalist space. Thus he often seems to be floating outside the crowded and alien world in which he finds himself trapped. The city is foreign to him, and the surrounding geographical space has long been appropriated by the white culture. Since he had never known where he came from, he can only enter a healing reservation space through fantasy.

Thus, perceiving horizontal space as hostile and alien, John tries to find salvation in vertical space. He has heard about the legendary Mohawk construction workers in New York City and seeks to find a sustaining identity in emulating them: "They were crazy bastards, walking across girders without safety harnesses, jumping from floor to floor like they were Spiderman's bastard sons. There were three or four generations of Mohawk steelworkers. Old Mohawk grandfathers sat around Brooklyn brownstones and told stories about working on the Empire State Building. They scared children with tales of relatives, buried alive in building foundations, who came back to haunt all of the white office workers" (132–33).[6]

Ironically, the way John articulates his admiration of the construction workers merely serves to emphasize the degree to which his consciousness is controlled by white culture. He describes them as the illegitimate sons of a white superhero, who, like most superheroes, is a projection of an urban consciousness (Spiderman does not leap from cliff to cliff but from skyscraper to skyscraper). John is perceptive in envisioning them as the "bastard sons" of urban culture—New York City, while benefiting from their bravery, nevertheless viewed them as inappropriate intruders into white urban space, just as the Seattle of Alexie's novel views the "tribe" of homeless Native Americans who haunt its streets.

The ancestors of the construction workers have, in fact, been buried alive in the edifice of American society, and *Indian Killer* is, in part, about the ghosts of Native Americans returning in order to obtain some long-deferred revenge. Still, while John does become an excellent worker on a Seattle skyscraper, to the point of frightening his co-workers with a bravery that seems suicidal at times, it is finally impossible to identify him as the "Indian killer" even though his foreman does so. Like a good detective writer, Alexie plants false clues throughout the novel that seem to identify John as the killer. At times there seems to be something supernatural about him, as if he is indeed a kind of ghost. In one especially frightening scene, his adoptive parents, Daniel and Olivia, are asleep in their bedroom until both are awakened by a sensation of John's presence in the room. But he is not there, and Olivia is somewhat relieved until she goes downstairs to discover that someone has, in fact, been in the house and cut a slice from a leftover roast and dropped a carving knife "carelessly into the sink" (223).[7]

A comparable mode of supernaturalism typifies the segments of the novel devoted to the kidnapping of the white boy Mark Jones. In the first of these, the narration focuses on the killer as he resolves to carry out the kidnapping. He is tormented by the sense that more than one murder is necessary: "The killer also needed trophies, the bloody scalp nailed to the wall, the shrine-in-progress. . . . The killer would have to send a message that would terrify the world" (150). Watching Mark playing competitive games with other white boys at a playground and consistently dominating them, he is certain that Mark will become a "powerful man" (151), like the powerful white men who have historically subjugated his people and who control the dominant capitalist structure. He enters the Jones house at night while the boy and his mother are sleeping, actually kneels to pray for a moment beside the sleeping mother, and then carries away Mark. Once again he leaves behind him two white feathers. His unseen presence in the Jones house, particularly the moment when he kneels beside the sleeping mother, foreshadows the later scene in Daniel and Olivia's bedroom.

In the second scene involving the young boy, the killer is depicted while planning to scalp the child alive, again obsessed with carrying out an act that will shock and consequently change the world. The language here conveys one of the most significant of all the clues in the novel, but one whose relevance will not become clear until its concluding scene: "The scalping was just preparation, the prelude to something larger. The killer knew that the kidnapping of Mark Jones was the true beginning, the first song, the first dance of a powerful ceremony that would change the world" (192). At the end of the novel, it becomes clear that the "dance" referred to here is the ghost dance of Wovoka. But in an abrupt and never fully explained reversal, the killer decides not to inflict any physical harm on Mark and, again functioning as if invisible, returns the boy to the arms of his sleeping mother. This time he slips into the Jones house past a police officer assigned to guard it (the police officer is distracted by his reading of a Tony Hillerman novel); as before, he leaves behind him two owl feathers.

The ability to slip unseen in and out of physical spaces seems to link the killer in these scenes with John Smith. John believes that he too was kidnapped away from the reservation, and he could be seen here as performing yet another kind of "private vengeance." Interestingly, John convinced himself when he was twenty that he was pregnant, and he still mourns his "failed pregnancy." This obsession represents, in part, John's attempt to identify with his unknown reservation mother. Moreover, as long as one equates him and the "Indian killer," it can be argued that the killer ultimately resolves not to harm Mark Jones because he, believing that he is also the victim of a kidnapping, comes to identify with the young white boy. Alexie could be signaling such an identification in the parallelism of prosaic last names of John and his victim.

But toward the end of the novel, Alexie develops a number of clues that point away from John as the killer. For instance, John finally decides that "the man in the white jumpsuit" who carried him to the helicopter in his birth fantasy must be his sacrificial victim: "John knew that the man in the white jumpsuit was to blame for everything that had gone wrong. Everything had gone wrong from the very beginning, when John was stolen from his Indian mother. That had caused the first internal wound and John had been bleeding ever since, slowly drying, until he was just a husk drifting in a desert wind" (379). John's epiphany that the "man in the white jumpsuit" must be his victim is evidence that he is still locked in his fantasy and thus unlikely to kill a real human being. Moreover, as we will see, a climactic scene involving John and one of the other suspects exonerates John as the "Indian killer."

Reggie Polatkin, the second major suspect in the novel, is, in different ways and for different reasons, as frightening and embittered a character as John Smith. He has managed, though, to retain a stronger hold on reality. The son of a white father, ironically named Bird, and a Spokane Indian woman, Reggie is "the mysterious urban Indian, the college student, the ambitious half-breed, the star basketball player, the Indian who would make a difference" (90).[8] However, the early hope associated with Reggie has already dissipated when the novel opens. He is no longer a college student, having been expelled from the University of Washington over an altercation with his white adviser, Dr. Clarence Mather. Initially, he and Mather are bonded by their racial and cultural ambivalence: "[Reggie] had immediately felt a strange kinship with the white man who wanted to be so completely Indian. Reggie was a half-Indian who wanted to be completely white, or failing that, to earn the respect of white men. Mather and Reggie were mirror opposites. Each had something the other wanted, and both had worked hard to obtain it" (135–36).

Mather is the prototype of the white academic who seeks advancement by appropriating the culture and literature of minority ethnic groups. There is thus an intensely cynical element in his racial ambivalence. As is evidenced in the names John Smith and Bird, Alexie not uncommonly assigns ironic names to his characters. Mather's name is probably intended as an allusion to

Cotton and Increase Mather, the Puritan divines notorious for their racial intolerance and determination to enforce their harsh and judgmental Christianity on "the new world."[9]

The altercation that destroys Reggie's devotion to Mather and results in his expulsion from college originates in Reggie's belated refusal to support Mather's appropriation of Indian culture. He is nevertheless so taken with Mather for a time that he allows the white professor to use him as a way "to obtain entry into the Seattle urban Indian community" (136). But Reggie rebels when Mather refuses to erase a tape that he has made of an elderly Spokane woman telling her family history. Reggie insists that the taped story "belongs to the family," while Mather views it as "a very valuable anthropological find" (137). In the characterization of Mather, Alexie has a good deal of satiric fun with the white academy's systemic appropriation and distortion of Native American cultures. Even when Mather actually stumbles onto some defining truth, he misses its import because he can only think in terms of Western cultural theory. He, for instance, intuits a mythological dimension of the Indian killer, perceiving it as a cumulative manifestation of the historic need of the Native American for private vengeance. But he can only approach the implications of this insight from an abstract perspective that renders it meaningless, calling the killer a "revolutionary . . . construct" (246). Mather stores his tapes in the basement of the university's anthropology building, where they are swallowed up in chaotic disorganization: "Boxes of various artifacts were stacked in tall piles. A maze of doors, small rooms, and hallways. Some rooms had not been opened since the early part of the century, and exploring the basement involved a contemporary sort of anthropology. The basement even had its own mythology. Chief Seattle's bones were supposedly lost somewhere in the labyrinth. And the bones of dozens of other Indians were said to be stored in a hidden room" (139).

Alexie does not miss the obvious possibilities of using such a setting for a supernatural scene that, until he undercuts it with comic overtones, recalls John Smith's unseen presence in his adopted parents' bedroom and the killer's invasions of the Jones household. Mather is alone in the basement sitting at a desk and listening to the tape of the Indian woman's story when the lights abruptly go out and he hears mysterious noises. The comic overtones take over when, in terror, he leaps up from the desk, begins running, and knocks himself unconscious when he crashes into a "low overhang" (141). At this point the scene resembles not so much the moments involving John Smith and the killer as an episode in which Truck Schultz, Alexie's parodic incarnation of Rush Limbaugh, finds himself in a fog-shrouded alley and senses a malignant presence near him. Alexie's implied reader is intended to enjoy the descriptions of the two thoroughly cynical white men terrified by what might be nothing.

Reggie's bitter experiences with white men do not begin with Professor Mather. His white father, Bird, had begun sadistically to inculcate in Reggie a self-hatred based on his Indian blood when he was only ten years old. Using physical and emotional abuse, Bird forced a distorted white imperialist version of history on Reggie until the boy came "to believe that he was successful because of his father's white blood, and that his Indian mother's blood was to blame for his failures" (94). In school he associated with white children and was an eager protégé for Mather, but after his emotional break with Mather and expulsion from the university he transforms his self-hatred into hatred of white people. In one scene, Reggie, accompanied by two other men, assaults and tortures a young white man who has wandered onto the "Indian Heritage High School football field." In a grim parody of Mather's appropriation of the Indian woman's story, he tapes the victim's cries of pain during the assault. The assault is a re-creation from the opposite perspective of the savage history lessons that Reggie experienced with Bird. He first calls his victim Truck Schultz, the racist radio commentator in the novel, and then says, "You look like one of those professor types. . . . I mean, with that fucking goatee, you look like a professor" (258). In the horrific attack, Reggie first identifies himself as Ira Hayes and then as Black Kettle. He is thus exacting revenge on several levels, including the personal, the racial, and the historic.

Especially in connection with this revenge scene, Reggie's final appearance in the text might be seen as strong evidence that he is the Indian killer. In it he has, on a lonely highway, hitched a ride with an elderly white man to whom he tells the story of Captain Jack, a Modoc Indian who tried to resist the U.S. Army until he finally surrendered and was executed: "So Captain Jack surrendered and they hung him. They hung him, cut off his head, and shipped it to the Smithsonian. . . . They displayed Jack's head like it was Judy Garland's red shoes or something. Like it was Archie Bunker's chair. . . . Captain Jack should never have surrendered. He should've kept running and hiding. He could have done that forever" (409).

The reader's final glimpse of Reggie nicely encapsulates his alienation and isolation. After letting his passenger out of his truck, the white man asks, "So, where are you running to?" Reggie's response is to point "up the highway . . . north or south, east or west . . . toward a new city, though he knew that every city was a city of white men" (409). Even while attempting to flee from white people and his own pervasive rage, Reggie inwardly knows that there is really no place to run to, no space (horizontal or vertical) that the white man has not appropriated.[10]

Reggie's cousin Marie points the way to the third major suspect in the novel. She insists from the first that the killer is white, arguing that the white killer, in scalping his victims and leaving behind the owl feathers, is, in a most calculated manner, attempting to provoke violent retaliation against Seattle's homeless Indians. That Truck Schultz, in his talk radio program, calls for such retaliation on an almost daily basis would seem to vindicate Marie's theory. The text subtly points to a particular white character as a possible killer.

Jack Wilson is a white writer of detective fiction who has created a Native American protagonist named Aristotle Little Hawk, "the very last Shilshomish Indian, who was a practicing medicine man and private detective in Seattle" (162); Alexie is obviously having some fun here at the expense of a number of white writers, from Charles Brockden Brown to James Fenimore Cooper to Tony Hillerman).[11] Wilson is a kind of mirror image of Reggie. He grows up an orphan and decides that he can acquire a sense of family by assuming a Native American ancestry. Inexplicably, he comes, in his loneliness, to identify with Native American culture and is incensed even as a child by distortions of it in American popular culture. In high school he discovers a means of appropriating for himself an Indian identity, telling his principal, "I'm part Shilshomish Indian. . . . I looked it up. There was an old medicine man named Red Fox who lived in a shack on Bainbridge Island. Back in the 1920s or something. His Indian name was Red Fox, but his American name was Joe Wilson. My dad used to say that Joe Wilson was his great-uncle" (158). The absurdity of Wilson's claim is emphasized by the name of his Indian "ancestor," virtually the same as that of the African-American comic Redd Foxx.

As an adult, Wilson becomes a police officer specializing in investigation of violent crime. He is irresistibly drawn to the homeless Indian community of Seattle, discovering there a means of requisitioning a Native American identity. Well aware of Wilson's real ignorance about their culture (he simply assumes that all the Native Americans in Seattle, no matter their tribe, are interchangeable), the Indians mock his pretensions of a shared cultural identity, referring to him condescendingly as "Casper the Friendly Ghost" (180).

Alexie saves some of his sharpest satire for Wilson's evocation of the Indian detective Aristotle Little Hawk. The second Aristotle Little Hawk novel becomes a "regional best seller" (162) and is taught by Professor Clarence Mather as an important example of Native American literature. (This, along with everything else about Mather, enrages Marie Polatkin, Reggie's cousin, who is briefly enrolled in Mather's "Introduction to Native American Literature class" [57]). In creating Aristotle Little Hawk, Wilson is attempting to wed white cultural images of a gothic Native American mysticism with a valorization of Western rationalism. His detective will bring both a supernatural and a rational perspective to the solving of crimes—who could ask for anything more?

The names—Shadow and Casper the Friendly Ghost—that Wilson is seriously and satirically given recall the Indian killer's ability to move unseen from space to space. Moreover, his familiarity with the police and police work enable him to prowl relatively unnoticed along Seattle's darkened streets. Especially when one considers that "Jack Wilson" was the "white Christian" name of Wovoka, the creator of the ghost dance, his fragmented identity seems a clue that he is indeed the killer. It ultimately becomes clear, however, that, except in a symbolic sense, he cannot finally be so identified. As with Reggie, the very fragmentation of his sense of self renders him incapable of undertaking the kind of crime spree described in the novel. Wilson does not want to kill Native American culture; instead, he fantasizes about becoming part of it, not realizing the degree of cultural appropriation involved in his claiming to be a Native American and writing about them. Wilson is, like John Smith, most frightening in his sheer innocence, his detachment from the complex world around him.

Both Wilson and Smith are eliminated as suspects in the novel's climactic scene. In it, Smith has kidnapped Wilson, brought him to an upper floor of the as-yet-unfinished "last skyscraper in Seattle" (403), and tied him to a wall; as the scene opens, he is threatening to kill him. In pleading for his life, the terrified Wilson manages to say all the wrong things. When he claims to be an Indian, John perceptively wonders if Wilson knows "the difference between dreaming and reality. How one could easily become the other" (403). Despite his own paranoia, John comprehends the dangerous and culpable nature of such innocence and tells Wilson that "you're the one who's responsible" (404). Finally, in a line that can be taken as a thematic statement of the novel, he begs Wilson, "Let me, let us have our own pain" (411). Then he slashes his captive across the face, leaving him with a kind of mark of Cain, and says before stepping off the skyscraper to plunge to his death, "No matter where you go . . . people will know you by that mark. They'll know what you did" (411). What Wilson, and indeed the dominant white culture, did was to distort, diminish, and try to steal the cultural legacy of a people.

This scene emphasizes the special vulnerabilities of both Smith and Wilson. It makes clear that the only person Smith was ever going to be able to kill was himself and that Wilson is hardly violent or dangerous. Thus, on the surface, the novel seems to end with the mystery still unsolved and can be most appropriately classified as an anti-detective novel. Alexie has some narrative fun by leading the reader in false directions concerning the identity of the killer. In this way he turns the conventions of the detective novel against the reader by seeming to withhold a resolution of the text's central mystery. But a brief last chapter contains not a solution of the mystery but an ominous final clue that is anticipated several times in the novel, twice through the character of Truck Schultz, the popular radio voice of white racism and bigotry.

In a chapter symbolically titled "Fire Starter," Schultz uses the murders for his own demagogic purposes. Referring to Indians as "children," Schultz complains that they "have rights that normal Americans do not enjoy" (208). He then appropriates an infamous line from Philip Sheridan, giving it his own unique twist: "The only good Indian Killer is a dead Indian Killer" (209). As he does throughout the text, Schultz, in valorizing white oppression of the First Nations, is lobbing a bomb into a Seattle already on the verge of explosion. While he does not actually start the symbolic fire at the center of the novel, he certainly contributes fuel to it. In a subsequent tirade he again endorses the victimization of Native Americans. After asserting that Native Americans have historically responded to white benevolence "in the only way they know: violence," he offers a theory about the identity of the Indian killer. Calling the killer "a distillation of [Native American] rage," he argues that the murderer is "pure evil, pure violence, pure rage. He has come to kill us because we have tried to help him" (346). In Truck's false binary of white good–Indian evil, any killer of white people must necessarily be a malevolent being acting only from the most perverse of motivations. He thus adds even more fuel to the symbolic fire.

Ironically, a comparable theory of the nature of the Indian killer comes from a demented, homeless Indian woman named Carlotta Lott, who shows John Smith a knife and then delivers a prophecy of vengeance against white people that will be brought about through "bad magic" involving her own "time machine" (253). As with John himself, Carlotta's Indian identity has been contaminated by white popular culture—Wovoka meets H. G. Wells. Moreover, she has been driven mad by homelessness, oppression, and rage. But the novel's concluding one-paragraph chapter indicates that her prophecy should not simply be dismissed. Entitled "Creation Story," the chapter begins by evoking "a full moon" and "a cemetery on an Indian reservation." The killer is first shown sitting "alone on a grave," but then he begins to sing and dance "for hours, days," and soon he is joined by "a dozen Indians, then hundreds, and more, all learning the same song, the same dance. . . . The killer never falls. The moon never falls. . . . [A nearby] tree grows heavy with owls" (419–20). In this concluding image, the killer is depicted as being the spirit of Wovoka come again to drive the white man into the sea. He is an image of a long-deferred "private vengeance," of the "bad magic" promised by Carlotta.

This final shift into a metaphoric and supernatural narrative mode may seem jarring in the context of the controlled realism of most of the text. Such realism is essential to the writing of a detective story, where, however momentarily inexplicable, things must never seem implausible. In this abrupt turn to the metaphoric, Alexie confirms what has been previously hinted at— he is deconstructing the detective novel form. It is then appropriate that the identity of the Indian killer is never revealed, is finally evoked on a purely metaphoric level. Alexie's novel is concerned most of all with depicting an unresolved sacrificial crisis residing at the very heart of American culture. Native American vengeance remains frustrated largely because the powerlessness of Indian culture prevents it from being enacted. Moreover, even the hint of Indian violence (the Indian killer may be, as Marie Polatkin insists, a white man) evokes a retaliatory white violence fed by the white media.

After adopting John, Olivia and Daniel Smith sought an Indian to baptize the infant and found "the only Indian Jesuit in the Pacific Northwest," Father Duncan, who is described as "an irony, an Indian in black robes" (13). The priest later takes John to the Chapel of the North American Martyrs in downtown Seattle. There John sees stained-glass images of "Jesuits being martyred by Indians": "Bright white Jesuits with bright white suns at their necks. A Jesuit, tied to a post, burning alive as Indians dance around him. Another pierced with dozens of arrows. A third, with his cassock torn from his body, crawling away from an especially evil-looking Indian. The fourth being drowned in a blue river. The fifth, sixth, and seventh being scalped"

(13–14). Father Duncan's reaction to the images is startling. He describes them to John as being "beautiful" (14) and then says, "You see these windows? You see all of this? It's what is happening inside me right now" (15).

While Sarah Quirk argues, on the basis of this passage and his subsequent mysterious disappearance into the desert, that Father Duncan is the actual Indian killer,[12] it seems safer to see him as a projection of John's paranoia. In either case, he encapsulates the bloody history of the European–Native American conflict, and his response to the stained-glass windows foreshadows the metaphoric ending of the novel. Duncan, in an aesthetic revision of the sacrificial crisis, equates beauty with retaliatory violence, with private vengeance on a massive scale. This envisioned violence, which so dominates the consciousness of John Smith as well as Reggie Polatkin, constitutes the novel's fourthspace. A repressed rage contaminates both the material and mental spaces of their experience and thus distorts any potential they might have for imagining a redemptive thirdspace. The novel's metaphoric conclusion seems to imply that this is true for American culture as a whole.

9

"The Battle of Bob Hope" and "The Great Elephant Zap"

Robert Stone's *Dog Soldiers*

Robert Stone's *Dog Soldiers* (1974) is a fictional investigation of the consequences of the United States's disastrous twentieth-century imperialist adventure in Vietnam and of the debased spaces which resulted from that adventure. After an extended section set in Vietnam, the narrative focus of *Dog Soldiers* shifts for the remainder of the novel to the United States. This narrative approach is central to two interrelated emphases of the novel: the destructive effects on the Vietnam landscape of the American invasion of that Asian nation, and the spiritual and mental consequences of that involvement for the United States. In essence, Stone's novel is an examination of the forced Americanization of Vietnam and the resultant Vietnamization of the United States.

The epigraph to *Dog Soldiers* is taken from a passage in Joseph Conrad's *Heart of Darkness* in which Marlowe summarizes the horror of his expedition up the Congo: "I've seen the devil of violence and the devil of greed and the devil of hot desire; but, by all the stars! these were strong, lusty, red-eyed devils that swayed and drove men—men, I tell you. But as I stood on that hillside, I foresaw that in the blinding sunshine of that land, I would become acquainted with a flabby, pretending weak-eyed devil of a rapacious and pitiless folly." Stone applies Conrad's phrase for nineteenth-century British imperialism—"a flabby, pretending weak-eyed devil of a rapacious and pitiless folly"—to the U.S. military intervention in Vietnam, and in his novel he creates four central characters who together represent a (re)creation of Conrad's embittered and murderous Kurtz. The four constitute a cumulative characterization that is every bit as morally reprehensible as Conrad's insane visionary and that personifies the corrupt imperialism which bequeaths a degraded fourthspace to the American landscape. *Dog Soldiers* is devoted to a depiction of an insane "devil of violence" that traveled from the United States across the Pacific to Vietnam and then returned home. A "devil of greed" is involved in Stone's novel as well, since the plot is centered in the international drug trade.

Two central concepts developed by Henri Lefebvre in *The Production of Space* are helpful in explicating Stone's novel. *Dog Soldiers* is a graphic study of the ways in which violent assault on physical space originates in mental space, which then controls physical space while simultaneously corrupting social space. Building on this initial delineation of three kinds of space, Lefebvre proceeds to a discussion of the violence inherent in what he calls "abstract space," which he defines as "the space of the bourgeoisie and of capitalism" and describes as "bound up . . . with exchange (of goods and commodities, as of written and spoken words, etc.)." He comments that "it hardly seems necessary to add that within this space violence does not always remain latent or hidden. One of its contradictions is that between the appearance of security and the constant threat, and indeed the occasional eruption, of violence" (57). Later, Lefebvre approaches this idea from a different, though related, direction: "The violence that is inherent in space enters into conflict with knowledge, which is equally inherent in that space. Power—which is to say violence—divides, then keeps what it has divided in a state of separation; inversely, it reunites—yet keeps whatever it wants in a state of confusion" (358). Clearly, nineteenth-century British imperialism was a defining example of capitalism's power to divide and then control space through violence. In *Dog Soldiers,* the U.S. involvement in Vietnam is treated as a reenactment of that historical moment, with drugs and with violence itself constituting the essential commodities being exchanged.

The assault of American imperialism on Vietnamese space is dramatized graphically through flashbacks that constitute defining moments in the psychological developments of two of the novel's central characters. One of these, Ray Hicks, the most complex character in the novel, is serving his third hitch in the Marines. Hicks believes that his age and experience have bequeathed him a special role, the professional, the model for the younger marines of the war. Yet at one critical point he is unfaithful to this self-imposed role and commits what he later views as an act of dereliction of duty. "In a mood of vague disgruntlement," he allows several of the men under his command to go into town to attend a Bob Hope performance: "It was not, in the circumstances, a serious dereliction but it called for reprisal; reprisal came in the form of an undesirable patrol, which resulted in what Hicks had come to call the battle of Bob Hope. Almost every man in his platoon who had seen Bob Hope died in it. He himself was shot and flown to Okinawa. At the end of the year his hitch expired and he walked" (75–76). The association Hicks makes between the Bob Hope performance and the "undesirable patrol" is, of course, completely arbitrary. Such magical thinking is hardly uncommon for Hicks.

The battle of Bob Hope assumes major symbolic importance in Stone's novel. In World War II, Korea, and Vietnam, Hope performed for American troops and then relayed his performances back to the United States by means of radio and television. For the homefront, he thereby put a comic "American" face on foreign spaces occupied, in however a fragile manner, by the U.S. military. This surface of comic patriotism was intended, in part, to hide, to mask, the brutal reality of all the undesirable patrols in all three wars—the American soldiers seen on television laughing at Hope or Jerry Colonna were clearly alive and well and offered proof that the wars would end well for the United States and that war was normal, even featuring entertainment. Of course, in the case of Vietnam, such comic reassurance proved to be an illusion.

In the context of Lefebvre, it is worth noting that in the undesirable patrols, as in other Vietnam battles, U.S. soldiers died in a space foreign to the experiences of the vast majority of Americans. The sending of U.S. troops to Vietnam was an invasion of a nation by what Lefebvre defines as the inherent violence of the "abstract space" of American capitalism. One legacy of this invasion was the exportation of American consumerist culture to Vietnam and the resulting assault on a complex and ancient culture by American popular culture. The battle of Bob Hope anticipates the scene in Stanley Kubrick's 1987 film *Full Metal Jacket,* in which U.S. Marines march into combat singing the theme to the children's television program *The Mickey Mouse Club.* Both depict an assault of the cultural heritage of Vietnam by an immature and superficial American consumerism. As a companion invasion to the military one, the exportation of consumerism—itself a form of imperialist violence—to Vietnam irrevocably changed the physical and social spaces of that country. Moreover, as evidenced by the characterization of Ray Hicks, the war devastated the cumulative mental space of the many American military men and women who served there. They had been at the forefront of the violent exportation of Bob Hope culture to Southeast Asia, and not surprisingly they brought the legacy of that violence home with them.

The physical and social spaces of the America of *Dog Soldiers* feel like combat zones; certainly violence is rampant in them, and a surreal fourthspace is born out of that violence.

The other important Vietnam flashbacks in *Dog Soldiers* are projected through the memory of the second of its central male characters, John Converse. Converse and Hicks represent two sides of Stone's cumulative Kurtz. One critic calls Converse "the ultimate dog soldier of the novel, the man who would do anything to be a living dog rather than a dead lion" (Solotaroff 224). He embodies an ineptitude rooted in a longing for self-annihilation that almost destroys him and everyone close to him. The roots of Converse's self-loathing precede his Vietnam experience. A professional writer, he once wrote a successful play about the Marine Corps. Subsequently, though, he worked for seven years writing sexually oriented sensationalist stories for a sleazy tabloid called *Nightbeat* published by his father-in-law, Elmer Bender, until, after publishing an exposé of the sexual impotence of the playboy socialite Porfirio Rubirosa, Converse suffered a debilitating attack of paranoid anxiety. His paranoia became so extreme that he considered suicide. After seven years of cynical compromise, he has come to doubt his professional, and even human, worth. There are strong overtones of the created persona of Ernest Hemingway in the Converse characterization. Converse's one honest literary effort was, like so much of Hemingway's fiction, an exploration of the cult of machismo, of an imagined heroic masculinity. Having betrayed his art, Converse doubts his sexual adequacy and, like Hemingway, becomes enamored of the prospect of release through self-annihilation.[1]

Rather than killing himself, Converse resorts to a desperate cure and begs his father-in-law to send him to Saigon as a correspondent, desperately hoping that exposure to the suffering of those in Southeast Asia might revive his artistic integrity. Almost immediately, however, the reality of war and death in Vietnam turns Converse's dream into a nightmare: "One bright afternoon near a place called Krek Converse had watched with astonishment as the world of living things transformed itself into a single overwhelming act of murder. In a manner of speaking, he had discovered himself. Himself was a soft shell-less quivering thing encased in a hundred and sixty pounds of pink sweating meat. It was real enough. It tried to burrow into the earth. It wept" (24). It can hardly be surprising that an America mentally obsessed with death brings death to the physical and social spaces of Vietnam and that this American obsession will then be transferred home to the United States.

Hicks and Converse personify two ways in which this complex phenomenon unfolds.

In fact, both of them are aware of the moral implications of the U.S. military intervention in Vietnam. In response to it, Hicks adopts a code of violence derived from an inevitably confused appropriation of Nietzschean philosophy and the Japanese code of the samurai. In contrast, Converse looks at Vietnam from a perspective of traditional humanism: "There were moral objections to children being blown out of sleep to death on a filthy street. And to their being burned to death by jellied petroleum. . . . [But] moral objections were sometimes overridden by larger and more profound concerns. One had to take the long view. It was also true that at a certain point the view might become too long and moral objections appear irrelevant" (41). Vietnam serves as an education in "the long view" for Converse. In the space of the massive, violent destruction and death that he witnesses, "moral objections" have come to seem "irrelevant." Converse's Vietnam education is a metaphoric encapsulated vision of traditional Western humanism's perversion by the nineteenth-century imperialist agenda and its failure to prevent a long list of twentieth-century horrors, including World War I, World War II, the Holocaust, Hiroshima, and the Vietnam War.

"The last moral objection that Converse experienced in the traditional manner" is his response to what comes to be known as "the Great Elephant Zap," in which the U.S. military command reaches the extraordinary conclusion that "elephants were enemy agents because the NVA used them to carry things" and orders an air assault on the animals: "All over the country, whooping sweating gunners descended from the cloud cover to stampede the herds and mow them down with 7.62-millimeter machine guns" (41). One could not ask for a better example of Lefebvre's analysis of the capacity of abstract imperialism to commit violence against a dominated space. That the assault on the elephants comes from the air exemplifies Lefebvre's concept of the relationship of "vertical" space and "horizontal" space (236). It is especially appropriate to envision imperialist domination from the perspective of verticality, since the power by which it is manifested descends from above on subjugated colonial space. Thus the elephants, a part of the natural physical space of Vietnam, are attacked technologically from above. In Lefebvre's view, "technological activity and the scientific approach" inevitably wage war on nature: "They seek to master it, and in the process they tend to destroy it; and, before destroying it, they misinterpret it" (108–9). Thus, in Stone's novel, the U.S. military command actually convinces itself that elephants, a part of the Vietnamese landscape, possess the reasoning power necessary to be "enemy agents" and must therefore be destroyed. A final twist of Stone's irony is that the planes depend on "cloud cover" in the first stage of their assault on the elephants.

From this moment, Converse comprehends that fear is the defining truth of his identity: "I am afraid, Converse reasoned, therefore I am" (420). An identity based on fear is obviously not conducive to a desired macho persona. To deal with his inherent shame, the fictional Converse, in contrast to the real Ernest Hemingway, chooses drugs instead of suicide. In a world as fundamentally violent and irrational as that in which the Great Elephant Zap occurs, drug addiction seems to make sense: "and as for dope, Converse thought, and addicts—if the world is going to contain elephants pursued by flying men, people are just naturally going to want to get high. . . . He had confronted a moral objection and overridden it. He could deal with these matters as well as anyone" (42). In fact, he cannot deal with these matters well at all, and in the present tense of the novel he demonstrates just how inept he is.

Converse sets the novel's central plot in motion by deciding to engineer a shipment of heroin from Vietnam back to the United States. Not surprisingly, the drug deal is compromised from the start. He asks Hicks to smuggle three kilos of heroin from Vietnam to California. When the two meet to discuss the proposal, Hicks informs Converse that, a year earlier, he had encountered one of the latter's former girlfriends, one Mary Microgram, in San Francisco. Mary Microgram—the mechanical, impersonal sound of her name is symbolically important—told Hicks that Converse had referred to his old friend and former war companion as "a psychopath." Converse does not even attempt to deny the allegation and offers the flimsy excuse that, while he was with Mary, he "was very fucked up." Hicks, in a deliberate understatement, responds that "it's outrageous. . . . I was hurt" (55). As the relatively few critics who have written about *Dog Soldiers* point out, Hicks cannot simply be dismissed as a psychopath; his characterization is considerably more complex than that, as are his motives in agreeing to smuggle the heroin into the States. The complexity of Hicks's characterization and motivation are, in fact, central to the underlying vision of Stone's novel. Still, his comment to Converse about being "hurt" implies a barely repressed need for revenge against Converse, a need that the "journalist" will fuel through the nearly suicidal incompetence with which he has planned the entire drug-smuggling operation. Also significant in all this is Converse's careless willingness to proceed with his dangerous plan in partnership with someone whom he regards, at least to some degree, as a psychopath.

Throughout their conversation, gunfire is heard in the background, but the two characters choose simply to ignore it. The gunfire becomes a metonymic representation of the war that surrounds them and of the American invasion of Vietnam from which they plan to profit by illegally importing the heroin to the States. It also encapsulates the violence on which the invasion of Vietnamese space was predicated and which underlies the entire novel. Throughout the scene, their dialogue is revelatory of the deadly unreality of what they are planning: "'You're mad,' Hicks told him, 'a great mind—warped—twisted.' It was an old movie line they had played with twelve years before in the Marine Corps. Converse seemed particularly elated. He raised his glass. 'To Nietzsche.' They drank to Nietzsche. It was adolescence. A time trip. Another burst of fire came from the opposite shore" (56). Hicks is the self-defined Nietzschean in *Dog Soldiers;* but as Robert Solotaroff has pointed out, the entire novel illustrates the destructive consequences of a misappropriation of Nietzsche's pronouncement that God is dead: "The good news, according to Nietzsche, is that man is now free to re-create himself heroically. The bad news, according to *Dog Soldiers,* is the variety of uses to which this newly conscious ethical freedom is put by people unmoored from a belief in God and the Judeo-Christian system of ethics that depends upon Him" (*Robert Stone* 63). One might amend Solotaroff's analysis by saying that the novel depicts individuals and a culture unmoored from any abstract beliefs except a fantasy of masculinity achieved through violence. *Dog Soldiers* illustrates with a narrative coldness that has troubled some critics the destructive nature of an immature cult of masculinity that was an essential factor in the tragic U.S. involvement in Vietnam. Indeed, Converse and Hicks are time tripping here and doing so in a fundamentally irresponsible way. They are attempting a moral abdication that underlies such grotesque actions as the Great Elephant Zap. It is also not insignificant that they play with dialogue from an old movie—American films representing one of the defining forms of American popular culture.

The ultimate source of the heroin that Converse and Hicks decide to smuggle into the United States is "Colonel Tho, whose heroin refinery was the fourth largest building in Saigon" (24–25). The partnership between Converse and Tho, who remains invisible in the novel, is symbolically important, representing the complex alliance of the U.S. and South Vietnamese governments and military structures, an alliance that was essential to the invasion of the natural space of Vietnam by the abstract space of American capitalism.

In the smuggling plan, Converse is to find someone to move the heroin to Berkeley, California, where it will be kept by Converse's wife until some friends pick it up. In discussing the transaction with Converse, the go-between, a woman named Charmian, implies that the so-called friends have CIA connections, a fact that she assures Converse guarantees the essential safety and ultimate success of the enterprise. Not surprisingly, Hicks is troubled by the vagueness of all of this, as Converse certainly should have been. The principal friend turns out to be a sadistic federal agent named Antheil, who represents the third, and the most thoroughly corrupt, of the four characters who constitute Stone's cumulative (re)creation of Conrad's Kurtz. Antheil plans from the first to appropriate the heroin himself with the help of two unambiguously psychopathic henchmen named Danskin and Smitty. Frank W. Shelton effectively summarizes the significance of Antheil and his two agents for Stone's narrative strategy: "The most corrupt people in *Dog Soldiers* represent the law, which is the supposed seat of order and authority in society. The feeling of paranoia gives the reader . . . a sense of claustrophobia" (74).

Paranoia and a propensity for murderous rage are central to the characterization of Hicks. In a paradoxical way, his outbreaks of rage elevate him above Antheil, who, in his relatively few appearances in the novel, consistently exhibits an emotional coldness that borders on the inhuman. Early in *Dog Soldiers*, Converse's wife, Marge, is rescued—along with the heroin, of course—from Antheil and his agents by Hicks. She spends virtually the rest of the novel on the run with her rescuer and becomes his lover. In the novel's conclusion, Marge offers Converse a summary evaluation of Hicks and of his motivations in risking his life to come to their aid: "He's not a sane person. . . . And he's not very bright. Sometimes . . . people do simple-minded things like that. They take a chance to help their friends" (306). Like Converse's reference to Hicks as a psychopath, Marge's judgment is simultaneously accurate and inadequate.

Perhaps above all, Hicks personifies the dangerous potential of a cult of masculine heroism, an essential factor in the U.S. military intervention in Vietnam. Hicks has concocted a philosophy out of appropriated and oversimplified bits of Nietzschean and Zen philosophy underscored by the mythology of American popular culture. Converse, the intellectual, introduced

Hicks to Nietzsche at a time when Ray had only read Ray Bradbury's *The Martian Chronicles* and Mickey Spillane's *I, the Jury*.[2] Hicks manifests the same kind of propensity for macho violence that characterizes Spillane's detective fiction and which underscored the American assault on Vietnam space. Hicks is later sent to Japan, where he becomes involved with a Japanese woman, adopts a philosophy vaguely reminiscent of Zen, and starts to think of himself "as a kind of samurai" (75). His involvement with the Japanese woman indicates his addiction to a white male fantasy of the submissive Asian female, the destructive consequences of which have been explored by several Asian-American writers, perhaps most memorably David Henry Hwang in *M. Butterfly* (1988). More importantly, his constructing a code of belief out of partially understood and uncritically assimilated bits of Nietzsche and Asian philosophy reveals a dangerous kind of unsophisticated and uncritical thought.

Hicks's philosophy, moreover, has a distinctly American thread. Late in the novel, Dieter Bechstein, Ray's onetime spiritual mentor in a New Mexico commune and the fourth part of Stone's cumulative Kurtz, offers an interesting extended analysis of his former protégé. "[Ray is] a serious man, like your President. . . . He's a total American," Dieter first comments (270). Truly, Ray is very serious, in fact deadly so, and like the U.S. government during the Vietnam era, he is arrogant and philosophically unsophisticated. Dieter then summarizes Hicks as follows: "He's trapped in a samurai fantasy—an American one. He has to be the Lone Ranger, the great desperado—he has to win all the epic battles single-handed. . . . It may not be a very original conception, but he's quite good at it" (272). While one must remember Dieter's own self-confessed corruption by American values, this evaluation of Hicks is perceptive.

Hicks has taken Nietzsche's doctrine of the superman and the Japanese celebration of the samurai warrior and wedded them to the American myth of the heroic outlaw, the avenging cowboy-sheriff. Such an unlikely mixture leads to a self-righteous sense of being outside and above any established laws and of the necessity of forcing a perverted male vision of order and authority onto the world. As Maureen Karagueuzian writes, "the plot of *Dog Soldiers* . . . parallels America's involvement in Vietnam" (65); one can add that the combination of an annihilation-seeking Converse, a cynical and brutal Antheil, the intellectually advanced but corrupt Bechstein, and, most of all, the self-proclaimed American mythic hero Hicks encapsulates the kind of thinking that led inexorably to this involvement.

A perverted sexuality is a key element in Hicks's personality. Ironically, it is precisely this perversion that leads Marge to surrender herself to him sexually. She quickly recognizes in Hicks a kind of man she has seen before, most probably in the San Francisco pornographic movie theater where she is employed: "Deprivation—of love, of mother's milk, of calcium, of God knows what. This one was sunburned, usually they were pale. They always had cold eyes. They hated women" (95). When he makes a sexual advance, "she could not make herself move. Her only act of resistance was to look at him, and what she saw repelled every instinct with which Marge associated her heart. His eyes seemed as flat as a snake's. There was such coldness, such cruelty in his face that she could not think of him as a man at all" (95). Like her husband, Marge is in truly in love with a longed-for oblivion, and she finds Ray's inhuman coldness literally and figuratively irresistible.

The text seems to imply a repressed homoerotic attraction between Converse and Hicks, an attraction that neither will acknowledge. One passage describes Hicks's emotions after meeting with Converse to plan the drug transaction: "Hicks knew very few people for whom he had ever felt anything like love, and Converse—whom he had not seen for twenty hours in the past ten years—was one of them. Seeing Converse again had made him feel good and young again in a simple-minded way; as though all the plans and adolescent fantasies they had shared in the service might take on some kind of renewed near-reality" (74). To a degree, then, the entire heroin-smuggling episode is on Ray's part a kind of repressed "adolescent fantasy" that disguises his erotic attraction to Converse. When one remembers Karagueuzian's observation that the novel's plot "parallels America's involvement in Vietnam," it seems that *Dog Soldiers* is a kind of allegory of imperialist rape.[3] In the context of Hicks's repressed homoerotic attraction to Converse, the former's seduction of Marge takes on added complexity. One can see it in part as revenge for Converse's reference to Ray as being a psychopath; one can also see it as an indirect form of sexual intercourse with Converse himself, something that Ray can never admit, most of all to himself, desiring.

It is worth pointing out that, until meeting Marge, Ray's sex life has been increasingly devoted to masturbation: "He preferred it to prostitutes because it was more sanitary and took less time" (114). Thus, emotional commitment to a woman has no role in sex for Ray; he wants erotic fulfillment to be simultaneously self-centered and impersonal. Fantasy is crucial to his sexual identity, but he could never admit a fantasy that would involve genuine commitment, especially not commitment to Converse or to any other male. All of this leads to a psychological complexity that will have him betray Converse by sleeping with Marge and then, at the end of the novel, rescue both of them.

At one point the novel diagnoses Ray as suffering from "accumulated venom" and says that the venom is "fouling his blood" (84–85). This fouled blood causes Hicks to periodically and violently lash out at others. For instance, after disarming Antheil's henchmen, Danskin and Smitty, who have come to steal the heroin from Marge, Ray indulges in something of an orgy of torture of the especially inept and deplorable Smitty, remarking as he does so, "I just can't leave him alone . . . I love him" (102). Hicks is of course echoing the kind of ironic tough-guy dialogue found in novels by his beloved Mickey Spillane and Raymond Chandler and Dashiell Hammett as well. But his equation of physical torture and love explains much about his essential characterization and, on a symbolic level, about the rape of Vietnamese space as well.

In a final stream-of-consciousness passage, Ray, as he half walks and half crawls across the New Mexico desert attempting to get the heroin to John and Marge, remembers the pain and suffering of his past. He grew up in "the Booth Women's Shelter in Chicago, North Side, Wisconsin Avenue," where his mother worked in the kitchen and where, like the rest of the children, he learned the necessity of lying and creating a false persona (234). In the shelter, Ray was introduced to the mythology of the Marine Corps: "That's the Training School tradition, you join the fucking Marines whether you want to or not. The social worker'll shame you into it. When you get down to Parris Island you'll recognize the other kids from the Training School because they steal" (325). In this chain of thoughts, Ray, without realizing its full implications for himself or for the nation or for Vietnam, understands the cynicism involved in the Marines' recruiting of the lower classes. Shame and a desire to belong to a group with a code of pride were essential elements in Ray's becoming a marine.

Hicks's childhood shame is further explained in his failure at the shelter to control his bladder and the subsequent punishment he received: "At the Training School, he was still pissing his pants at thirteen. He'd carry the underwear around with him, hidden, afraid to put it in the laundry bag because it was labeled. Hid it under the bed and then did the same with the next pair. Oh, my God, two pairs of them all pissed on, they'll beat the shit out of me" (326). The unwanted child bedwetter, terrified by beatings, will long for power in a distinctly male community devoted to violence. Shelton perceptively points out that, for Ray, "love, as is true of almost all relationships in his life, is translated into power" (78). No wonder there is such "accumulated venom" stored up in him. Until it was provided by a German priest who contemptuously tossed a fifty-cent piece to Ray and told him to take in a movie, one ingredient was lacking for the young boy Ray to be able to focus his need for power and comradeship. Ray obeyed and saw Cecil B. DeMille's 1935 film *The Crusades,* with its glorification of medieval England's invasion of the Middle East and repression of the infidels. As an adult he will participate in another crusade, this time an American one, against another alien culture.

Yet despite his psychopathic behavior and his sexual betrayal of Converse with Marge, Hicks does finally rescue John and Marge in an act that is, to some extent at least, heroic. Moreover, he has himself been betrayed by Converse's incompetence in formulating the heroin transaction—an incompetence that introduced the cynical and murderous Antheil into the equation. Shelton argues that Hicks is "in a strange way . . . ethical" (77) and offers the following summation of the character: "For all his admirable qualities as a man of action, [he] is a stunted human being" (77–78). In fact, Hicks's morality is so centered around a destructive code of masculine violence that he seems more "stunted" than admirable. Still, Shelton is not altogether inaccurate in his assessment of the Nietzschean samurai warrior. It is not, then, inappropriate that Hicks's dying fantasy is one of becoming a kind of secular Christ who willingly takes on the pain of everyone.

In contrast to Hicks, there is nothing ambiguous in Stone's characterization of Antheil, who seems almost an allegorical representation of evil and corruption. Until the end of the novel, Antheil's viciousness is largely dramatized indirectly through the actions of his henchmen, Danskin and Smitty, both of whom are experts in brutality and physical torture. It was, in fact, precisely for such expertise that Antheil originally recruited them. The savagery of both is so extreme as to border on black comedy, as is true of comparable figures in the detective fiction of Spillane, Chandler, and Hammett. But Antheil himself dominates the novel's concluding scene. In company with a corrupt Mexican law enforcement officer, he tracks down the wounded and dying Hicks in order to regain the heroin. Realizing that things have gone too wrong for him to be able simply to return to the unnamed federal agency for which he works, Antheil plans to seek sanctuary in company with Charmian: "Others had left the service in circumstances as potentially compromising. In the place to which he planned to repair with

Charmian, he might do them service from time to time, should they discover him. He had many friends there, and no one would trouble him. It was a country where everybody did it" (340). The country where he plans to seek refuge is unnamed, but the novel's implication is clear: in America and by extension Vietnam, everybody does, in fact, "do it." Antheil's unnamed "country" functions in the novel as a metaphor for the debased fourthspace that was bequeathed to the United States by its involvement in Vietnam and which pervades Stone's text. The corrupt federal agent instantly strikes up a deal with Angel, the Mexican law enforcement officer, and concludes that "it was not venality that made [Angel] a crook, merely tradition. Antheil reflected that his service had brought him in contact with many people and cultures other than his own" (341). The clichéd sound of this is both intentional and ironic. Antheil's real culture is a truly international corruption and violence that has its roots in the United States. He also remembers a saying he once heard: "If you think someone's doing you wrong, it's not for you to judge. Kill them first and let God do the judging" (342). By assuming a godlike position, Antheil has become one of the Conradian devils who inflict tragedy on Vietnam and transform the United States into a debased fourthspace.

Dieter Bechstein, the fourth part of Stone's cumulative Kurtz, like Marge Converse, is a parodic embodiment of the 1960s counterculture. In the 1960s he founded a commune in the New Mexico desert.[4] He was also an early mentor of Ray Hicks, and the complex mixture of admirable and murderous qualities that characterizes Hicks's psychology is dramatized in the relationship of the two characters. Dieter seems to have begun the commune with idealism, a legitimate desire to provide sanctuary and identity for young people who lacked both. But like his disciple Ray, he is unable to handle power and allows it to corrupt everything he does. Later, Dieter shouts to Marge that "life belongs to the strong" (231).

What saves Dieter morally, at least to a degree, is his awareness, and his confession to Marge of the nature and the process of his corruption. He was corrupted, he says, by the American dream. Observing a secular world in which truly visionary voices were lacking, he stepped in and, for a time, believed that he had been anointed as the voice of some primal "Energy." But, he says, "I was sitting up here [in the New Mexico mountain commune] hearing it [the cosmic 'Energy']. . . . What they wanted . . . I had. I knew! So I thought, a little push, a little shove, a little something extra to shake it loose. And I ended up as Doctor Dope" (272). Ultimately, Dieter is killed by Ray, whose reaction afterward is typically cold: "Damn it, if you're going to make a gesture, you have to have some grace, some style, some force. You have to have some Zen. [Bechstein] certainly fucked his gesture" (315).

The surreal fourthspace that pervades the novel is most overtly evoked in a climactic scene at Bechstein's commune. Antheil and his henchmen are attempting to invade the commune and thereby recover the heroin when Hicks carries out a bizarre resistance to the invasion. He turns on the surrealistic lighting and sound systems Bechstein had installed in the commune, and the landscape of the commune becomes a space every bit as "unreal" as the Vietnam of the battle of Bob Hope or the Great Elephant Zap. One detail that highlights the existential absurdity of what might be called the Great Commune Battle is a loudspeaker message that echoes throughout the confrontation: "Form is Not Different From Nothingness. . . . Nothingness is Not Different From Form. They are the same" (300).

In order to begin the counterassault against Antheil and his law enforcement agents, Hicks has to crawl through an extended underground Indian shelter. Inside it he encounters numerous scrawled messages and graffiti. At one point, Stone utilizes this underground commentary as metafictional commentary on his novel—for instance, one graffiti message reading "There Are No Metaphors" can be taken as emphasizing that, like realist and naturalist fiction in general, *Dog Soldiers* is structured through metonymy rather than metaphor. In one section of the underground Indian shelter, Hicks encounters graffiti derived from popular culture that echoes the earlier allusions to Bob Hope: "The place into which he had descended was the Dick Tracy Room; the lamp shone on Dick's neat rep tie and on the base of his mighty chin. Next to him there were portraits of Flyface and Flattop and Vitamin Flintheart" (294). Dick Tracy, the relentlessly heroic comic-strip police officer, is a grotesque twentieth-century urban re-creation of the Lone Ranger and the other Wild West heroes.

In crawling through the old Indian shelter, Ray is, in a telescoped manner, reenacting his childhood in the Booth Women's Shelter, and it is hardly surprising that he emerges in a murderous state of mind. Here three chronotopes—Ray's childhood in the shelter, his Vietnam years, and his experience in the Indian shelter—merge into one. Ray emerges from the womb of the Indian shelter into death rather than life. It is fitting, given the ironic nature of the rest of the text, that Hicks, in his act of heroic defiance, gets himself killed and loses the heroin to Antheil. He is, after all, not truly a Nietzschean superman, a samurai warrior, the Lone Ranger, or Dick Tracy. He is a dog soldier who manifests psychopathic tendencies.

The Great Commune Battle culminates a number of passages in the novel that parallel American spaces with the devastation wrought in Vietnam. Driving from Los Angeles to Bechstein's New Mexico commune, Ray and Marge pass through an uninhabitable desert in which abandoned and wrecked automobiles constitute the primary evidence of previous human habitation. The heroin itself becomes another kind of degraded fourthspace in *Dog Soldiers*—when shooting up, Marge feels herself float free from the restrictions of physical and social space. Finally, the novel contains an allusion to the popular television science-fiction program *Lost in Space* (267), and it depicts natural and social spaces in Southeast Asia and the United States that have been assaulted by the violence of abstract capitalist space and through which Stone's characters, who are most profoundly "lost," mindlessly wander, creating destruction in their wake. In such a universe, it is only appropriate that Antheil, who embodies the most ruthless and cynical part of the novel's cumulative Kurtz, should ultimately triumph. Certainly, in the novel, Robert Stone epitomizes Kathryn Hume's description of American fiction writers since 1960 as "the Generation of Lost Dreams" (292).

"I Hope You Didn't Go into Raw Space without Me"

Bret Easton Ellis's *American Psycho*

At one point in Bret Easton Ellis's 1991 novel *American Psycho*, the protagonist-narrator, Patrick Bateman, receives a phone call from his sometime fiancée, Evelyn. Once again Bateman has broken a date with her, and Evelyn, angered at and frustrated by Bateman, as she is for most of the novel, asks, "Where *were* you tonight? I hope you didn't go into Raw Space without me" (220). On a literal level, Raw Space is the name of one of the numerous Manhattan restaurants that Ellis's characters discover in the novel, but it also serves as a metaphor for the intertwined mental and social spaces of the novel.

Few novels in recent years have been as controversial as *American Psycho*, both because of the extreme violence that dominates the text and because that violence is largely directed against female characters.[1] At times one feels that Ellis is deliberately writing the most politically incorrect novel imaginable. But as signaled in the restaurant name, Ellis has higher ambitions than sheer sensationalism. He is intent in *American Psycho* on exploring the mental spaces of characters so dehumanized by the American consumerist society that they seem at times to be inhuman, to be zombies with high-paying jobs and dressed in expensive clothing. He then describes the world in which such characters live in a narrative mode that falls somewhere between literary naturalism and surrealism. In fact, Ellis's narration explores the point at which excessive naturalistic documentation of violence inevitably takes on surrealistic overtones.

The "raw space" of *American Psycho* has two interrelated dimensions. Approximately the first third of the novel is devoted to relentlessly and repeatedly describing the superficial consumerist culture of Bateman and other affluent male New Yorkers with Wall Street jobs. As resolutely as anyone in Hemingway, the male characters in *American Psycho* follow a code, the central ingredients of which are obsession with designer-name clothing and other consumer items, pursuit of hedonistic pleasure, and ridicule of women and the poor. In drunken conversation they reduce women to female body parts and engage in competitive banter about material possessions. The second dimension of the novel's raw space is a desolate and depressing urban-scape that exists just outside the realm of affluence in which Bateman and his friends ordinarily move. Ruth Helyer describes this realm of raw space: "[It] is represented as a desolate and dirty urban landscape, inhabited by penniless beggars, showing the other side of the obscene wealth of the [novel's] yuppie traders" (738). This grim urban landscape must exist in order for Bateman and his associates to function as they do, epitomizing as it does the emptiness and barrenness of their spiritual and intellectual lives.

The novel's initial focus on the first of these two realms of raw space is dominated by extensive lists of brand names and absurdist dialogue that at times become indistinguishable from the kind of monotonous prose one finds in restaurant, entertainment, and travel guides. In the midst of all this, the text drops hints about Bateman's horrific secret identity. It soon becomes clear that Bateman is, or fantasizes himself to be, a serial killer specializing in the torture, mutilation, and murder of women. As Kathryn Hume has pointed out, much of the horrific impact of *American Psycho* comes from its unmediated first-person narration. There is nothing between the reader and a first-person narrator, who is on some level clearly mad. There is thus no external "normal" vision in the text, almost no recognition that such a rational and controlled norm exists. All of this is complicated by the possibility—increasingly raised in the second half of the novel—that Bateman's acts of violence may be limited to his imagination. One might compare the unmediated nature of Ellis's narration to that of Hubert Selby Jr. in *Last Exit to Brooklyn* (1964), a relentless exploration of lower-class dehumanization and violence.

While Bateman's violence is primarily directed against women, it is worth noting that his first victim is a homeless male. Throughout the first half of the novel, cruel teasing and taunting of the homeless are major pastimes of the protagonist's affluent male acquaintances, activities from which Bateman largely abstains until his confrontation with an especially passive and abject beggar named Al. Bateman first demands that Al explain to him why he has no job: "Were you drinking? Is that why you lost it [your job]? Insider trading? Just joking. No, really, were you drinking on the job?" (129). In fact, Bateman is hardly joking and is truly interested in how the homeless man lost his job. As he continues to question Al, the protagonist's curiosity turns to outrage. After an insincere promise to help the man, Bateman begins to insult him, raving about the beggar's "stench" and ordering him to "stop crying like some kind of *faggot*" (130). Then, with no transition, the protagonist adopts a tone of mock compassion: "Al . . . I'm sorry. It's just that . . . I don't know, I don't have anything in common with you." After this expression of mock commiseration, Bateman's pent-up rage abruptly explodes, and after calling the beggar "a fucking loser" he cuts out Al's eye with a knife and then repeatedly stabs him. As a last gesture, he injures the beggar's pet dog.

The scene is crucial to an understanding of the text as a whole. Bateman's curiosity about how Al came to be in his current desperate condition signals the protagonist's deep-seated fear of losing the affluent lifestyle he enjoys. Thus his questions to the homeless man all posit some blame for Al, some mistake or addiction that led to Al's downfall. Much of Bateman's subsequent rage in the scene is the result of the beggar's refusal to accept any blame and his explanation that he was "laid off" (130). Most importantly, Al's plight raises the specter of powerlessness; it potentially makes Bateman, who worships power above all else, briefly confront his own vulnerability. This is why Ellis's protagonist must quickly deny that he has anything in common with Al. Should a sharp economic downturn come about, he just might have. June Howard has argued persuasively that a central feature of late-nineteenth-century naturalism was a deep-seated fear of proletarianization. Frank Norris, Stephen Crane, Theodore Dreiser, and Jack London, she believes, were writing out of a desperate need to maintain middle-class status. For the affluent characters of *American Psycho*, the pervasive dread is of being plunged into the lower depths of urban raw space. A central irony of the text is that, on the surface, Bateman appears more liberal and compassionate than his friends. In one key early scene, he objects to some anti-Semitic conversation in which they are involved.

In suggesting that Al is an alcoholic, Bateman unintentionally frightens himself by introducing the possibility of a damaging addiction as contributing to the man's desperate condition. If his murders are in fact real, no one could be engaged in a more destructive addiction than Bateman. His insults to the homeless man concerning his stench followed by his mock apology represent the protagonist's insistence that he and the beggar are, in some qualitative, objectively verifiable way, different. They are not; they merely represent contrasting positions in a consumerist social structure. Lefebvre's discussion of the inherent violence of abstract capitalist space is relevant here: "Abstract space, the space of the bourgeoisie and of capitalism, bound up as it is with exchange (of goods and commodities, as of written and spoken words, etc.) depends on consensus more than any space before it. It hardly seems necessary to add that within this space violence does not remain latent or hidden. One of its contradictions is that between the appearance of security and the constant threat, and indeed the occasional eruption, of violence" (57).

The repetitious, and ultimately tedious, references to commodities and brand names in *American Psycho* allude to the violence that resides just beneath the surface of such an empty capitalist structure, and Bateman functions in Ellis's novel as the embodiment of that violence. Like his business acquaintances, Bateman has tried to equate the wearing of expensive clothing with recognizable brand names and the abuse of individuals in a subordinate social position with security and invulnerability, but he can never escape awareness of his own vulnerability to fluctuations in the capitalist system and, even more frightening, to death. Thus he tries to defeat death by killing women and the poor, by attempting to take control of death in order to manipulate it for his own ends. The affluent social class to which he belongs lives off the blood of the economically oppressed. It is thus appropriate that the first murder he commits is of a homeless man.[2]

That Bateman irrationally insults the homeless man as a "faggot" is significant as well. Homosexuals are, in urban America, not uncommonly targets of random assault. Moreover, Bateman must be aware of the monstrosity of his own sexuality. A cult of masculine aggression and exploitation of women is as central to the identities of Bateman and his friends as are the wearing of expensive clothes and the possession of the latest technological toys. Again Lefebvre is helpful here. In *The Production of Space* he posits three central "formants" of abstract capitalist space, the third of which is "the phallic formant": "Metaphorically, it symbolizes force, male fertility, masculine violence. . . . Phallic erectility bestows special status on the perpendicular, proclaiming phallocracy as the orientation of space, as the goal of the process—at once metaphoric and metonymic—which instigates this facet of spatial practice" (287). A state of permanent, and constantly gratified, erection is the dream of Bateman and his friends, and they equate such an ideal with identity and self-worth. Women thus become mere accessories to this projected virility. By their sheer existence, homosexuals thus defy the deification of the phallic that is so central to *American Psycho*'s abstract capitalist space. They seem to mock everything in which Bateman and his acquaintances believe.

Lefebvre argues that abstract capitalism is inherently castrating:

> [The space] where nature is replaced by cold abstraction and by the absence of pleasure, is the mental space of castration (at once imaginary and real, symbolic and concrete): the space of a metaphorization whereby the image of the woman supplants the woman herself, whereby her body is fragmented, desire shattered, and life explodes into a thousand pieces. Over abstract space reigns phallic solitude and the self-destruction of desire.
>
> The representation of sex thus takes the place of sex itself, while the apologetic term "sexuality" serves to cover up this mechanism of devaluation. (309)

A striking aspect of *American Psycho* is its depiction of the pleasureless and desperate lifestyles of Ellis's affluent characters. Many seek temporary oblivion through drugs, and all of them continually and unsuccessfully seek an antidote for their boredom in new restaurants and clubs. There is, moreover, no instance of remotely pleasurable sexual contact in the novel; one reads instead of horrifying and disgusting rapes, mutilations, and murders of women. By dehumanizing women, by reducing them to fragmented body parts, Ellis's men have symbolically castrated themselves by distancing themselves from women as human beings. They thus exist in a state of profound solitude, the inhabitants of a thoroughly debased fourthspace that emerges out of the merger of the consumerism they worship and the spiritually annihilating urban space in which they exist.

One of the most amusing aspects of *American Psycho* is the frequency with which the male characters fail to recognize each other. Focusing only on what the other, whether male or female, is wearing, they have exiled themselves to the superficial. In such a world, characters only have to change clothes to become interchangeable. True eros is so banished from their world that they don't even desire it. Lefebvre discusses the relationship between the phallic formant and the visual: "Abstract space is doubly castrating: it isolates the phallus, projecting it into a realm outside the body, then fixes it in space (verticality) and brings it under the surveillance of the eye" (110). In such a world, the basic dishonesty and superficiality of advertising flourish: "Confined by the abstraction of a space broken down into specialized locations, the body itself is pulverized. The body as represented by the images of advertising (where legs stand for stockings, the breasts for bras, the face for make-up, etc.) serves to fragment desire and doom it to anxious frustration, to the non-satisfaction of local needs. . . . the female body [is] transformed into exchange value, into a sign of the commodity and indeed into a commodity *per se*" (310).

The sheer desperation that characterizes Bateman's assaults on women is perhaps a result of his inability as a true disciple of the superficiality of consumerism to discover a complete, a real, woman anywhere. He can only see expensive clothing covering fragmented body parts. Paradoxically, the hedonistic culture that Ellis depicts is most distinguished by its absence of genuine pleasure.

Another paradox in the novel is that, despite their affluence, neither Bateman nor his acquaintances ever seem to work. Bateman is shown in his office in a few scenes, but these merely accentuate his commitment to a superficial space that dehumanizes women; and while the male characters sometimes identify each other by where they work, this seems to be primarily a mode of identifying true initiates (this isn't difficult, since virtually everyone in the novel, except of course for the homeless, is an initiate). A detailed depiction of the working life of these characters would have offered the reader some relief from the claustrophobic feeling of the text.

But as the sheer excess of the murder scenes demonstrates, Ellis intends to offer no such relief. It would be difficult to think of a novel that is more committed to an invocation of violent excess. The descriptions of the murders are so excessive that it comes as something of a shock to remember that they are largely limited to the second half of the novel. In the double context of the relative absence of discussions of work and the excessive descriptions of violence in *American Psycho*, we might do well to remember Georges Bataille's discussion of a human commitment to a realm of work, dominated by control and rationality, that is continually threatened by an underlying violence: "Man has built up the rational world by his own efforts, but there remains within him an undercurrent of violence. Nature herself is violent, and however reasonable we may grow we may be mastered anew by a violence no longer that of nature but that of a rational being who tries to obey but who succumbs to stirrings within himself which he cannot bring to heel" (40). Bataille adds that work demands the repression of violent impulses except on the occasion of "feast days" or in "games" (41). But he continues by arguing that their total repression is impossible. Work itself, he argues, based as it is on rationality, is in part a strategy for repressing such impulses and promises material rewards to those who succeed in repressing them. Such an ultimately impossible mandate of denial, Bataille insists, can only intensify a frustration that becomes thereby even more likely to erupt at some point into excess and violence. Thus, work and excess become the defining duality of human existence for Bataille.

In *American Psycho*, Ellis is concerned with one half of this duality: excess as manifested in violence. It is interesting that the male characters are involved throughout the novel in capitalistic games—in demonstrating their insider knowledge of consumer items and consumer spaces. Their relentless restaurant- and club-hopping constitutes what may well be the most depressing example of game-playing in American literature.

Since the novel is primarily limited to Bateman's perceptions, and since he is so thoroughly a product of an oppressive and superficial capitalist culture, the text pays very little attention to the New York, and indeed the world, that do, of course, still exist outside the raw space he inhabits. This is an ironic twist in the novel, since the mass media plays a major role in Ellis's narrative. Bateman, for instance, is addicted to a local television program called *The Patti Winters Show*, which focuses on initially superficial and then increasingly bizarre subject matter. Ellis is satirizing the breed of television programs most infamously represented by *The Jerry Springer Show* that exploit people who are willing to debase and humiliate themselves for the enjoyment of others. It is hardly surprising that Bateman, who is so obsessed with torturing and murdering others, should enjoy *The Patti Winters Show*.

Moreover, the fictional program embodies the perversion and castrating of a potentially powerful mass media with the potential to inspire dialogue that might result in affirmative change in American culture. One *Patti Winters* topic, "People Who Weigh Over Seven Hundred Pounds—What Can We Do About Them," somewhat humorously to be sure, underscores Carla Freccero's analysis of the ironic reassurance that is gained through making a serial killer the source of the novel's violence. The *Patti Winters* title is significant—it is not what can we do *for* such people, but what can we do *about* them? By falling outside a prescribed normal appearance, such individuals somehow threaten the social fabric and must, like the homeless, be dealt with.

Such determined superficiality inevitably leads to a cult of celebrity. Bateman virtually worships Donald Trump, arguably the prototype of the egotistic male who seeks to dominate and control space itself, and he is tremendously excited to learn that Tom Cruise has a penthouse apartment in the same building that he does. One *Patty Winters* show indirectly establishes a link between Bateman's veneration of celebrity and his violence against women: "The *Patti Winters Show* this morning was in two parts. The first was an exclusive interview with Donald Trump, the second was a report on women who had been tortured" (256). Bateman's lack of celebrity status is an element in the considerable self-hatred that functions as the dark side of his egotism and which finds an outlet in his assaults against women. In these assaults, whether real or imagined, Bateman has descended into perhaps the most terrifying of all the debased fourthspaces examined in this study.

Even Bateman occasionally notices, primarily in newspaper accounts, the world outside the metaphoric Raw Space that he inhabits, and what he reads confirms what he observes in the barren and depressing cityscape through which he travels on his way to the affluent realm of raw space. Near the end of the novel, he is shown reading the *New York Post:* "The *Post* this morning says the remains of three bodies that disappeared aboard a yacht last March have been recovered, frozen in ice, hacked up and bloated, in the East River; some maniac is going around the city poisoning one-liter bottles of Evian water, seventeen dead already: talk of zombies, the public mood, increasing randomness, vast chasms of misunderstanding" (383). The pervasive irony of the novel is underscored in Bateman, the real or pretend serial killer, feeling outrage that some "maniac" is going around poisoning Evian bottles, a crime that personally threatens him (in one early seduction scene a bottle of Evian is present). Throughout the novel, he is largely successful in denying the insanity of his own thoughts and actions while condemning even minor indiscretions in others.

Despite its obvious journalistic insignificance, the *Post* account of grotesque New York violence and talk of zombies points to an important symbolic subtext of the novel. As more than one critic has pointed out, *American Psycho* echoes and parodies several fictional genres, most noticeably the gothic.[3] And as the walking dead, zombies are an appropriate symbolic representation of Bateman and the other characters of Ellis's novel who seem to lack any kind of spiritual or emotional identity.

Perhaps even more than zombies, vampires have long been central to literary gothicism and especially to film evocations of it. The extreme focus on blood in *American Psycho* inevitably recalls such texts as Bram Stoker's classic *Dracula* (1897) and all the subsequent cinematic vampires. Metaphorically, vampirism represents a promising approach to *American Psycho*. The classic vampire needs to drain blood from others in order to survive, and Bateman often seems submerged in the blood of his victims. Moreover, a perverted eroticism has always been a barely submerged element in fictions and films about vampires. The erotic, certainly present in Tod Browning's 1931 film version of Stoker's novel, has become more overt in the numerous subsequent *Dracula* movies. Yet even though Bateman engages in graphically described sexual activities with women before murdering them, *American Psycho* is an almost militantly nonerotic text. The descriptions of the various sex acts in which Bateman participates convey most of all the depressing and debased tone of pornography, a genre of which Bateman is inordinately fond. Ellis may well be conducting a kind of experiment here; he may be interested in demonstrating the potential of excessive graphic description to transform the usual eroticism of vampire fiction into a kind of anti-eroticism. In their spiritual emptiness, their entrapment in a hideously debased fourthspace, Bateman and his associates replicate "the undead" of vampire mythology.

There are other metaphoric overtones of Bateman's murderous assaults of women. Bateman's dismembering of the women he murders and his symbolic immersion in their blood arises from his desire to possess for his own gratification literally every part of them, to assault them internally as well as externally. Barry Keith Grant writes that in "*American Psycho*, the emphasis on the details of female victimization work [*sic*] to show a disturbing picture of a besieged white phallocentrism. Bate*man's* mutilations of women are grotesquely graphic exaggerations, overtly monstrous depictions, of the treatment of women within patriarchy" (27).

In their conversations, Bateman and his male companions always reduce women to body parts, and Bateman effectively takes the implications of their dialogue to a literal level. Throughout the novel, attractive women are referred to as "hardbodies" and "pussies," and Bateman is obsessed with possessing on a sexual level, and on a literal level, the private parts of female bodies. One extreme example of this possessiveness, which may also signal that his assaults exist only on the fantasy level, comes near the end of the novel: "In my locker in the [gym] locker room at Xclusive [Bateman's health club; he is a fitness fanatic] lie three vaginas I recently sliced out of various women I've attacked in the past week. Two are washed off, one isn't. There's a barrette clipped to one of them, a blue-ribbon from Hermes tied around my favorite" (370). The improbability of anyone actually being able to hide three vaginas in a gym locker room is obvious. The fact that Bateman hasn't washed the blood off one of them echoes the implicit association in vampire texts between the blood of female victims and menstruation, a natural female body function that most probably simultaneously repels and attracts Bateman, who is constantly at war with any threat to his own bodily cleanliness. Not surprisingly, he is also especially fond of anal intercourse.

It should also be pointed out that in gay literature written since the 1980s blood is often associated with the AIDS epidemic; and, as Helyer points out, a gay subtext is present in *American Psycho*. Bateman and most of his male acquaintances are intensely homophobic and obsessed with proving their own heterosexuality. It would be possible to read *American Psycho* as a kind of coded novel about the AIDS epidemic, as has been done with the vampire fiction of Anne Rice and the 1987 film *Fatal Attraction*.

Most of all, *American Psycho*'s male characters fear death, and all of their veneration of affluence—their obsession with wearing the correct clothes and owning the newest and most expensive technological devices—represents a desperate and doomed attempt on their part to believe that death cannot touch them. Thus, in acts that are rooted in a kind of absurdist existentialism, Bateman attempts to protect himself from death by killing others. Such an attempt is, of course, doomed, and his grasp of any kind of reality steadily disintegrates as the novel nears its conclusion. Significantly, the last words of the novel echo Jean-Paul Sartre's play *No Exit*.

The climactic moment in Bateman's accelerating madness, and a crucial clue (among others) that some, if not all, of the protagonist's multiple murders have occurred only in his mind, comes in a wildly improbable scene near the end of the novel. In it, Bateman shoots a street entertainer who plays the saxophone (it is worth noting that the protagonist ordinarily kills with a knife). Not surprisingly, so public a murder attracts a police squad car that begins to chase after the fleeing Bateman, who commandeers a cab driven by "a young Iranian guy." The cabbie begs Bateman not to shoot him, a plea that prompts Bateman to kill him: "I impatiently mutter 'fuck yourself' and raising the gun to his face, pull the trigger, the bullet splatters his head open, cracks it in half like a red watermelon against the windshield, and I reach over him, open the door, push the corpse out, slam the door, start driving" (348–49). The police pursue the protagonist until he crashes the cab into "a karaoke restaurant called Lotus Blossom" (349), at which point he engages in a gun battle with two sets of policemen in two squad cars and shoots one policeman and blows up one of the squad cars by firing a bullet into it.

The sheer improbability of all this is obvious (it reads like a parody of chase scenes in innumerable urban cop movies), and Ellis's lack of high seriousness in the scene is emphasized by one of Bateman's thoughts during the chase: "I shot a saxophonist? a *saxophonist?* who was probably a *mime* too? for *that* I get this?" (350). Moreover, after the gun battle with the police, the narrative point of view abruptly switches to third person for the only time in the novel (except for the celebrity profiles, one of which immediately follows this chapter). In this brief third-person narrative, Bateman escapes into the building that houses his firm after momentarily confusing it with another building. Once inside the lobby, he shoots a nightwatchman and a janitor before boarding an elevator to his office, from which he tries to call his lawyer in order "to make public what has been, until now, my private dementia." When Bateman gets, instead of the lawyer, a recording requesting that he leave a message, he proceeds to do so: "I leave a message, admitting everything, leaving nothing out, thirty, forty, a hundred murders" (352).

The sudden and brief shift to third-person narration in this climactic scene is important in two related ways. As the novel progresses, Bateman becomes increasingly aware that he is in a state of mental deterioration. In fact, from the first he is quite frank and analytical when discussing the profound inhumanity that resides at the core of his being:

> There wasn't a clear, identifiable emotion within me, except for greed, and, possibly, total disgust. I had all the characteristics of a human being—flesh, blood, skin, hair—but my depersonalization was so intense, had gone so deep, that the normal ability to feel compassion had been eradicated, the victim of a slow, purposeful erasure. I was simply imitating reality, a rough resemblance of a human being, with only a dim corner of my mind functioning. Something horrible was happening and yet I couldn't figure out why—I couldn't put my finger on it. (282)

Like Sartre's Roquentin in *Nausea*, Bateman is thoroughly trapped in materiality, in facticity. In contrast to Roquentin, however, Bateman attempts to transpose the nausea he feels at his entrapment onto the external world, the world of raw space. But the most significant aspect of all of this is Bateman's recognition that "something horrible" is happening, that he is undergoing a process of depersonalization.[4] The rapid shift from first to third person in the climactic chase sequence is evidence of the accelerating nature of this process.

There is other evidence of Bateman's disintegrating hold on reality in the novel. The kind of absurd, over-the-top detail that characterizes the chase scene intensifies in the last third of the novel. This becomes especially evident in the description of Bateman's acts of cannibalism. One chapter, "Tries to Cook and Eat Girl," describes the protagonist's frustrations in attempting to do what the title specifies and ends with this: "Maggots already writhe across the human sausage, the drool pouring from my lips dribbles over them, and still I can't tell if I'm cooking any of this correctly, because I'm crying too hard and I have never really cooked anything before" (346). The impersonality of the chapter title is significant—it reads as if Bateman is describing the repugnant and unbelievable actions of someone other than, and outside of, himself.[5]

The essential ambiguity of Bateman's murders leaves open at least three possible readings: all of the murders (including the final shootout with the police) actually occur; Bateman killed some limited number of people and has fantasized the rest in an obsession to become the number one serial killer ever (a projection of the capitalist competition that dominates the novel); or all of the murders are sheer fantasy. The implausibility and over-the-top detail in the last third of the novel make the first alternate unlikely, but the text makes it impossible to choose between the second and third. This ambiguity is central to the surreal fourthspace of the Bateman murders.

Most of the deliberate ambiguity here involves the murder of one of Bateman's business associates, Paul Owen. The murder of Owen is essentially different from the other killings in the novel; prompted by professional jealousy, it does not manifest the sheer randomness that characterizes the protagonist's assaults on women and the homeless. After killing Owen and disposing of his body in an especially gruesome manner, Bateman then commits other murders in his victim's apartment. In probably the most puzzling and intriguing scene in *American Psycho,* Bateman, shortly before the end of the novel, returns to Owen's apartment to find that it has been thoroughly cleaned, with all evidence of the protagonist's brutal assaults removed. Moreover, a real estate agent named Mrs. Wolfe is showing the apartment to a couple.

Baffled and obviously concerned, Bateman asks whether the apartment belongs to Owen or not. Mrs. Wolfe, only after "a long pause," responds that it does not. During the exchange, Bateman becomes aware of a television commercial playing in the background: "A man holds up a piece of toast and tells his wife, 'Hey, you're right . . . this margarine really *does* taste better than shit.' The wife smiles" (369). Mrs. Wolfe next asks Bateman whether he saw the apartment ad "in the *Times*," and after Bateman responds that he did, she informs him that there "was no ad in the *Times*" and then twice suggests that he leave without making "any trouble." As he does so, Mrs. Wolfe warns him not to return to the apartment (368–70).

Tony Williams, among others, reads this complex scene as indicative of the complicity of the surrounding capitalist system in Bateman's activities, and this interpretation would certainly explain Mrs. Wolfe's hostility to Bateman.[6] She may throw out the red herring about the *Times* ad as a means of identifying Bateman as the man who has appropriated Owen's apartment as a space for murder. In an alternate reading, Mrs. Wolfe may simply be concerned that the obviously distraught Bateman, who is carrying a surgical mask when he enters the apartment, may ruin the real estate deal that she is in the process of closing. The clear unreality of the television commercial would substantiate this interpretation, though it does, of course, leave open the question of who cleaned up the apartment and disposed of the murder evidence.

To further complicate the Owen motif in the novel, Bateman begins to hear rumors that the rival he believed he killed has been seen in London. The rumors culminate in the protagonist's second attempt to confess his killings to his attorney, Harold Carnes. Their conversation typifies the black humor that characterizes the entire text. Approaching Carnes at a party, Bateman asks him whether he got the earlier phone confession, only to have the attorney dismiss it as a joke. Moreover, Carnes continues the motif of mistaken identity that runs throughout the novel: "Davis, . . I am not one to bad-mouth anyone, your joke *was* amusing. But come on, man, you had one fatal flaw: Bateman's such a bloody ass-kisser, such a brown-nosing goody-goody, that I couldn't fully appreciate it. Otherwise it was amusing" (387). Carnes's assault on Bateman's self-identity continues when he tells "Davis" that Bateman "could barely *pick up* an escort girl." When Bateman insists that he is, in fact, Bateman and that he did indeed kill Paul Owen, the attorney responds that he recently had dinner with Owen in London (388).

Given the text's ongoing motif of mistaken identity, it is, of course, possible that Carnes had dinner in London with someone whom he believed to be Paul Owen, and one thing that does seem clear about Bateman is that he is attractive to women and has little trouble "picking up" anyone. Still, especially in context with the other rumors that Bateman hears asserting that

Owen is still alive, the scene can be interpreted as supporting the fantasy reading of the text.

One almost buried clue to all this is Bateman's comment that he has been the cause of five abortions. To the degree that Ellis means this as a negative comment on the ease of abortion in contemporary urban America, one understands another dimension of NOW's hostility to the novel. But it is more meaningful to take the abortion reference as a comment about the selfishness and irresponsibility of Bateman and the consumer culture in which he thrives. Repressed guilt about the abortions may lie at the root of Bateman's fantasies about murdering women, if indeed they are fantasies.

Ellis's deliberate cultivation of ambiguity is also relevant to the novel's mock gothicism. As horror writers have long realized, nothing is ultimately so terrifying as the unknown. In this context, as Ruth Helyer points out, Edgar Allan Poe seems a likely influence on the novel. Bateman recalls Roderick Usher and other Poe protagonists who desperately and unsuccessfully try, through confession, to stop themselves from perpetrating horrific acts. The primary reason why Bateman's confession attempts repeatedly fail is that all his associates are too self-centered to listen to what he is saying. There are, moreover, two variations on the confession motif in the novel. First, Bateman is obsessed with serial killers and tries to get others in raw space restaurants and bars interested in them. But again, his listeners are too absorbed in superficiality to pay serious attention to him. In one such instance, an acquaintance deliberately mocks Bateman's fascination with serial killers and pretends to think Leatherface from *The Texas Chainsaw Massacre* is called "Featherhead" (153). It is revealing that the acquaintance refers to a fictional killer here, adding that "I don't want to know anything about Son of Sam or the fucking Hillside Strangler or Ted Bundy or Featherhead, for god's sake" (153). There is a serious aspect to this—a central tenet of Ellis's aesthetic is that Ted Bundys and Hillside Stranglers do actually exist even if Leatherface and Patrick Bateman do not, and someone had *better* be interested in them. Primarily, though, the scene underscores the impossibility of getting anyone to listen to Bateman. In this respect, Ellis's aesthetic parallels Cormac McCarthy's in *Child of God.*

The second variation of the confession motif is for one of the secondary characters in the novel to verbally assault Bateman in extreme language that is, in fact, quite accurate without the speaker's knowing it. In one such instance, an exasperated Evelyn, who has once again been stood up and insulted by Bateman, explodes at him. She calls him "pathological," "inhuman," and "a ghoul," an accusation of inhumanity that echoes Bateman's own earlier confession to the reader. Late in the novel, Tim Price, Bateman's best friend, who, earlier in the novel, has disappeared into a tunnel in a club called appropriately enough the Tunnel, abruptly resurfaces in the protagonist's office and affectionately says to Patrick: "You're a madman, Bateman. A total animal" (384).[7]

At least by the end of the novel, Bateman does indeed seem to be a madman. He himself offers the best analysis of the kind of madness that afflicts him when he experiences a defining vision: "Justice is dead. Fear, recrimination, innocence, sympathy, guilt, waste, failure, grief, were things, emotions, that no one really felt anymore. Reflection is useless, the world is senseless. Evil is the only permanence. God is not alive. Love cannot be trusted. Surface, surface, surface was all that anyone found meaning in . . . this was civilization as I saw it, colossal and jagged" (375). Thus, Bateman himself provides the most important description of the debased fourthspace that the spiritual barrenness of an urban landscape plagued by extreme violence produces. For Bateman's friend, violence itself exists on the margins of work and play; for Ellis's protagonist, however, it increasingly takes over the center of his consciousness whether he actually kills anyone or not.

Bateman proceeds to analyze the effects of living in such a "civilization" on himself: "*I simply am not there.* . . . Myself is fabricated, an aberration. I am a noncontingent human being" (377). The precise meaning of "noncontingent human being" is somewhat difficult to grasp, but it seems to imply a (non)existence that lacks any relation to anyone or anything else, a surface existence completely without meaningful ties to the world outside the individual ego. That Bateman is aware of his condition, and regrets it, supports Steven Jay Schneider's argument that remorse is a central motif in the novel.

Tim Price's report of his experience in the tunnel is quite succinct: "It was . . . surprising. . . . It was . . . depressing" (384). This seems an understated metafictional comment. *American Psycho* is intensely shocking and considerably more than just "depressing." The reader, through submersion in Ellis's tunnel of raw space, is left wondering and unnerved; the novel is fiction at its most assaultive. It explores the degree to which evocations of violence, in America's media-saturated culture, can still shock, or even be meaningful.

11
Violence and Family Structures

Violence rooted in excess and distorted, even perverted, modes of masculinity has been a defining concern of this study, which has, except for Allison's *Bastard Out of Carolina,* focused on texts by male writers. It must be stressed, however, that several important women novelists have dramatized the traumatic effects of male violence, especially on women, children, and family structures. Indeed, this motif has dominated the fiction and much of the nonfiction of Joyce Carol Oates from the beginning of her career, thus her fascination with boxing. Three other important women novelists have conducted especially memorable explorations of fourthspaces rooted in male violence, and in all three cases they have focused on the destruction such violence has had on families.

In *A Thousand Acres,* her 1992 Pulitzer Prize–winning novel, Jane Smiley explores a fictional space that is, at least on the surface, comparable to Allison's envisioned small-town South Carolina. Smiley's rural Midwest is also controlled by patriarchal values that celebrate the family. The patriarchal domination in her text extends to a natural landscape superficially subjugated by a male technology that perverts and distorts it. This perverse domination of nature is related, in the text, to the legacy of rape and incest that has been denied and covered up in the Cook family. Thus some of the most perceptive critical discussions of Smiley's text have approached it from the critical perspective of eco-feminism.[1]

Perhaps the second dominant focus in criticism of *A Thousand Acres* has been on the ways in which Smiley's plot is built on inversions of the essential story in *King Lear;*[2] the ramifications of these inversions are essential to the perverted fourthspace evoked in the text. In the present tense of the novel,

Smiley's Iowa farm patriarch, Larry Cook, has, through cunning and ruthlessness, amassed a thousand acres of farmland and has thereby become a much respected, even a venerated, figure in the surrounding farm community. He is also the widowed father of three adult daughters, each of them warped by the violence they experienced as children at the hands of Larry. Ginny, who functions as the novel's narrator, remembers the brutal physical violence that Larry inflicted on her and her sister, but she has survived by denying the anger it made her feel.

Rose, in contrast, is openly angry at, and resentful of, her father, and in the course of the novel she forces Ginny to confront a deeply repressed memory—that Larry sexually abused her when she was a child, as he did Rose. The violence of such abuse has inevitably marred the psyches of the sisters and made adult relationships intensely difficult for them. Moreover, the violations and resulting anger have taken their physical toll as well. When the novel opens, Rose has lost her right breast to cancer and is undergoing chemotherapy for the disease, which will, before the novel ends, take her life. Ginny, who badly wants children, has experienced five miscarriages, and her husband, Ty, has made it clear that he does not want her to become pregnant again. Rose and Ginny—Regan and Goneril as victims—are two natural allies against their father, but at one point Ginny actually tries to poison Rose over a young man with whom they both have affairs.

Seeming to have escaped comparable physical and psychological damage, Caroline, the youngest Cook daughter and the novel's inversion of Shakespeare's Cordelia, is a young lawyer living in Des Moines who made it clear while still a child that she would, as soon as possible, escape farm life. It soon becomes apparent that her professional success and apparent psychological intactness have come at great cost. She is emotionally cold and selfish, incapable of sustaining any personal relationship except with her father. Moreover, she closes her mind to any information that might complicate her unrealistic image of the Cook family, refusing to believe Rose's testimony of sexual abuse by her father. After initially quarreling with her father over a plan he suggests for legally passing on his thousand acres to his daughters, she then aligns herself with Larry in a protracted lawsuit that ultimately reveals to the neighboring farmers the illusion of Cook family stability and causes Ginnie and Rose to become communal outcasts.

Throughout the novel, the suppressed Cook family history of abuse and the barely suppressed anger resulting from it surface in instances of violence. Initially the violence appears indirectly, in the form of illness (Rose's cancer and Ginnie's miscarriages), but ultimately it manifests itself in more direct ways. In addition to Ginnie's attempted poisoning of her older sister, violence shatters Rose's marriage. Her husband, Pete, long the subject of Larry Cook's criticism and condemnation, commits, while drunk, an act that results in the blinding of a neighboring farmer and then dies after driving his pickup into a water-filled quarry. It is impossible to know whether his death is an accident or suicide.

In Smiley's text, the violence that haunts the Cook family and indeed the entire farm community is envisioned as rooted in the earth itself. Ginnie learns that her miscarriages were caused by drinking well water poisoned by nitrates from fertilizer runoff. She further discovers that the poisonous effect of such nitrates on well water has been documented for a decade or more but has been covered up, like Larry Cook's sexual abuse of his daughters. The poisoned well water parallels Ginnie's attempted poisoning of Rose—in fact, she learns the cause of her miscarriages from the young man with whom she and Rose are both having affairs.

The poisoned water is only one instance of the rape of the earth in Smiley's novel, in which a crucial synecdoche for the patriarchy's assault of nature is introduced early. Ginnie remembers that the fertile farmland of the novel rests upon a sea of water invaded and subjugated by the area's prosperous farmers, who proceeded to lay a system of tile within it. The tiles, "long snakes of plastic tubing," have been instrumental in the farmland, producing "more acres of a better crop, year after year, wet or dry." Ginnie perceives that "however these acres looked like a gift of nature, or of God, they were not" (15).

In fact, this hidden earth invaded by "long snakes of plastic tubing" functions as the novel's perverted fourthspace. Ginnie observes further that "the grass is gone, now, and the marshes, 'the big wet prairie,' but the sea is still beneath our feet, and we walk on it" (16). But the walk is short-lived. Ultimately, the violated sea swallows first Larry Cook's sanity and then his life, the lives of Rose and her husband, and Ginnie's unborn children and finally her marriage. It would have swallowed her too had she not fled. The fourthspace beneath the earth images the violent past of the Cook family, which will soon erupt on the surface of the novel. It is representative of Rose and Ginnie's violated and poisoned wombs and, more sweepingly, of the patriarchal domination of a farm community that has sacrificed saving truths for prosperity.

In *Beloved* (1987), Toni Morrison, working from a historic incident, famously (re)created an escaped slave mother who murders her own daughter rather than allow the child to experience the abuse and degradation of slavery. Morrison's fiction is dominated by fictional African-American families torn apart by racism, poverty, patriarchal oppression, and self-hatred. Her first novel, *The Bluest Eye* (1970), centers around the ironically named Breedlove family (they breed anything but love), which is severely warped by a self-hatred rooted in racism, poverty, and a white-defined popular culture. The Breedloves live in an abandoned store in a Lorain, Ohio, ghetto "because they were poor and black, and they stayed there because they believed they were ugly. Although their poverty was traditional and stultifying, it was not unique. But their ugliness was unique. No one could have convinced them they were not relentlessly and aggressively ugly" (38).

In an afterword written for the 1994 Plume paperback edition of the novel, Morrison defines the thematic focus of *The Bluest Eye*. She writes that her inspirations for Pecola Breedlove, the tragically destroyed figure at the heart of her text, were twofold. First she remembered an African-American classmate from elementary school who longed to have blue eyes and concludes that "implicit in her desire was racial self-loathing" (210). Wondering how such a damaged self-image came about, Morrison moves to a discussion of the "Black is beautiful" movement of the 1960s. She points out that the movement's slogan would have been a redundancy if African Americans had not been programmed to believe that they were not, and could not be, capable of beauty: "The assertion of racial beauty was not a reaction to the self-mocking, humorous critique of cultural/racial foibles common in all groups, but against the damaging internalizations of assumptions of immutable inferiority originating in an outside gaze" (210).

The individual members of the Breedlove family have been victimized by this outside gaze in more or less direct ways. Most directly assaulted is Cholly Breedlove, who in turn rapes his daughter, Pecola. As a young man in the South, Cholly was himself metaphorically raped. He was having sexual intercourse for the first time with a young woman named Darlene at night in a wooded area when two white hunters abruptly appeared shining a flashlight on them. Cholly's immediate reaction was to cover himself and Darlene, but the hunters ordered him to complete the intercourse, one of them commanding Cholly to "get on wid it, An' make it good, nigger, make it good" (148). Rendered impotent, he was unable to consummate the act. The momentary sexual impotence prefigures his impotence to control and direct the rest of his life. Moreover, he subsequently directs his hatred at Darlene and, in fact, at all women.

As a baby, Cholly was literally thrown on a trash heap by his mother and raised by a great-aunt who died shortly before the incident in the forest with Darlene. Seeking something to alleviate his pain and humiliation and give himself a sense of stability, he seeks out his father, who, when they meet, rejects him, refusing to interrupt a game of craps. Subsequently, Cholly becomes "dangerously free" (159). Having determined that no certainty is possible for him and that all extreme experiences, especially those involving violence, are equally open to him and equally meaningless, he lives a desperate existence: "He could go to jail and not feel imprisoned, for he had already seen the furtiveness in the eyes of his jailer, free to say, 'No, suh,' and smile, and smile, for he had already killed three white men. Free to take a woman's insults, for his body had already conquered hers. Free even to knock her in the head, for he had already cradled that head in his arms. . . . He was free to live his fantasies, and free even to die, the how and when of which held no interest for him" (159).

Cholly marries a young southern woman named Pauline, a more indirect victim of the outside gaze. Hampered by a slight limp since stepping on a rusty nail at the age of two, Pauline suffers much more from her brainwashing by white popular culture and especially the movies. After marrying Cholly and becoming pregnant, she retreats to her private sanctuary, a movie theater in which she indulges her fantasies of a secure and comfortable existence like that lived by the white actors she sees on the screen. She is wrapped up in a film starring Clark Gable and Jean Harlow when, while eating a piece of candy, she loses a tooth. Black, pregnant, slightly crippled, she has nevertheless been able to maintain a fantasized identity with film gods and goddesses like Gable and Harlow until the loss of the tooth, an accident that plunges her into the desperate reality of her life. After the loss of her tooth and consequently of her fantasy of possessing the beautiful and luxurious life of movie stars, Pauline's private thirdspace, the darkened movie theater, is transformed into a fourthspace that, like the rest of her life, taunts her with messages of her ugliness and inferiority.

Pauline's life gets increasingly desperate when Cholly takes her to live in Lorain, where she believes the older black residents of the community look down on her. Trapped in this isolation and soon the parents of two unwanted children, she and Cholly assault each other psychologically, emotionally, and even physically until they find themselves living in the desperate fourthspace of the abandoned store. She only finds some sense of order and stability by working in the kitchen of a middle-class white family. When her daughter, Pecola, whom she openly views as irreparably ugly, invades this space, Pauline physically assaults the young girl. Pauline's physical assault of Pecola foreshadows Cholly's subsequent drunken rape of his daughter, a sexual assault that occurs at least twice.

As a consequence of all this, Pecola, the final and most indirect victim of the outside gaze, is driven insane and mentally retreats to her own imaginary fourthspace which she shares with an equally imaginary friend. In the fourthspace of her madness, Pecola possesses not just blue eyes but the bluest eyes. Her madness is a metaphoric representation of the fourthspace of the abandoned storefront, which a drunken Cholly eventually burns down, leaving his family literally on the streets of a truly pervasive fourthspace, the ghetto in which the Breedloves are trapped.

Morrison's first novel is crowded with victims of the outside gaze—in fact a little too much so, since several of them seem to be primarily plot devices arbitrarily thrust into the narrative. Her subsequent novels are characterized by a stronger aesthetic unity, and this is especially true of her 1973 novel, *Sula*. In this novel, Morrison depicts another ironically named family plagued by violence. This time the most immediate agent of violence is female, a much stronger woman than Pauline Breedlove, but one also damaged by economic suffering and rage against an inadequate husband. Eva Peace, the matriarch of the Peace family, is surely one of the most complex and, at times, frightening mothers in literature, a character who cannot be comprehended within a context of conventional Western morality.

Barbara Hill Rigney describes Eva as possessing a "power symbolic of her function as the phallic mother to destroy as well as to create life" (93). One of her acts of destruction, burning her son, Plum, to death after soaking him with kerosene, is a genuinely shocking fictional moment. Plum has returned from World War I, hopelessly addicted to heroin and progressively retreating to irresponsible and even childlike behavior. Later explaining her murderous action to her older daughter, Hannah, Eva recounts her difficulties in giving birth to Plum and then in keeping him alive as a child: "It was such a carryin' on to get him born and to keep him alive. . . . and look like when he came back from that war he wanted to git back in. . . . After all that carryin' on, just gettin' him out and keepin' him alive, he wanted to crawl back in my womb and well. . . . I ain't got the room no more even if he could do it. There wasn't space for him in my womb. . . . I had room enough in my heart, but not in my womb, not no more. I birthed him once. I couldn't do it again" (71).

Eva then recounts her dread of Plum someday entering her room and actually trying to crawl back into her womb. While the oedipal implications of all this are obvious, more is involved. Rigney, echoing Karla Holloway and Stephane Demetrakopoulos, identifies most of the frightening African-American mothers in Morrison's fiction, which most certainly includes Sethe of *Beloved*, as incarnations of the "Great Mother [of Africa], the giver of both life and wisdom, who is *nommo*, the creative potential and the sacred aspect of nature itself" (68–69). But Morrison's Great Mother figures, like nature itself, possess the power to destroy as well as to create. Moreover, Eva has been victimized by the phallic power of patriarchal society, especially after being abandoned with three children by her irresponsible husband, symbolically nicknamed BoyBoy, who is himself a victim of white racism and oppression. Left to keep her children alive however she can, and lacking the symbolic phallus of white patriarchy, Eva at one point disappears for a time and then returns with one leg missing. The rumor is that she sold the leg, having thus sacrificed a limb to overcome her lack of the symbolic phallus. As Cholly Breedlove transfers his hatred of the white hunters and racist American society into rage against Darlene and all women, Eva Peace transfers her pain and resentment over her literal dismemberment by the white-controlled socioeconomic structure into a pervasive refusal to show affection to her family, a refusal that, as with Plum, sometimes explodes into violence.

Eva's granddaughter, the Sula of Morrison's title, evolves into something of a reincarnation of Eva and inevitably becomes her grandmother's mortal enemy. The violence associated with Sula is primarily actualized in her assault on social norms, both of her immediate African-American society and of the larger white society into which she dares to intrude. Morrison describes Sula as living an "experimental life," which seems to imply a determination to experience everything that will not restrict her freedom. She emulates Eva's attempt to repress all feeling; and, when she finally fails to do so, she is destroyed. Violence comes to plague Sula early. As a young girl she is the accidental cause of the drowning of a young boy and then watches, with apparent lack of feeling, as her mother, Hannah, who has withheld love from her, burns to death (an event that echoes Eva's burning of Plum). As a young woman Sula briefly leaves the African-American community in which she grows up, only to return and be transformed into the communal scapegoat. She finally dies when a sexual affair causes her to experience the one emotion she has always denied, love, and an accompanying need for possession.

There are a number of physical and metaphoric fourthspaces in *Sula*, beginning with the Bottom, the black community in which the novel is set. The ironically named Bottom is situated at the top of a hill, a living space assigned to its early settlers by the surrounding white community, itself an amorphous space that sets in motion the violence of the novel through racism and economic oppression that are, in turn, manifested by the amputation of Eva's leg. The house in which three generations of the Peace family reside is a smaller but no less frightening fourthspace, a place where love has surrendered to repressed rage—a rage made overt in the fiery deaths of Plum and Hannah.

Finally, as several critics have noted, the dates in which the main events of the novel transpire are crucial. The essential plot takes place between 1919 and 1941, thus encompassing the end of one world war and the beginning of another. Besides Plum, a shell-shocked character named Shadrack is a mental casualty of World War I. In a tragic echo of the Pied Piper story, Shadrack eventually leads a number of the characters to death in the collapse of a tunnel. The black residents of the Bottom have been denied participation in building the tunnel, though workers have been desperately needed, and it is doubly ironic then that many of them die in it while being led by the war casualty Shadrack, who has attempted to control death by founding a National Suicide Day. Thus the two world wars function as metaphoric fourthspaces and symbolically bequeath their violence to the citizens of the Bottom. In this context, it should be pointed out that a comparable echoing of World War II is central to *The Bluest Eye,* the fictional present tense of which is 1941. In both novels, the allusions to war are tied to an eco-feminist perspective with the male technology of warfare assaulting the earth itself.

A less distant though still removed fourthspace threatens the survival of family structures in the fiction of Edwidge Danticat. Memories of their Haitian past, a past dominated by a legacy of almost inconceivable government-sanctioned violence and economic depredation, haunt the characters of Danticat's *Breath, Eyes, Memory* (1994) and *The Dew Breaker* (2004). In both texts, the oppressive Haitian past constantly threatens to actualize itself in violence, the origins of which are distinctly male. In *Breath, Eyes, Memory* the legacy of male violence is dramatized through a custom, the enforcement of which is entrusted to mothers. Early in the novel, the mother of the female protagonist of the novel, an immigrant to the United States and New York City, describes her personal experiences of the custom while a young girl in Haiti: "When I was a girl, my mother used to test us to see if we were still virgins. She would put her finger in our very private parts and see if it would go inside. Your Tante Atie hated it. She used to scream like a pig in a slaughterhouse. The way my mother was raised, a mother is supposed to do that to her daughter until the daughter is married. It is her responsibility to keep her pure" (60–61). The mother then tells her daughter, Sophie, that this custom of "testing" only stopped for her after she was raped by a stranger, an assault that resulted in Sophie's birth. Such "testing" is itself a form of sexual violation, and while mothers are entrusted with carrying it out, they do so at the behest of men who are obsessed with female purity, at least until they commit rape.

In an afterword, Danticat writes a letter to her protagonist, Sophie, allegedly composed "*while sitting on the edge of my grandmother's grave, an elevated tombstone in the high mountains of Leogane* [the Haitian village in which Sophie, her mother, and her aunt Atie were raised], *overlooking a majestic lime-colored mountain range.*" Danticat goes on to explain that "*this is one place in the world where I belong. This is the place that I most wished as a home for you too*" (235). Tragically, Sophie is unable to remain in the beautiful mountains of Leogane. Brought to the United States as a young girl and thereby leaving the protection of her beloved Tante Atie, she cannot ultimately escape the destructive legacy of Haiti, a legacy realized in the rape that resulted in her birth and the ritual "testing" suffered by her mother and aunt.

Danticat's concluding letter makes it clear that Sophie is destined to carry with her a symbolic identity that threatens to engulf her identity as an individual character: "Your experiences in the night, your grandmother's obsessions, your mother's 'tests' have taken on a larger meaning, and your body is now being asked to represent a larger space than your flesh. You are being asked . . . to represent every girl child, every woman from this land that you and I love so much" (236). The "large space" referred to here has several dimensions in which the internal and external become inextricably combined— the vaginas of all the Haitian children who have been both literally and figuratively raped through the custom of "testing," the male-dominated Haitian society that gave rise to both, and the legacy of such rape that haunts the characters of Danticat's novel. Such a complex fourthspace is almost impossible to transcend, and it is thus not surprising that Sophie's mother "tests" her when she falls in love with an older man or that, when Sophie returns to

Haiti to see Tante Atie, she finds an island under constant threat from the Tonton Macoutes, the terrorist enforcers of the Duvalier government.

The Haitian legacy of male violence is more immediately dramatized in *The Dew Breaker*, in which the male protagonist is a former Tonton Macoute prison guard infamous for his sadistic torture of political prisoners. In the novel's present tense, the former guard, identified early as Mr. Bienaime but referred to simply as "he" for most of the novel, lives a deliberately secluded life as a barber and landlord in Brooklyn, avoiding as much as possible close contact with other Haitian immigrants. His face disfigured by a long scar, he has told his daughter, Ka, that he was a prisoner in Haiti and that the scar resulted from his being tortured by Tonton Macoute guards. In the opening section of the novel, Bienaime makes a "Negative Confession" to Ka, an act of contrition from the Egyptian *Book of the Dead*, from which he used to read to her. In the confession, Bienaime tells Ka that he was, in fact, never a prisoner, but a "dew breaker," one of the Tonton Macoute terrorists who arrived in the early morning to take someone away to prison or burn down his house, thus disturbing the morning dew. The "dew breaker's" long-standing obsession with *The Book of the Dead* is revealing. In Haiti he functioned as an agent of death, and subsequently he has been haunted by guilt for his past crimes.

After this opening section, the focus of the novel shifts to several Haitian immigrants, all suffering from direct or indirect pain and all tortured by memories of their lives in Haiti. It is interesting that not all of these characters come in contact with Bienaime. One is a nurse named Nadine who is haunted by desperate letters from her impoverished family still trapped in Haiti and by the suffering of the cancer patients she treats. Another is a seamstress who, since immigrating to the United States and settling in Brooklyn, has moved repeatedly because she believes that a former Tonton Macoute prison guard, who may or may not be Bienaime, is following her into whatever neighborhood she chooses to reside. As is appropriate for a reader of *The Book of the Dead*, Danticat's "dew breaker" protagonist functions as an embodiment of the horrific Haitian past and of death itself.

In a powerful concluding section entitled "The Dew Breaker," the history of Bienaime's recruitment by the Tonton Macoutes and his brutal actions as a prison guard are fully disclosed:

> He liked questioning the prisoners, teaching them to play zo and bezik, stapling clothespins to their ears as they lost and removing them as he

let them win, convincing them that their false victories would save their lives. He liked to paddle them with braided cowhide, stand on their cracking backs and jump up and down like a drunk on a trampoline, pound a rock on the protruding bone behind their earlobes until they couldn't hear the orders he was shouting at them, tie blocks of concrete to the end of sisal ropes and balance them off their testicles if they were men or their breasts if they were women. (198)

Most shocking here is not the details of torture but the information that the former guard "liked" it, that he enjoyed being an agent of pain and death.

The final revelation of "The Dew Breaker" section concerns the origin of the scar that disfigures Bienaime's face. Having arrested a minister who dared speak out against the Duvalier government on television, the prison guard, identified in this scene only as "the fat man," is savagely interrogating his prisoner when the minister suddenly counterattacks with the spiked end of a broken chair leg. The minister aims for "the fat man's" eye but instead leaves a deep gash that extends from Bienaime's check to his jaw. Enraged, "the dew breaker" shoots and kills the minister, only to learn subsequently that the government had decided to free his victim because of the public outrage caused by his arrest. Now with his face bleeding profusely, he must flee the government himself. He rushes out into the night, where he is rescued by the minister's sister-in-law Anne, who has raced to the prison hoping to help her brother-in-law. Anne mistakes the guard for a tortured prisoner who has escaped. He lets her believe this, and after they are married she helps him flee the country, only revealing the truth to her after she comes to America.

In *The Dew Breaker*, the ironically named Bienaime functions as a personification of the fourthspace of a cruel and oppressive Haitian past that none of the novel's characters can escape, even those who, like his daughter Ka and the nurse Nadine, never directly experience it. He also embodies the fourthspace of painful death, of which he was all too often the agent—he is, in fact, his own *Book of the Dead*. It is thus appropriate that he is almost never named in the novel, generally referred to as "he" or, in the concluding section, "the fat man." He is a grotesque and impersonal force, a threat hanging over the lives of the other characters and shattering their dreams of love and family. His cruel past and his lies ultimately alienate him from his own daughter, whom he has chosen to name for an imagined concept from his favorite book—"the body's companion through life and after life [who] . . .

guides the body through the kingdom of the dead" (17), his kingdom in which the novel's other characters are trapped.

Smiley, Morrison, and Danticat have, from a feminist or womanist perspective, created a powerful body of fiction in which they imagine their own destructive fourthspaces, ranging, in the realm of physical space, from the buried but invaded earth beneath rich Iowa farmland, to an abandoned storefront in an urban ghetto, to a hill community ironically known as the Bottom and a house inhabited by a violence-plagued family named Peace, to a remembered Haiti that haunts those who have fled it for New York but who have never, and will never, escape it. As in the ten texts discussed in the preceding chapters of this study, all of these physical spaces take on social and mental manifestations and become degraded representational spaces.

Finally, another "family structure," this time evoked by a male writer, merits brief discussion. In his cult novel *Fight Club* (1996), Chuck Palahniuk envisions an even more hyperreal masculine space than Ellis's in *American Psycho*. Violence is, in Palahniuk's case, the entire raison d'être for the imagined fourthspace. *Fight Club*, which inspired a cult film of the same name, is centered around an arbitrarily constructed family that is ultimately revealed to be almost completely illusionary. The novel's unnamed narrator (brilliantly played by Ed Norton in the film version) works at a bureaucratic job he hates, a job that essentially involves helping insurance companies deny claim benefits, deciding whether it is cost-effective to institute recall proceedings against demonstrably dangerous consumer products and, in other comparable ways, helping corporations defraud the public. The novel opens with the young man about to shoot himself in the face and remembering the events that led him to this desperate decision. Plagued by insomnia, the narrator has become a "fake" who attends support groups for people suffering from terminal illnesses, where he encounters a young woman named Marla Singer, herself a "fake," and is attracted to her.

But Marla is hardly his strongest attraction, that honor being reserved for another young man, Tyler Durden, whom he significantly meets at a nude beach. Durden works as a waiter and glories in hiding disgusting matter in the food he is about to serve and, as a film projectionist, in splicing pornographic images into family and children's films. The images are so brief that they can only be apprehended subliminally, but nevertheless they leave their audience severely disturbed. *Fight Club*'s popularity among young and especially young male readers is due to its deliberately over-the-top satire of the excesses of American corporate culture, and Tyler embodies an imagined rebellion against corporate America. It is Tyler who introduces the narrator to the concept of fight clubs, underground venues in which young men engage in bloody fights in which there are no rules except that they are conducted in secrecy—"the first rule about fight club is that you don't talk about fight club" is a refrain repeated throughout the novel. Thus the narrator and Tyler seek out secluded buildings in which to stage the fights at night. The concept of the fight club functions as the dominant example of Lefebvre's representational space in the novel, with the abandoned buildings in which the fights take place functioning as examples of Lefebvre physical space.

In the narrator's memory, he, Marla, Tyler, and a growing band of followers take up residence in another such space, an abandoned and dangerous building on Paper Street that is awaiting demolition. In this house Tyler instigates Project Mayhem, a systemic campaign of sabotage against the city's commercial and financial centers. This campaign is foreshadowed by Tyler's raids on the trash containers of medical centers to steal the collagen that has been suctioned out of the bodies of women and his then transforming the stolen collagen into soap. He comes to refer to himself as the "Paper Street Soap Company" (78). The parallels between Tyler's soap manufacturing and the Nazis' notorious practice of making soap out of concentration camp victims illustrate the provocatively extreme nature of Palahniuk's satire of corporate America.

Increasingly in the final third of the novel, after Project Mayhem is instituted, the narrator is shaken when people identify him as Tyler Durden. Thus the revelation at the end of the novel that Durden and the house on Paper Street exist only in the narrator's feverish psyche is hardly a surprise. More shocking is the accompanying revelation that the narrator has in fact shot himself in the face and is incarcerated in some kind of institution. The imagined violence of Project Mayhem serves as a synecdoche of the violence of his self-inflicted wound. The narrator's initial encounter with a nude Tyler on a nude beach cannot be reduced to a simple indication of homosexual feelings on the part of the narrator (though that does seem to be a subtext in the novel). More importantly, it represents his naked encounter with, and recognition of, his repressed, rage-filled self. His rage is also clearly associated with an intense self-loathing, and the two emotions culminate in the attempted suicide that leaves him alive but horribly disfigured.

In *Fight Club*, the Paper Street house and Project Mayhem are imagined fourthspaces devoted to the enactment of violence, reflections of the damaged fourthspace of the narrator's consciousness. The Paper Street "family structure" itself constitutes a degraded fourthspace. At the conclusion, the reader can be certain that the narrator of the novel exists, while Tyler and the plethora of recruits for Project Mayhem who begin to fill the house near the end of the novel do not. The degree of Marla's reality is more difficult to determine. What is important is that, even in his fantasy, the self-loathing narrator loses her to his alter ego, Tyler. Of course, the fantasized fight club, a floating underground space, constitutes the novel's principal fourthspace. A construct rather than a reality, as it turns out, fight club is a celebration of mindless male violence, echoing the history of boxing in the United States as a not always legitimate masculine sport—exclusively masculine until recently, that is.[3]

The most fascinating aspect of all the texts discussed in this study is the imaginative way they evoke fourthspaces existing at the margins of physical, mental, and cultural spaces. Violence is consistently the activating force behind their emergence (the cancer in the breast of the woman in Inverness), and almost without exception it negates the possibility of any saving affirmation for the characters depicted in the novels. Moreover, while all of them are inherently complex, since they exist only at the margins and since they contain some admixture of concreteness and abstraction, they occupy different levels on a hypothetical scale of complexity.

The fourthspaces imagined in the ten novels discussed in the preceding chapters can be divided into dominant and subordinate fourthspaces. Of the dominant fourthspaces, the Ground Zero of Johnson's *Angels*, a merger of physical and mental or psychological spaces; the United States of Stone's *Dog Soldiers*, a violence-cursed United States invaded and made almost unrecognizable by the violence that it has inflicted on Vietnam; and Ellis's "raw space," a grotesque intermingling of consumerist culture and a dehumanizing urbanscape (echoed on a hypertextual plane in Palahniuk's *Fight Club*)—all of these occupy comparatively low levels on this hypothetical scale of complexity. Physical space can be said to be the sphere out of which they all emerge. Occupying a similar scale position is the mythology of the Boatright males in *Bastard Out of Carolina*, a debased jumble of bricolage rooted in the cumulative mental space of the novel's characters. Slightly more complex is the surreal fourthspace of Alexie's *Indian Killer*. Its origins are cultural and physical, the genocide of the Native American and a resulting Indian mythology of revenge haunting the white-dominated urban landscape of Seattle. Similar is the fourthspace that emerges out of the intermingling of the

New Hampshire woods soaked with the blood of animals killed by suburbanite invaders, a mythic prehistory of savage Pleistocene hunters, and a submerged Vietnam subtext in Banks's *Affliction*. The origins here are physical and cultural—regional mythology and the heritage of a violent U.S. foreign policy.

The fourthspaces evoked in Cormac McCarthy's *Outer Dark* and *Child of God* are more complex. They are grotesque mergers of physical, mental, social, and cultural spaces, an Appalachia plagued by nomads devoted to ritual sacrifice, a fourthspace that leaves Culla Holme trapped in a nightmarish landscape in which dreams cannot be distinguished from reality and which transforms Lester Ballard into a murderous scarecrow wrapped in the skin of his victims. The most complex of the dominant fourthspaces is that found in DeLillo's *End Zone*. It has a physical origin (the west Texas desert), a cultural origin (the game of football), a mental origin (the doomed struggle of Gary Harkness to find transcendent meaning), and, encapsulating them all, a linguistic origin (DeLillo's exploration of the meaninglessness of language). Only in Nordan's *Wolf Whistle* does one discover a dominant fourthspace that allows, or even emphasizes, a transcendent affirmation. After depicting a grotesque fourthspace rooted in the physical (a vulture-haunted Mississippi Delta) and the cultural (a racist mythology), Nordan manages to bring a sense of hope to this surreal landscape through the narrative mode of magic realism.

The secondary fourthspaces in these novels grow out of the dominant ones and serve to particularize, parallel, or extend them. Rolfe's escapist narration in *Affliction* is inspired by his need to deny the murderous Whitehouse family legacy, but ironically it results in his contributing to the destruction of his brother. It is a failed attempt to find escape in the margins of social space through imaginative reconstruction. The fundamentalist Christianity depicted in *Bastard Out of Carolina* proves to be almost as inherently repressive and destructive as the Boatright family myth. Both emerge out of the margins of cultural space. Heroin addiction in *Dog Soldiers* represents an attempt to flee social space by escaping to the extreme margins of mental space. So does the hideous space of Bateman's murders, whether real or imagined, in *American Psycho*. Finally, the cultural nightmare of nuclear language in *End Zone* can only be approached through the extreme margins of language itself.

In diverse and imaginative ways, all the texts discussed in this study explore the origins and ramifications of violence, especially as it manifests itself in the United States of the second half of the twentieth century. The insights they provide could hardly be more relevant to a country increasingly saturated in, and obsessed with, violence. We want our violence to be simultaneously graphic (such popular films as the innumerable versions of *Halloween* and *Friday the 13th*) but reassuringly removed from the middle class (television programs like *Cops*). This desire to immerse ourselves in gore from a reassuring distance is increasingly transformed into a national foreign policy that instinctively seeks solutions through the ultimate violence of warfare. In their explorations of the spaces of violence, the texts examined here may provide no final answers, but they do provide clues to the origins of our national obsession with the excess that is violence, especially as it relates to images and cults of masculinity.

Notes

Chapter 1

1. For a thorough and eloquent history of the lynching of African Americans, see Dray.

Chapter 2

1. For a good summary of the biblical sources of McCarthy's title see Arnold 46.

2. One especially memorable such scene occurs when the "innocent" Gene Harrogate, violator of melons and planner of inept criminal schemes, passes beneath the window of a "viperous" evangelist who calls down a curse upon him (*Suttree* 106).

3. Arnold relates the circular structure of *Outer Dark* to Culla's doomed flight from judgment: "His sin still unspoken, his guilt yet unnamed . . . Culla, wandering in his state of nothingness, seems fated to return again and again to the site of his sin" (54).

4. I am borrowing this term from Richard Wertime's discussion of the symbolic significance of the street gang that serves as the central unifying structure in Hubert Selby Jr.'s *Last Exit to Brooklyn*.

5. The most important application of the number three is obviously to the three outlaws, the "grim triune," and they are indeed a dark parody of the Trinity, bringing violence and death instead of hope and salvation. Culla's thrice-repeated denial that he is Charon may well be intended to echo Peter's denial of Christ.

6. Especially in view of McCarthy's later revisionist novels about the American West, it is possible that "the man with no name" is a veiled reference to the protagonist played by Clint Eastwood in the 1964 Sergio Leone "spaghetti Western," *A Fistful of Dollars*. The Eastwood character also appears out of nowhere with a mission to punish evil. Since Eastwood, though of unknown origins, is a heroic figure in the film, such an allusion would be in keeping with the parodic subtext of McCarthy's novel.

7. William C. Spencer applies an allegorical reading to the three outlaws. Picking up on the Old Testament feel of the novel, he argues that "the three marauders of *Outer*

Dark comprise a triple allegory of evil, with the bearded leader symbolizing lawless authority and destruction, Harmon [the only one of the three named in the novel] representing violence, and the idiot corresponding to ignorance" (76). He adds that "like the God of the Old Testament, the bearded one of the three is an authoritarian. He gives all the orders; he clearly is in charge at all times. Furthermore, like the Father of the Holy Trinity, he acts as judge and as a dispenser of 'justice'" (74).

8. The text makes overt the biblical overtones of this scene through dialogue that recalls early floods and fires that have threatened the community.

9. By the exclusion of African Americans from this list of victims, one is again reminded of Jarrett's discussion of the strong differences between McCarthy's Appalachia and the race-dominated and history-plagued South of Faulkner and other writers.

10. The scene inevitably recalls the aborted river crossing in Faulkner's *As I Lay Dying*. Again, Bloom's ideas about the ephebe's need to "appropriate the precursor's landscape for himself [*sic*]" (105) through creative "(mis)reading" are relevant to any discussion of the relationship between the fiction of Faulkner and McCarthy.

11. In a perceptive discussion of the shifting levels of narrative perspective in *Child of God*, Bartlett discusses the cinematic aspects of the text, pointing out that Lester is sometimes viewed as in a cinematic "freeze frame."

12. The kind of difficulty that confronts a writer like McCarthy, for whom shock effect is a central element in his chosen aesthetic, can be seen in the fact that a realistically staged act comparable to those performed by the "demented gentleman" can be seen in the most recent Hannibal Lecter film, *Hannibal*. Even though the movie was made almost three decades after McCarthy wrote his novel, one could argue that his appropriation of cinematic narrative techniques constitutes McCarthy's recognition of film's advantage over fiction in evoking purely visceral reactions. It has, after all, been a long time since Buñuel imaged the slicing open of an eyeball.

Chapter 3

1. This echoes a common dilemma for Banks's young males—for instance, *Rule of the Bone* (1995) recounts a twentieth-century Huck Finn who, during an extensive quest for a redemptive father figure, encounters only sexual predators and other comparably debased older males.

Chapter 4

1. One assumes that Campbell does not find surprising the 2001 vote in Mississippi to retain the Confederate flag as the official state banner. See Whitfield for a detailed account of the Emmett Till murder.

2. Needless to say, a white critic must be conscious of a parallel kind of appropriation in writing about a white novel concerning the subject.

3. Although he plays a relatively minor role in *Wolf Whistle*, Sugar Mecklin is the

narrative focus of much of Nordan's fiction. His cumulative characterization often possesses what seem to be autobiographical elements.

4. Sweet is another recurring Nordan character, and his and Sugar's nicknames constitute affectionate satire of the southern glorification of the male child and of the male in general.

5. The arrow-catching trope is one of the best jokes in Nordan's novel. Arrow catching is a boys' team sport at Arrow Catcher High School because of the inevitability inherent in the town name and as a complement to other violence-based male sports like football. Arrow-catching teams consist of two members, one who shoots the arrow at the sky and one who tries to catch it when it descends. This is, in part, a parody of male initiation rituals and of the power of names to define behavior.

6. In "A Body in the River," an essay included in *Boy with Loaded Gun,* Nordan reveals a factual basis for the Smokey Viner episode. He writes that, after the recovery of Emmett Till's body, cruel jokes were common among the boys in his high school. The main one is incorporated into *Wolf Whistle:* "The joke was that this nigger had tried to steal a gin fan and swim across the river with it and drowned himself" (79). Like the fictional Smokey Viner, an anonymous young man abruptly put an end to the joke by announcing that he "was for the nigger." In an ironic postscript to this anecdote, Nordan tells of contacting the now-adult boy only to have him say that he doesn't remember anything about the incident. This may be another reason why Nordan mutes the optimism of *Wolf Whistle's* ending.

7. In his biography of Martin Luther King Jr., Oates provides some chilling details about the aftermath of the Chaney, Goodman, and Schwerner murders that constitute part of the social and cultural landscape Nordan is describing. Ultimately "twenty-one local whites including [Neshoba County] Sheriff Lawrence Rainey and Deputy Sheriff Cecil Ray Price" were arrested by the FBI for the murder of the three civil rights workers, but "a conviction was impossible in this bastion of white supremacy; the governor and attorney general announced that they would not prefer charges." Later eighteen of the suspected men were indicted in Meridian, Mississippi, "on charges of conspiring to deprive the victims of their civil rights. But U.S. District Judge W. Harold Cox . . . an avowed segregationist who compared Negro voter applicants to chimpanzees, dismissed or reduced the charges to misdemeanors. . . . Free on bond, Rainey and the others became heroes in white Mississippi, and Confederate flags sprang up around the federal building in a symbolic taunting of national authority" (300).

8. As a further example of the novel's absurdist humor, the Prince of Darkness is so known from childhood, and the title has nothing directly to do with the funeral home that he runs.

Chapter 5

1. More than one critic has observed the obvious autobiographical elements in *Bastard Out of Carolina;* see, e.g., Hart (esp. 173–75) and Donlon.

2. See Donlon and Irving for two other perceptive discussions of the relationship between storytelling and queer identity in *Bastard Out of Carolina.*.

3. In something of a parallel point, Cvetkovich emphasizes the performance overtones of the scenes. It is as if Bone must objectify herself through fantasy performance in order to save herself.

Chapter 6

1. In this context, the tendency of "pro-business" conservatives to describe environmentalists as being weak and effeminate is especially revealing.

2. Howard, in discussing Hubert Selby Jr.'s *Last Exit to Brooklyn,* argues that since "in this . . . later period naturalism is inevitably a *re*invention, and no doubt serves new purposes, I suggest that critics identify this novel as latter-day naturalism not only because of its pessimism but because it does indeed have crucial structural similarities to naturalist novels of an earlier period" (166). *End Zone* constitutes an even more dramatic "*re*invention" of naturalism than Selby's novel.

3. Paul Civello has perceptively discussed *End Zone* as a naturalistic text. He sees DeLillo's novel as representing the end of the "Zolaesque experimental novel" (*American Literary Naturalism* 140). Zola, Civello reminds the reader, gave the novelist a new paradigm of "scientific" order that was essentially a restatement of Christian "dualism": "DeLillo . . . demonstrates in *End Zone* that Christianity and classical science are two sides of the same construct, that the demise of the one necessitates the demise of the other. Both are dualistic, the Christian dualism of spirit/flesh and God/humanity paralleling the scientific separation of object and subject and the discreteness of parts. Moreover, Christian teleology recapitulates linear causality; Christian history is a one-way linear progression beginning with the Creation and ending with the Apocalypse" (125–26). Civello, then, argues that DeLillo's text depicts the undermining of both the Christian and the scientific paradigms of order by a postmodern "entropy" that can only lead to chaos. Gary Harkness and the other characters in *End Zone* cannot create a new sense of order because the separateness of their selves from the physical world has been revealed as an illusion, leaving them no center from which to construct resistance to a "world of force" (139).

4. For instance, there is Robert E. Lee Prewitt's accidental blinding of a boxing opponent in James Jones's *From Here to Eternity,* an incident that results in Prewitt's attempting to renounce boxing.

5. Keesey's *Don DeLillo* contains an informative discussion of these secondary characters.

6. Mark Osteen writes persuasively about the significance of motel rooms and deserts as extreme spaces in DeLillo's fiction: "Deserts and motels: one prefigures the landscape after a nuclear holocaust, and the other reflects the terminal condition of the American aesthetic spirit. DeLillo's ascetics end their tales in one or both of these terminal sites. The desert is harsh, unforgiving—and clean. . . . Motels represent in DeLillo's novels an almost irresistible urge to create sterile spaces, to destroy history by demolishing its ar-

chitectural symbols. Often DeLillo's motels are found in the desert, and thus they do not interrupt its sterility so much as internalize that terminal geography. . . . A motel room is an indoor desert; it is another locus of terminality" (146).

Chapter 7

1. In the context of *Angels,* "thirdspace" constitutes a revisionist appropriation of Edward Soja's definition of the term. One of the most disturbing aspects of *Angels* is Johnson's creation of a thirdspace for the economically marginalized that has been appropriated by the capitalistic system and thereby transformed into a nightmarish and closed level of spatial perception.

2. I am using the terms "bricolage" and "bricoleur" in the sense that Lévi-Strauss defined them, especially in the introductory chapter of *The Savage Mind.*

3. The deceptively simple style in which *Angels* is written might lead a careless reader to overlook its conscious intertextuality—in addition to Eliot, the novel contains overt allusions to Yeats, Henry James's *The Wings of the Dove,* and Wallace Stevens's "Sunday Morning," among others. Moreover, at one point Johnson seems to be introducing his own condensed version of the "newsreel" technique that John Dos Passos perfected in *Manhattan Transfer* and *U.S.A.*

4. One is obviously meant to recall the Sybil of Cumae from Petronius's *Satyricon,* whose desire to die is quoted as an epigram to "The Waste Land."

5. For instance, Dwight Snow, the "mastermind" of the aborted bank robbery, fills his cap with tinfoil as protection against "E-rays."

Chapter 8

1. Aware of the problematic nature of the terms especially for a white critic like myself, but seeing no satisfactory alternative, I use "Native American," "Indian," and "First Nations" interchangeably in this study. Alexie consistently uses the term "Indian."

2. For a valuable discussion of the urban roots of the British detective novel, see Raymond Williams, *The Country and the City.*

3. The three suspects are narrative devices through which Alexie can misdirect the reader. As with most characters in detective plots, they are overtly artifacts existing primarily for purposes of plot development. In the subsequent discussion, however, it will be necessary to adopt a convention of their "reality" in order to demonstrate the specific ways in which they do and do not correspond to the implied identity of the killer. This device is especially necessary, since Alexie does not conclusively solve the mystery at the heart of his text.

4. Based on his willingness to have fun with Native American traditions, especially in *The Lone Ranger and Tonto Fistfight in Heaven* and *Reservation Blues,* Alexie's position in contemporary Native American fiction can be compared to that of Philip Roth in Jewish-American fiction in the 1960s.

5. Alexie's reference to Scrabble offers rich opportunities for postmodernist critical

analysis. Language itself, and specifically the English language, has both positive and negative implications in the context of *Indian Killer*. In writing treaties and in other dealings with Native Americans, the white government often seemed to view language as a kind of game, the rules of which it could change when it became convenient to do so. Thus the English language became an instrument of deception and oppression in historic dealings between the government and Indian tribes. Moreover, the novel's origins are undeniably European and, as a literary form that assumes private, individual creation and reception, contrasts strongly with art forms that are historically based on orality and that are communal in nature. In his evocation of Scrabble as the reservation game, Alexie seems to be having some satiric fun with the idea of language, and again specifically of the English language, as a kind of deadly game that Europeans used as a mode of imperialist oppression and appropriation. On the other hand, the deconstruction of language— the perception of signs as arbitrary and fluid, as outlined in the theories of Saussure, Derrida, and Foucault—has been appropriated as a mode of challenging established and dominant cultural systems, including the traditional Western novel. It is at least interesting that, in his fantasy of a happy reservation life, John Smith is fascinated with the indeterminacy of language: "A word like democracy can become rain instead. That changes everything. John can read a phrase from his history book and change it to 'Our Founding Fathers believed in rain'" (45).

6. See Mitchell for a fascinating discussion of the Mohawk construction workers in New York City.

7. The scene seems to be a reconstruction of the opening of the 1981 film *Halloween II*. In all his writing, Alexie makes heavy use of popular culture, generally for satiric purposes.

8. Basketball as an illusory arena for Native American achievement is a recurrent motif in Alexie's fiction.

9. More amusingly, Mather's department chair is named Faulkner. Alexie is most likely having some fun here with Faulkner's depiction of Sam Fathers in "The Bear" as a diminished noble savage as well as with the academy's long-standing veneration of the Mississippi novelist, who was himself so obsessed with issues of racial identity.

10. Interestingly, Reggie is at one point depicted watching John Ford's 1956 film *The Searchers* on television. The text supplies a brief and, in the specific context of Reggie's racial hatred, chilling plot summary of the film: "Natalie Wood had been kidnapped by Indians, and her uncle John Wayne had spent years searching for her. He planned on killing her if he ever found her, because she had been soiled by the Indians" (319).

11. One could have a great deal of fun examining the implications of the historical fondness of white writers and film producers to balance stereotypes of ethnic villains with corresponding characterizations of ethnic "super sleuths." This is especially evident in popular-culture representations of Asians. To balance, for instance, Fu Manchu, Sax Rohmer's Chinese cruel master criminal played in films by the British actor Boris Karloff, the vicious and cowardly "Japanese soldiers" in World War II propaganda films that may well have reached their nadir in Ray Enright's *Gung Ho!* (1943), and the Vietcong in Michael Cimino's *The Deer Hunter* (1978), there are Charlie Chan and Mr. Moto, the

Japanese detective created by the white novelist John P. Marquand and played in films by the Austrian Peter Lorre.

12. In an unpublished paper written for my graduate course in Multicultural American Literature.

Chapter 9

1. Maureen Karagueuzian has drawn an extensive parallel between *Dog Soldiers* and Hemingway's *The Sun Also Rises*. She compares Converse to Hemingway's Jake Barnes, noting especially that since his involvement in the invasion of Cambodia, Converse has been sexually impotent. In fact, Stone leaves the details of Converse's psychological impotence as vague as Hemingway does Barnes's physical wound: "Bad things had happened [in Cambodia] . . . and he had not had it together" (*Dog Soldiers* 16). Karagueuzian's parallel of Stone's and Hemingway's novels involves more than just the characterizations of Converse and Barnes: "One of the clichés of literary history is that *The Sun Also Rises* shattered our romantic illusions about war and love. Indeed, generations of educated Americans were to pattern themselves after Hemingway's characters, freed—in some measure by his nihilism—to work out their own standards. *Dog Soldiers* describes what has been done with that freedom: the United States is at war, fighting on the 'wrong' side, and the kind of excitement that was once reserved for sex has been transferred to drugs" (67).

2. Critics of *Dog Soldiers* consistently and accurately point out that the characterizations of John and Marge Converse and of Marge's father, Elmer Bender, symbolize the failure of the American "Old" and "New Left." In the novel's present tense the publisher of a tabloid scandal sheet, Bender "was a veteran of *New Masses* and the Abraham Lincoln Brigade" (*Dog Soldiers* 23). Marge's mother committed suicide with her lover during the McCarthyism hysteria, and Marge has protested against the Vietnam War. Robert Solotaroff writes that "in the novel's morphology of soured idealists, Marge most obviously models the failure of the traditional left" (*Robert Stone* 66).

3. Leslie Fiedler's classic analysis of American romantic fiction as a kind of extended adolescent male fantasy in *Love and Death in the American Novel* (1966) seems especially relevant here.

4. Quoting Stone, Robert Solotaroff locates the site of Bechstein's commune: it "is northern New Mexico lifted up and placed on the Rio Grande" (*Robert Stone* 56).

Chapter 10

1. See Freccero and Iannone for important discussions of the controversy surrounding Ellis's novel, and especially of the efforts of the Los Angeles chapter of the National Organization of Women to have it suppressed or at least censored.

2. In this context, it is interesting that Richard Lehan interprets Stoker's *Dracula* as a kind of imperialist nightmare in which the non-European world threatens to turn upon the imperial West and drain away its lifeblood (95).

3. For instance, Ruth Helyer writes that *"American Psycho* . . . leaks into differing categories, demonstrating characteristics of comedy, autobiography, spoof horror, bleak social commentary, conventional horror, and pornography" (741).

4. Schneider argues, through a comparison of *American Psycho* to Zola's *Thérèse Raquin,* that this self-awareness on Bateman's part is evidence of a sense of remorse that elevates him beyond complete monstrosity.

5. Tony Williams is especially perceptive in relating the real or imagined cannibalism in the novel to Bateman's participation in a consumerist society: "Bateman's entire philosophy may be defined by 'You are What You Consume' or 'The Personal is the Commodity,' which ironically apply both to his later cannibalist tastes and objectification of his chosen victims. Bateman's world is also one where Roland Barthes's insights into the nature of capitalist co-optation and inoculation now rule" (409).

6. Williams also connects Mrs. Wolfe's name with the rat that Bateman uses to torture one of his victims to argue that the novel belongs to the tradition of animal imagery in literary naturalism.

7. It seems obvious that Ellis, in Price's descent into the Tunnel's tunnel, is echoing Alice's experiences in the rabbit hole.

Chapter 11

1. See, e.g., Carden.

2. See, e.g., Schiff and Keppel.

3. In his film about female boxing, *Million Dollar Baby,* Clint Eastwood seems to believe that he must make the boxing matches especially brutal and bloody because they are between women and thus potentially not sufficiently realistic and gratifying.

Works Cited

Allison, Dorothy. *Bastard Out of Carolina.* New York: Penguin, 1992.

———. *Trash.* New York: Penguin Plume, 2000.

Alexie, Sherman. *Indian Killer.* New York: Warner Books, 1996.

Arnold, Edwin T. "Naming, Knowing, and Nothingness." *Perspectives on Cormac McCarthy.* Ed. Edwin T. Arnold and Dianne C. Luce. Jackson: U of Mississippi P, 1999. 43–57.

Banks, Russell. *Affliction.* 1989. Harper Collins Perennial, 1990.

Bartlett, Andrew. "From Voyeurism to Archaeology: Cormac McCarthy's *Child of God.*" *Southern Literary Journal* 24 (Fall 1991): 3–15.

Bataille, Georges. *Erotism: Death and Sensuality.* Trans. Mary Dalwood. San Francisco: City Lights Books, 1986.

Bell, Vereen M. *The Achievement of Cormac McCarthy.* Baton Rouge: Louisiana State UP, 1988.

Bloom, Harold. *The Anxiety of Influence: Theory of Poetry.* London: Oxford UP, 1973.

Borges, Jorge Luis. *The Aleph and Other Stories.* New York: Penguin, 2000.

Campbell, Bebe Moore. "Boy in the River." *Time* 8 Mar. 1999: 35.

———. *Your Blues Ain't Like Mine.* New York: Putnam, 1992.

Carden, Mary Paniccia. "Remembering/Engendering the Heartland: Sexed Language, Embodied Space, and America's Foundational Fictions in Jane Smiley's *A Thousand Acres.*" *Frontiers* 18 (1997): 181–202.

Ciuba, Gary M. "McCarthy's Enfant Terrible: Mimetic Desire and Sacred Violence in *Child of God.*" *Sacred Violence: A Reader's Companion to Cormac McCarthy.* Ed. Wade Hall and Rick Wallace. El Paso: Texas Western P, 1995. 77–86.

Civello, Paul. *American Literary Naturalism and Its Twentieth-Century Transformations.* Athens: U of Georgia P, 1994.

———. "Don DeLillo." *Dictionary of Literary Biography.* Vol. 143, *American Novelists since World War II.* Ed. James R. Giles and Wanda H. Giles. Detroit: Gale, 1996. 14–36.

Clontz, Ted. "Wilderness City: The Post-WWII American Novel." PhD diss., Northern Illinois U, 2003.

Cvetkovich, Ann. "Sexual Trauma/Queer Memory: Incest, Lesbianism, and Therapeutic Culture." *GLQ* 2 (1995): 351–77.

Danticat, Edwidge. *Breath, Eyes, Memory.* 1994. New York: Random House Vintage, 1998.

———. *The Dew Breaker.* New York: Knopf, 2004.

Deardorff, Donald L., II. "Dancing in the End Zone: DeLillo, Men's Studies, and the Quest for Linguistic Healing." *Journal of Men's Studies* 8 (Fall 1999): 73–82.

Debo, Angie. *A History of the Indians of the United States.* Norman: U of Oklahoma P, 1970.

DeLillo, Don. *End Zone.* New York: Penguin, 1972.

———. *Mao II.* New York: Penguin, 1991.

Dickens, Charles. *Domby and Son.* New York: Knopf/Everyman's Library, 1994.

Donlon, Jocelyn Hazelwood. "'Born on the Wrong Side of the Porch': Violating Traditions in *Bastard Out of Carolina.*" *Southern Folklore* 55 (1998): 133–44.

Dray, Philip. *At the Hands of Persons Unknown.* New York: Random House, Modern Library, 2003.

Ellis, Bret Easton. *American Psycho.* New York: Vintage, 1991.

Evenson, Brian. "McCarthy's Wanderers: Nomadology, Violence, and Open Country." *Sacred Violence: A Reader's Companion to Cormac McCarthy.* Ed. Wade Hall and Rick Wallace. El Paso: Texas Western P, 1995. 41–48.

Fiedler, Leslie. *Love and Death in the American Novel.* 1966. New York: Stein and Day, 1975.

Foucault, Michel. *Madness and Civilization: A History of Insanity in the Age of Reason.* Trans. Richard Howard. New York: Random House Vintage, 1998.

Freccero, Carla. "Historical Violence, Censorship, and the Serial Killer: The Case of *American Psycho.*" *Diacritics* 27 (Summer 1997): 44–58.

Frye, Northrup. *Fables of Identity: Studies in Poetic Mythology.* San Diego: Harcourt Brace/Harvest, 1963.

Girard, René. *Violence and the Sacred.* Trans. Patrick Gregory. Baltimore: Johns Hopkins UP, 1979.

Grant, Barry Keith. "American Psycho/sis: The Pure Products of America Go Crazy." *Mythologies of Violence in Postmodern Media.* Ed. Christopher Sharrett. Detroit: Wayne State UP, 1999. 23–40.

Hart, Lynda. *Between the Body and the Flesh: Performing Sadomasochism.* New York: Columbia UP, 1998.

Helyer, Ruth. "Parodied to Death: The Postmodern Gothic of *American Psycho.*" *Modern Fiction Studies* 46 (Fall 2000): 725–46.

Holloway, Karla F. C., and Stephane Demetrakopoulos. *New Dimensions of Spirituality: A Biracial and Bicultural Reading of the Novels of Toni Morrison.* New York: Greenwood P, 1987.

Howard, June. *Form and History in American Literary Naturalism.* Chapel Hill: U of North Carolina P, 1985.

Hume, Kathryn. *American Dream, American Nightmare: Fiction since 1960*. Urbana: U of Illinois P, 2002.

Iannone, Carol. "PC and the Ellis Affair." *Commentary* 92 (July 1991): 52–54.

Irving, Katrina. "'Writing It Down So That It Would Be Real': Narrative Strategies in Dorothy Allison's *Bastard Out of Carolina*." *College Literature* 25 (1998): 94–107.

Jarrett, Robert L. *Cormac McCarthy*. New York: Twayne, 1997.

Johnson, Denis. *Angels*. 1983. New York: Random House Vintage, 1989.

Jones, James. *From Here to Eternity*. New York: Scribner, 1951.

Karagueuzian, Maureen. "Irony in Robert Stone's *Dog Soldiers*." *Critique: Studies in Modern Fiction* 24 (Winter 1983): 65–73.

Keesey, Douglas. *Don DeLillo*. New York: Twayne, 1993.

Keppel, Tim. "Goneril's Version: *A Thousand Acres* and *King Lear*." *South Dakota Review* 33 (Summer 1995): 105–17.

Kowalewski, Michael. *Deadly Musings: Violence and Verbal Form in American Fiction*. Princeton, NJ: Princeton UP, 1993.

Kramer, Lawrence. *After the Lovedeath: Sexual Violence and the Making of Culture*. Berkeley: U of California P, 2000.

Lang, John. "Lester Ballard: McCarthy's Challenge to the Reader's Compassion." *Sacred Violence: A Reader's Companion to Cormac McCarthy*. Ed. Wade Hall and Rick Wallach. El Paso: Texas Western P, 1995. 87–94.

LeClair, Thomas. "Deconstructing the Logos: Don DeLillo's *End Zone*." *Modern Fiction Studies* 33 (Spring 1987): 105–23.

Lefebvre, Henri. *The Production of Space*. Trans. Donald Nicholson-Smith. 1974. Oxford: Blackwell, 1991.

Lehan, Richard. *The City in Literature: An Intellectual and Cultural History*. Berkeley: U of California P, 1998.

Lévi-Strauss, Claude. *The Savage Mind*. Chicago: U of Chicago P, 1996.

Luce, Dianne C. "Cormac McCarthy," *Dictionary of Literary Biography*. Vol. 143, *American Novelists since World War II*. Ed. James R. Giles and Wanda H. Giles. Detroit: Gale, 1994. 118–36.

Maher, Blake. "An Interview with Lewis Nordan." *Southern Quarterly* 34 (Fall 1995): 113–23.

Mailer, Norman. *The Armies of the Night*. New York: New American Library, 1968.

McCarthy, Cormac. *Child of God*. New York: Random House Vintage, 1973.

———. *Outer Dark*. 1968. New York: Random House Vintage, 1993.

———. *Suttree*. New York: Random House Vintage, 1979.

Mitchell, Joseph. "The Mohawks in High Steel." *Up in the Old Hotel*. New York: Random House Vintage, 1993. 267–90.

Morrison, Toni. *The Bluest Eye*. 1970. New York: Penguin, 1994.

———. *Sula*. 1973. New York: Random House Vintage, 2004.

Niemi, Robert. *Russell Banks*. New York: Twayne, 1997.

Nordan, Lewis. *Boy with Loaded Gun: A Memoir*. Chapel Hill, NC: Algonquin Books of Chapel Hill, 2000.

——. *Wolf Whistle*. 1993. Chapel Hill, NC: Algonquin Books of Chapel Hill, 2000.

Oates, Stephen B. *Let the Trumpet Sound: The Life of Martin Luther King, Jr.* New York: New American Library, 1982.

Ong, Walter J. *Fighting for Life: Contest, Sexuality, and Consciousness.* Ithaca, NY: Cornell UP, 1981.

Osteen, Mark. "Against the End: Asceticism and Apocalypse in Don DeLillo's *End Zone.*" *Papers on Language and Literature* 26 (Winter 1990): 143–63.

Palahniuk, Chuck. *Fight Club.* 1996. New York: Henry Holt, Owl Books, 1997.

Pynchon, Thomas. *The Crying of Lot 49.* New York: Harper and Row Perennial Edition, 1986.

Rebein, Robert. *Hicks, Tribes, and Dirty Realists: American Fiction after Postmodernism.* Lexington: UP of Kentucky, 2001.

Redding, Arthur. *Raids on Human Consciousness: Writing, Anarchism, and Violence.* Columbia: U of South Carolina P, 1998.

Reynolds, David. "White Trash in Your Face: The Literary Descent of Dorothy Allison." *Appalachian Journal* 20 (Summer 1983): 356–66.

Rigney, Barbara Hill. *The Many Voices of Toni Morrison.* Columbus: Ohio State UP, 1991.

Sandell, Jillian. "Telling Stories of 'Queer White Trash.'" *White Trash: Race and Class in America.* Ed. Matt Wray and Annalee Newitz. New York: Routledge, 1997. 211–30.

Schiff, James A. "Contemporary Retellings: *A Thousand Acres* as the Latest *Lear.*" *Critique* 39 (1998): 367–81.

Schneider, Steven Jay. "'I Guess I'm a Pretty Sick Guy': Reconciling Remorse in *Thérèse Raquin* and *American Psycho.*" *Aizen* 17 (2002): 421–32.

Shelton, Frank W. "Robert Stone's *Dog Soldiers:* Vietnam Comes Home to America." *Critique* 24 (Winter 1983): 74–81.

Smiley, Jane. *A Thousand Acres.* New York: Ballantine, 1992.

Soja, Edward W. *Thirdspace: Journeys to Los Angeles and Other Real-and-Imagined Places.* Oxford, UK: Blackwell, 1996.

Solotaroff, Robert. *Robert Stone.* New York: Twayne, 1994.

——. "Robert Stone." *Dictionary of Literary Biography.* Vol. 152, *American Novelists since World War II.* Ed. James R. Giles and Wanda H. Giles. Detroit: Gale, 1995. 216–31.

Spencer, William C. "Cormac McCarthy's Unholy Trinity: Biblical Parody in *Outer Dark.*" *Sacred Violence: A Reader's Companion to Cormac McCarthy.* Ed. Wade Hall and Rick Wallach. El Paso: Texas Western P, 1995. 69–76.

Stone, Robert. *Dog Soldiers.* Boston: Houghton Mifflin, 1974.

Wertime, Richard. "Psychic Vengeance in *Last Exit to Brooklyn.*" *Literature and Psychology* 24 (1974): 153–66.

Whitfield, Stephen J. *A Death in the Delta: The Story of Emmett Till.* New York: Free Press, 1988.

Williams, Raymond. *The Country and the City.* New York: Oxford UP, 1973.

Williams, Tony. "*American Psycho:* A Late-Twentieth-Century Naturalist Text." *Excavatio* 17 (2002): 403–20.

Index